LAW AND THE
QUEST FOR
JUSTICE

Law and the Quest for Justice

edited by

Marjorie S. Zatz
Doris Marie Provine
James P. Walsh

Contemporary Society Series

qp

QUID PRO BOOKS
New Orleans, Louisiana

Law and the Quest for Justice

Published in 2013 by Quid Pro Books.

ISBN 978-1-61027-163-9 (pbk.)
ISBN 978-1-61027-164-6 (eBook)

QUID PRO BOOKS
Quid Pro, LLC
5860 Citrus Blvd., Suite D-101
New Orleans, Louisiana 70123
www.quidprobooks.com

qp

Publisher's Cataloging-in-Publication

Zatz, Marjorie S.

    Law and the quest for justice / edited by Marjorie S. Zatz, Doris Marie Provine and James P. Walsh.

        p. cm. — (Contemporary society)

    Includes bibliographical references.

    ISBN 978-1-61027-163-9 (pbk.)

1. Justice. 2. Law—United States. 3. Civil rights. 4. Immigration. 5. Terrorism. 6. Judges—Judicial Process. I. Provine, Doris Marie. II. Walsh, James P. III. Title. IV. Series.

JC322.Z61 2013

        320'.03'5—dc22

        2013539392

CONTENTS

Dedicated to the memory of John P. Frank
and the
quest for justice he nourished in so many.

ACKNOWLEDGMENTS

The chapters in this book were initially presented as lectures in honor, and later in memory, of John P. Frank. We thank the authors for graciously collaborating with us to transform their spoken words into text, and Katherine R. Abbott, Heather Gough, and Eva Lester for their research assistance. We also thank the faculty, staff and students of Justice & Social Inquiry, now in the School of Social Transformation at Arizona State University, for their efforts over the years in making the lecture series so successful and in transcribing the lectures. Finally, our thanks to Joseph E. McGarry, the John P. Frank Memorial Steering Committee, and the law firm of Lewis and Roca LLP for their generous support.

LAW AND THE
QUEST FOR
JUSTICE

Social Justice, Law and Policy in Times of Uncertainty

Doris Marie Provine and Marjorie S. Zatz

Doris Marie Provine and Marjorie S. Zatz are professors of Justice and Social Inquiry and former directors of the School of Justice and Social Inquiry, now part of the School of Social Transformation, at Arizona State University. Each of them has published widely in the field of social justice and equality during distinguished careers as scholars, educators and academic administrators.

One of the strongest, brightest threads in the tapestry of human life is the desire for justice, if not for oneself, then for one's children. Consider the struggle that Oliver Brown and his family undertook to fight racially segregated public education in Topeka, Kansas. Mr. Brown was outraged that his seven-year-old daughter Linda—prohibited by law from attending a public elementary school with white third graders—was obliged to walk a mile through a railroad switching station to a bus stop. Each day she waited there for a school bus to take her to her racially segregated elementary school.

Mr. Brown asked to have his daughter enrolled in a white school in the summer of 1950, and thirteen other parents joined him in making this request. Topeka school officials turned them down. So, with the help of the National Association for the Advancement of Colored People, the parents sued the school district. They lost in the state courts, which applied the Supreme Court's long-standing "separate but equal" doctrine to reject their constitutional claim. The parents appealed to the United States Supreme Court, and after a lengthy process of briefs, arguments, and re-arguments, the Court returned a unanimous decision that racially segregated public schools violated the equal protection clause of the Fourteenth Amendment. The parents had won their case.

Yet the struggle for equality in public education did not end when this landmark case was decided. It may never end. Still, the Court's decision in *Brown v. Board of Education* set an important precedent challenging the unjust racial hierarchy that then prevailed in public education.[1] Black schools were not only separate from white ones—they received only 1/3 of the public resources available to white schools. *Brown* helped to change the terms of engagement in this struggle. Since then the terrain for critical engagement for

---

[1] 347 U.S. 483 (1954).

educational opportunity has broadened to include students disadvantaged by ethnicity, gender, physical disability, and other markers of social status. The advocates include people like Allan Cameron and Fredi Lajvardi, teachers at Carl Hayden High School in West Phoenix, Arizona. The district is poor, dreary, and 92% Latino. Cameron and Lajvardi yearned for their students to beat the stiff odds against success that face disadvantaged Latino youth in academic pursuits. They offered to sponsor anyone willing to compete in the third annual Marine Advanced Technology Education Center's Remotely Operated Vehicle Competition, a contest that is also open to college students, including, as it turned out, a team of 12 engineers and computer scientists from the Massachusetts Institute of Technology. The four Hayden High School students who stepped up to this challenge worked as a team for four months, raising money, begging materials, consulting experts, and thinking through the elements required to make a rapid, versatile, water robot. They built what turned out to be the winning entry in a hard-fought contest.[2]

The heartwarming story of these four young men has a somber side. Although all four had spent much of their youth in the United States, they were born in Mexico, an accident of birth that subjects them to the risk of deportation and cuts them off from many opportunities. Even as outstanding high-school graduates, they are not eligible for in-state tuition or financial aid in the public universities of their home state because of an Arizona law that bars undocumented residents from these benefits.[3] There are no constitutional protections against laws that discriminate in this way. The situation of these young men nevertheless disturbs a sense of justice in many people, reminding us that law and justice are not necessarily the same.

The Quest for Justice

The human preoccupation with justice is evident from a glance at any week's news events, or even the movie listings. The film industry is utterly dependent on the themes of injustice, justice restored, just deserts, fairness, and revenge for evil deeds. Heroes are heroes because they restore or impose justice on a

---

[2] The Carl Hayden Robotics team continues to excel. For a recent update, see also http://embedded.communities.intel.com/community/en/applications/blog/2012/04/12/robotics-in-arizona—carl-hayden-robotics-does-it-again.

[3] On June 15, 2012, the Obama Administration announced a Deferred Action for Childhood Arrivals program granting long-term U.S. residents who came to the United States as children deferrals from deportation for two years if they meet a set of requirements including currently being enrolled in school, having graduated from high school or obtained a GED certificate, or having been honorably discharged from the U.S. military. See Memorandum from U.S. Secretary of Homeland Security Janet Napolitano, "Exercising Prosecutorial Discretion with Respect to Individuals who Came to the United States as Children" (June 15, 2012), available at http://www.dhs.gov/xlibrary/assets/s1-exercising-prosecutorial-discretion-individuals-who-came-to-US-as-children.pdf. Although those who receive deferred action will generally receive work authorization if needed, state laws barring in-state tuition and financial aid remain intact.

disorderly universe, sometimes through violence and pain. Fiction reminds us that justice stands severely apart from simple order or mere pleasantness. The quest for this most fundamental ideal seems to reflect a powerful human longing that inspires not only artists of all types, but also activists and change-makers.

In daily life, away from movie scripts and escape fiction, nothing about justice is obvious. The quest for justice is perennial and elusive. It has been a potent source of disagreement and conflict throughout human history. Sometimes it seems as if we know no more about justice now than in the time of the ancient Greeks. Antigone's torment over how to respond to an unjust law is familiar on the contemporary scene. Aristotle's thoughts about when to treat people alike and when to treat them differently remain highly debatable. Aquinas, Kant, Bentham, and other classical philosophers have attempted to enlighten us. Justice remains a difficult concept, both in the abstract and in application. And yet it is the yardstick by which western civilization has long measured the law it enacts and the historical record as a whole. Reading that yardstick has always been challenging and subject to varying interpretations. There remains the lingering doubt that humans are up to this task.

The contributors to this book have devoted themselves to the cause of justice, and to the potential for law to promote positive social change. In the chapters that follow, they share their thoughts and experiences with real-world problems of justice. They are critical observers, undeceived by the illusion of permanency and simplicity that law often offers. They know that the struggle to make law achieve lofty goals is always more difficult than anticipated, and frequently unsatisfying. They have nevertheless made the pursuit of justice through law into their life's work, engaging the world as activists and educators. Here they deal with the law/justice problematic by framing their inquiry around discrete social issues with which they are deeply familiar.

Each of the chapters provides a canvass for drawing connections between law and justice that is both in-depth and accessible. These are essentially stories of legal struggle and conflict, but they are not all happy-ending stories. They illustrate pitfalls, as well as opportunities, in the use of law. Heroes can be found in some of these stories, and villains as well. But the villains in these accounts tend to be impersonal, bureaucratic, historically embedded, or simply us at our panicky worst.

Our guides in this investigation are sharp observers who are knowledgeable about the intricacies of law in contemporary society. They speak to us, not as philosophers, and not in an overly academic tone, but more informally, as people with a depth of relevant experience and knowledge that they would like to share. Their vast experience makes them well aware of how difficult it is to move closer to the sometimes ambiguous ideal of a more just society. Their accounts are valuable in part because of who they are and what they have achieved, as each author has made significant contributions to contemporary legal and political thought. Yet their essays also convey the difficulties and challenges inherent in pursuing social justice through the law.

As the chapters in this book demonstrate, the relationship between law and justice is complex. The idea that there is an eternal or natural law discoverable by the application of reason has generally been rejected in our era. We are left with law as a tool that grows out of the very passions and prejudices that we seek to tame through law. Judges are not aloof from the gritty groundedness of law. As Holmes famously said, "The prophecies of what the courts will do in fact, and nothing more pretentious, are what I mean by the law."[4]

Judicial intervention in public affairs has always been relatively frequent in the United States and is becoming more common around the world.[5] Thus it should not be surprising that the U.S. Supreme Court figures prominently in the chapters of this volume. But its prominence raises a question implicit in the volume as a whole: Is the considerable involvement of courts in contemporary issues that divide the nation—from health care to immigration—a good thing? Constitutional republics encourage deliberation by specifying, dispersing, and limiting the powers of government, but in the United States, unlike in many other democratic republics, courts at every level are empowered to hear constitutional cases, and they do so with regularity. This tends to make the American public rather sensitive to constitutional issues and ready to debate political questions in terms of constitutional rights and duties.[6]

The presence of a Bill of Rights in the federal constitution encourages public engagement with rights talk, offering grounds for a national conversation about justice. The Bill of Rights can be read, for example, as a kind of primer in personal freedoms. And that seems to have been the purpose of its drafters, who added the Bill of Rights after the main text of the Constitution had been drafted. They were evidently concerned that the new government that they had laid out would seem too powerful without a set of guarantees that acknowledge and protect individual liberties.

But the original Bill of Rights is not the only constitutional touchstone that is important in this volume. Another primary focus is on equality before the law as guaranteed by the Fourteenth Amendment. This provision came later, in 1868, provoked by the American Civil War. Congress adopted it,

---

[4] Oliver Wendell Holmes, Jr., "The Path of the Law," *Harvard Law Review* 10: 457 (1897), 457.

[5] See, e.g., Ran Hirschl, "The Judicialization of Mega-Politics and the Rise of Political Courts," *Annual Review of Political Science*, 11: 93-113 (2008).

[6] Steven H. Shiffrin, *The First Amendment, Democracy and Romance* (Princeton, NJ: Princeton University Press, 1993). Popular understanding of constitutional requirements does not always match the legal reality. See Jon Gould, *Speak No Evil: The Triumph of Hate Speech Regulation* (Chicago: University of Chicago, 2005).

along with the Thirteenth and Fifteenth amendments, to protect the newly freed slaves. The discussion about equality has broadened considerably beyond this original purpose, suggesting a certain alliance between constitutional guarantees, elegant in their simplicity, and deeply held American values.

Another major theme in this volume is the issue of the power of government and its potential to over-reach its legitimate bounds. Here a key reference is the Constitution itself, which was drafted with concerns about governmental abuse of power firmly in mind. The solution that the drafters adopted—division of powers across branches and levels of government and limitations on those powers—frames many disputes, including some discussed in this volume. Litigation and debates about state and municipal immigration legislation, for example, center on the power of these governments to enact legislation in an arena that has traditionally been occupied by federal law. Essays in this volume consider, not just the proper division of powers, but also the proper occasions for the unilateral exercise of federal authority.

The two major concerns discussed here can also be summed up without reference to Constitutional documents. They are: (1) *The problem of exclusion* on the basis of characteristics that should not be relevant in a society that guarantees equality; and (2) *The problem of the over-reaching state*. Our political system offers many possibilities for critical examination of, and debate about, both concerns.

Exclusion from desirable aspects of civic life on the basis of indelible characteristics has been a fundamental issue since the first European settlers arrived and began to displace the indigenous population. Slavery and its harsh and violent aftermath added new dimensions of exclusion and disadvantage. Gender, religious belief, disability, sexual orientation, and other grounds of exclusion have also become the basis for demands for equal treatment and inclusion in the full benefits of citizenship. The situation of non-citizens raises additional questions about inclusion and civic membership. In a globalizing world, the question becomes whether the whole idea of a civil contract between the individual citizen and a territorially defined state needs some revision to include basic rights for non-citizens.[7]

The second theme of this volume, the problem of balancing national security and other interests against the dangers of government intrusion into private life and civil liberties, also has a long history in the American nation. The attack on the World Trade Center and Pentagon brought the issue of government's power to find and fight its enemies to the fore in everyone's

---

[7] See, e.g., Linda Bosniak, *The Citizen and the Alien: Dilemmas of Contemporary Membership* (Princeton, NJ: Princeton University Press, 2006), Seyla Benhabib, *The Rights of Others: Aliens, Residents, and Citizens* (Cambridge, UK: Cambridge University Press, 2004), and Charis Kubrin, Marjorie S. Zatz, and Ramiro Martínez, eds., *Punishing Immigrants: Policy, Politics, and Injustice* (New York: New York University Press, 2012).

mind. The response of the legal system, which has been criticized as panicky and ineffective, nevertheless raises important justice issues worthy of political debate.

Finding the balance between government powers to protect the population and unwarranted intrusion into personal lives and beliefs is not just a matter for legal experts, as several authors in this volume note. They also warn us to beware of what social scientists call "moral panics," which occur when a nation loses its grip on rational discussion and debate. In these situations—e.g., the McCarthy Era, the panic over crack cocaine—legislators may enact laws and policies based on frenzied hype about public danger that has little basis in fact. The losses are serious for the American public. When fundamental freedoms are sacrificed in the name of safety, Americans lose something intangible, but basic to our way of life.

Crosscutting these themes are questions regarding the capacity of American political, economic, military, social, and legal institutions to adequately respond to the demands of contemporary society. These questions, which flow throughout the book, are not posed in vague abstractions, but rather in the context of concrete cases emblematic of fundamental justice concerns. The individual and institutional struggles described in this collection thus reflect the very messy tensions and contradictions inherent in a society trying to meet its multiple and often conflicting responsibilities in times of social change and uncertainty.

It may seems surprising that twelve essays, written over the course of that many years, would have enough internal coherence to belong together in a single volume. The essays were originally public lectures, designed to stand by themselves and produced without reference to each other. And yet they clearly belong together because they were inspired by one man's vision of law in a just society. That man was John P. Frank, a national leader in advocating for the rights of underdogs. He campaigned in various ways, including through litigation, for the importance of keeping freedoms alive. He showed by his own example the value of standing up for good causes. John Frank was a friend to all who joined in the effort. In Frank's view, law memorializes evolving concepts of justice and can be a tool to achieve justice.

Frank believed that lawyers could use law and litigation to appeal to the nation's fundamental values as inscribed in the U.S. Constitution. He contended that anyone, through public discourse, has the capacity to draw upon law in order to hold the nation's feet to the fire to produce positive social change. Such changes are not won easily or quickly, and sometimes they are not won at all, as the contributors to this volume would freely admit. But there is a positive spin in these essays, as there was in John Frank. Each of the authors knew Frank well; many of them worked with him. An Afterword to this volume introduces readers to John Frank's outstanding contributions to law, and to our society more broadly.

Organization of the Book

The book is organized into three sections. We begin with the *problem of exclusion* of some members of society from the full benefits of citizenship. The progressive opening up of civic membership to persons of color, to women, and to those disadvantaged by language or physical difficulties is a major achievement of our nation, but it is an achievement that has been fraught with sacrifice, including death. Full civic membership is also a goal not yet reached for some, and appears to be out of reach for others.

The Problem of Exclusion

We open this discussion with a chapter by Professor Charles Ogletree, Director of the Charles J. Hamilton Houston Institute for Race and Justice and a professor at Harvard Law School. Ogletree's chapter offers a wide-ranging history of racial oppression in the United States. He describes its current manifestation in racial profiling and one of the principal outcomes of profiling, stereotyping, and disadvantage: the mass incarceration of men (and increasingly women) of color in our prisons.[8] He also links this theme to discrimination in schools, juvenile justice, and refugee admissions. Yet Ogletree is an optimist, viewing racism as a disease, rather than a fundamental and unchanging aspect of American culture. He calls on the U.S. Supreme Court and on fellow scholars to develop more realistic and comprehensive responses to these problems, providing the reader with an enlightening tour of current thinking about race discrimination and its eradication.

Ogletree's broad overview of the problem of racial justice in contemporary American society provides a critical context for thinking about the U.S. Supreme Court's premier achievement in guaranteeing equal justice for African Americans, *Brown v. Board of Education*.[9] Looking back to *Brown*, Professor Jack Greenberg asks, what did it really achieve? Greenberg addresses this question from a vast well of experience, as a law professor and dean, as the former legal director-counsel of the NAACP's Legal Defense and Educational Fund for more than two decades, as a frequent and successful litigator before the U.S. Supreme Court, and, perhaps most importantly, as a surviving member of the legal team that attacked segregation in *Brown v. Board of Education* in the U.S. Supreme Court. Greenberg is proud of the Court's decision, not just because it began to undo the legacy of segregation that once prevailed by law and custom throughout much of the United States, but also because of the decision's symbolic importance. *Brown* legitimized the civil-rights claim that equality requires an end to separation by race. This

---

[8] See also Doris Marie Provine, *Unequal Under Law: Race and the War on Drugs* (Chicago: University of Chicago Press, 2007), and Michelle Alexander, *The New Jim Crow: Mass Incarceration in the Age of Colorblindness* (New York: New Press, 2010).

[9] 347 U.S. 483 (1954).

affirmation by a respected institution of government, Greenberg argues, made all the difference in the civil-rights struggle. He is sharply critical of those who would second-guess the decision on legal or logistical grounds because they miss a most important point: the moral vindication the case provided at a crucial time.

Brown v. Board of Education may have started a trend toward more inclusive beliefs about who belongs in American society, but it has been construed perhaps too narrowly. For example, the emancipatory potential of the *Brown* decision has never been applied to the legal oppression of Native Americans. The chapter that follows Greenberg's relatively optimistic assessment is by John Echohawk, a Pawnee Indian and Executive Director of the Native American Rights Fund. He traces the long history of injustice toward indigenous people in the United States, focusing particularly on treaties negotiated, then ignored, and on land claims unpaid by the federal government. The U.S. Supreme Court has played a sometimes supportive, and sometimes hostile, role in resolving Indian claims. Yet Echohawk is hopeful that litigation can resolve some of the injustices that Native Americans have endured. Beginning in the 1970s, a corps of Native American lawyers began to emerge. These lawyers have a well-thought out strategy for achieving their aims, and they are prepared to fight the necessary battles in the courts.

Echohawk's essay sets the stage for the final chapter in this section, which addresses the potential for litigation in ending historic discrimination against marginalized groups. The author, Antonia Hernández, is well situated to make such an assessment. She is the former president and general counsel of the Mexican American Legal Defense and Educational Fund and a long-time leader in the struggle to gain full citizenship for Mexican Americans and other marginalized groups. Hernández traces the evolution of ideas about who can be a full-fledged citizen, from the narrow founding-era base of white propertied males, to the contemporary reality of full citizenship for all who qualify by birth or naturalization. She is troubled by current tendencies at the subnational and federal level to restrict jobs and benefits for legal non-citizen residents and by the harsh treatment accorded people without legal residency. Fears about non-citizens have become even more pronounced since the 9/11 terrorist attacks. Hernández suggests that the United States needs more consistent and comprehensive policies to integrate and include immigrants so that it can compete effectively at a global level.

The Problem of the Over-Reaching State

The lethal attacks on New York's World Trade Center and the Pentagon in Washington, as Antonia Hernández notes, made a profoundly important impression on the United States, precipitating changes in the legal system and the administration of justice that are significant and troubling. *The problem of the over-reaching state*, typically understood as asking how far the state should go in attempting to guarantee public safety, frames the second section of this volume.

The opening chapter in this section is by the Pulitzer Prize-winning journalist, Anthony Lewis, whose name is familiar to long-time readers of *The New York Times*. Lewis focuses on the broadening of executive power that has been justified in the name of the need to fight terrorism, taking readers on a journey through the Bush administration's actions in the aftermath of the 9/11 terrorist attacks. The details suggest a shocking combination of unexplained arrest, detention, and denial of fundamental rights, including the right to communicate with one's family or lawyer. Citizens, as well as foreigners, have been held under these conditions, generally without explanation. Secrecy has been used to prevent independent review and the ordinary rules of criminal procedure have been cast aside. Lewis notes historical precedents, including the internment of Japanese Americans during the Second World War and the Alien and Sedition Acts in the early years of the new Republic. The lesson, he argues, is that we must be alert to such deviations from the rule of law inscribed in our Constitution, which sets forth a *limited* government, even—and perhaps especially—in dangerous times.

The theme of unwarranted government power and the capacity of legal institutions to stem its excesses also receive detailed analysis in a contribution by Geoffrey Stone, law professor and former dean of the University of Chicago Law School. Stone provides a broad historical sweep of free speech doctrine since the Founding era. He finds a distinctive and disturbing pattern: protections for dissenting voices decline and sometimes disappear in times of peril, the very times when critical advice from every quarter is most needed. The excuse for jailing, deporting, or discrediting these voices is always the same—the requirements of national security. Stone finds six major episodes of government suppression of civil liberties, noting that courts have avoided becoming engaged during these periods, reflecting their own immersion in the nation's fears. Stone is encouraged, however, by the Court's negative reaction to President Bush's extra-legal authorization of wiretapping of American citizens in the name of national security. He is hopeful that a culture of civil liberties is beginning to develop in which citizens—including Supreme Court justices—understand the importance of being skeptical about government's claims in times of peril.

Professor Judith Resnik's assessment is more somber. Resnik holds the Arthur Liman Professorship of Law at Yale Law School and has a long-standing interest in the exercise of government authority. Her contribution to the volume addresses the federal government's assertion that it can legitimately interrogate and confine people without charges and trial. Resnik details the conditions of confinement in Guantánamo Bay, a description that makes for chilling reading. Her analysis of the case law and actions on the ground make it clear that we have moved backwards in rights in this area since the Supreme Court's decision in *Miranda v. Arizona*.[10] This was the case that brought us the now-famous Miranda warnings and established the right of any person accused of a serious crime to have legal counsel, at the state's expense if necessary.

For a period of time, *Miranda* was celebrated for putting an end to highly coercive tactics designed to produce confessions. Torture by American authorities under the cover of law, it was believed, had been consigned to the dustbin of history. The 9/11 attacks appear to have cracked this foundation, however, suggesting the difficulty of sustaining justice in times of uncertainty and peril.

This section closes with an essay by Department of Homeland Security (DHS) Secretary and former Arizona governor Janet Napolitano. As a public administrator with awesome responsibilities to protect vital national security interests, Napolitano is concerned on a daily basis with finding the appropriate balance between national security and the protection of privacy and civil rights and liberties. The task is formidable, especially in light of the institutional challenges involved. DHS is a young agency of enormous size and scope. It has responsibility, for example, for ensuring aviation security on a worldwide basis for American travelers in addition to its better-known responsibilities for immigration control and disaster relief.

Napolitano details some of these complexities, providing a valuable perspective on the development of agency policy. As she demonstrates, the task of integrating rights protections into this giant agency begins with the structure of DHS itself. The agency includes an office of civil rights and liberties and a privacy office, but the challenge is to bring these voices and the concerns they represent into the planning and implementation stages of agency policy making. For Napolitano, security and liberty are mutually reinforcing and inextricably intertwined core values. Security, she argues, is a prerequisite for the exercise of rights. Yet it must not be an excuse to justify policies that undermine constitutional rights and liberties.

What Does the Future Hold?

The final section of the book looks to the future. What, these authors ask, does the future hold for us? Are we on track to resolve the problems of discrimination and exclusion based on race, gender, national origin, and other statuses? Are we close to establishing an appropriate balance between the branches of government, and are we protecting our security without endangering our fundamental civil rights and liberties?

This section begins with an essay by Harvard Law Professor Lani Guinier, a nationally recognized legal scholar whose work attracted the attention of President Bill Clinton. The President nominated Guinier to serve as

---

[10] 384 U.S. 436 (1966).

Assistant Attorney General for Civil Rights in 1993, a nomination that proved controversial and ultimately unsustainable. Guinier asks us to look beyond the current legal battles over the constitutionality and desirability of affirmative action programs to focus more attention on the conditions that produce inequality. Lack of racial and gender diversity in schools, public service, and employment is a sign that something is dangerously wrong, and desperately in need of fixing.

Racial or gender disproportion, Guinier argues, is like the proverbial miner's canary. Miners once relied on this sensitive bird to warn them of unsafe air and avoid the disaster of asphyxiation. To illustrate her point, Guinier cites the examples of women excluded from policing because of height requirements and African Americans dissuaded from college by costly student-loan requirements. A society that does not fully engage all of its members in the important tasks of its communal life, Guinier powerfully argues, is like that unhealthy coalmine—full of unnecessary dangers.

Recent years have seen a rising gap between rich and poor and a growing racial divide in income and net worth. These are global trends, and they are troubling. Robert Reich, a professor at the University of California at Berkeley and formerly Secretary of Labor under President Bill Clinton, addresses the question of whether the American economy will facilitate the effort to achieve a more just society, or will it prevent progress in that direction. He asks a simple, haunting question: Will our children live as well? In a time of economic turmoil and recession, this query could not be more pertinent. Will we be able to sustain the American Dream, the notion that hard work will allow anyone to achieve a middle-class lifestyle—if not for themselves, then for their children?

Reich traces the roots of the current deep economic recession to the 1970s, when hourly wages for men began to drop. The downward trend was at first masked by an increasing rate of women's employment and then by increased borrowing. But eventually the dimensions of the gap became clearer. An indication of the downward trend is the current vastly unequal distribution of wealth, with the top one percent taking home 34.6% of the national wealth in 2007, a proportion that increased to 35.6% two years later. The deep current recession can only be ended, Reich suggests, by investment in public goods—education, environment, transportation, health—that allow the poor to be more productive and thus better able to buy consumer goods. This "trickle-up" approach to the economy, Reich argues, is the key to providing a better life for our children, and it is a matter of social justice.

Institutions of government, as Reich points out, will have a significant say in whether our children live as well as their parents. In this context it is helpful to ask whether the decisions of the nation's highest court will help future generations live better. The Court is a dynamic institution, changing over time as its membership changes and in response to the demands of contemporary society. Linda Greenhouse, a well-known expert on the Supreme Court, offers her perspective in this volume. Greenhouse is knowledgeable about the Court's history and is thus in a position to offer insight about what to expect from it in the future. Like Anthony Lewis, she had a long and fruitful career with *The New York Times*, and like Lewis, she has been awarded the Pulitzer Prize for journalistic excellence.

Greenhouse writes here about how justices change in the course of their tenure on the Court. Drawing on her biography of Harry Blackmun and her knowledge of other justices, she argues that many Supreme Court justices do indeed significantly adjust their views in light of their lived experience. The changes are evident in their decisions, which often grow more skeptical of government assertions and more sensitive to the claims of individuals over time. This is true particularly for justices who have not worked in the nation's capitol prior to their appointment. The move to Washington, new friends, and the new position, Greenhouse speculates, make these justices more open to new ideas.

The final chapter is by Erwin Chemerinsky, Founding Dean of Law at the University of California, Irvine. Chemerinsky is an expert on the overlapping and sometimes conflicting powers of government at various levels. As he demonstrates, many of the most contentious social and constitutional issues facing us today—including debates over the constitutionality of Arizona's SB 1070, the individual mandate in the Affordable Care Act, and prohibitions on marriage equality for gays and lesbians—are framed in terms of states' rights. Yet as Chemerinsky argues persuasively, this type of hard-fought conflict between levels is not new. Drawing on earlier controversies, he shows that opponents of progressive change have often employed states' rights arguments to block legislation. A better approach, he suggests, is to consider our system of federalism as a way of empowering government to act at the appropriate level(s) to meet society's problems, rather than restraining the federal government from acting at all. As this essay and other contributions to *Law and the Quest for Justice* reveal so eloquently, we must learn from the past in order to most effectively meet current and future challenges.

In conclusion, this collection of essays examines the most hard-fought battles for justice in our country's history through the eyes of some of the nation's most acute social observers. These scholars speak from their own experience as expert observers and change-makers on the national and international scene. In the process, they remind us of the values and beliefs about justice that underlie the nation's founding. They clarify the risks to those values in social structures and institutions constructed to privilege some while excluding and disadvantaging others. They also remind us that in times of uncertainty and fear, when individuals and institutions feel threatened, there is a heightened risk that we will unnecessarily sacrifice civil rights and liberties. The most vulnerable among us, racial minorities, the poor, and the foreign-born, tend to lose the most in these situations.

Many of the authors learned these lessons from John P. Frank, the renowned legal scholar engaged in most of the major legal battles over the past century, including both *Brown v. Board of Education* and *Miranda v. Arizona*. The book concludes with an Afterword by John Frank's former partner, James Walsh, summarizing Frank's most notable achievements and his vision of a just society.

1

The Challenge of Achieving Racial Justice in the New Millennium

Charles J. Ogletree

Charles J. Ogletree is Jesse Climenko Professor of Law and Founding Director of the Charles Hamilton Houston Institute for Race and Justice at Harvard Law School. In 2008, the National Law Journal named Professor Ogletree one of the 50 Most Influential Minority Lawyers in America, and in 2009 he received the American Bar Association's Spirit of Excellence Award in recognition of his many contributions to the legal profession.

Contemporary discussions of justice and the challenges of achieving racial equality in the new millennium require us to straddle generational divides of meaning, knowledge and experience. As one means of crossing generational lines to talk about issues of race historically and contemporaneously, I will start with a scripture from the Bible: "The harvest has come, the summer has ended and we are not saved" (Jeremiah 8:20). It is, in a sense, one of the more prophetic sayings that relates to the issue of race in America. Some of us believe that the harvest has come, the summer has ended and we are in fact not saved. Some of us believe it is winter in America because of the way race is treated today. Some of us look back on the 20th century with a sense of frustration, disappointment, and a harsh dose of reality. We hear the echoes of W.E.B Du Bois, who told us: "The problem with the 20th century is the problem of the color line."[1] As the tortured history of race relations in America demonstrates, the problem of racism has not only persisted, but in some respects it has been exacerbated as we have moved into the 21st century.

The racial divide today can be graphically illustrated in the treatment of African Americans and others in the criminal justice system, and through our societal responses to issues of diversity and affirmative action. The problems are pervasive, but they are also capable of being resolved. It is well documented that minorities have been historically disadvantaged and excluded from participation in American society. As we look back, there has been some progress: we ended slavery and we were able to legally knock down Jim Crow laws. These things were very important. But we moved from these obvious racist practices to more subtle forms of discrimination, and race, racial discrimination and racial disparity are still very much central parts of the

---

[1] W.E.B. Du Bois, *The Souls of Black Folk* (Stilwell, KS: Digireads.com, 2005 (1st edition, Chicago: A.C. McClung & Co., 1903)), 11.

American landscape. The challenge is to not only acknowledge the benefits of racial progress over the centuries, but also to acknowledge the continuing burdens that race imposes on so many communities today.

The problems of race are national in character and are not limited to any one particular geographic community or any specific race or ethnicity. They are broad, powerful, and often overwhelming. Looking back historically, there are individuals in each generation who have captured the frustrations of the color line and confronted these powerful forces. For example, when we look back at the Declaration of Independence, which says *we hold these truths to be self evident that all men are created equal*, we recall the writing and advocacy of Frederick Douglass. Douglass was born a slave in Maryland. He was the product of a black woman and a white man—who probably was her master. Douglass would become a central figure in the abolition movement and a trusted friend of white abolitionists, even of the then soon-to-be president, Abraham Lincoln. After the Civil War, Douglass understood the goal was not simply racial integration. He also fought for the right for women to vote, saying that we all have to succeed if any of us are going to be successful.

In a powerful and eloquent address he gave one year on the Fourth of July, a time for this nation to celebrate its independence from England and celebrate the power of people, Douglass asked:

> What have I, or those I represent, to do with your national independence? Are the great principles of political freedom and of natural justice embodied in that Declaration of Independence? Do they extend to us? This Fourth of July is yours, not mine. What to the American slave is your Fourth of July? I answer: a day that reveals to him, more than any other day in the year, the gross injustice and constant cruelty in which he is the constant victim. To him, your celebration is a sham. Your boasted liberty an unholy license, your national greatness a swelling vanity, your sermons and thanksgiving, with all your religious parades and songs made to God, mere bombard, fraud, deception, impiety, hypocrisy, a thin veil to cover a crime which would disgrace a nation of savages. For revolting, barbarity, a shameless hypocrisy, America reigns without a rival.[2]

This speech was given in the early 19th century, before the end of slavery. Moving forward in time to the Emancipation Proclamation, many people thought that was the defining moment—of freeing the slaves, of promoting true equality and of striving towards racial equality in that millennium. And yet it did not create such equality.

W.E.B. Du Bois, one of the greatest philosophers of all time, had a differ-

---

[2] Frederick Douglass, "The Meaning of Fourth of July for the Negro: Speech at Rochester New York, July 5, 1852," *Frederick Douglass: Selected Speeches and Writings—The Library of Black America Series*, ed. P. S. Foner & Y. Taylor (Chicago: Lawrence Hill Books, 2000), 194.

ent view about the dilemma of race in America. What many people do not realize is that Du Bois, who was a native of Massachusetts, was a brilliant young man. At twelve years old he was a high school student and by the time he was fifteen, he was entering college at Fisk University. He also took up journalism, began to write for the *New York Globe*, and helped work in his local church. With a sophomore standing, he studied German, Greek, Latin, classical literature, philosophy, and other subjects. He then went on to Harvard and, in 1895, he became the first African American to receive a Ph.D. from Harvard. A few years later he wrote one of the most important books of our generation: *The Souls of Black Folk.* What he did, more than a century ago, is what we are doing now. He struggled with the issue of race: how do we choose between our black-ness and our American-ness? And he questioned why such a choice is necessary. He tried to answer these questions in powerful language that is as relevant in the 21st century as it was in the 20th century. Du Bois wrote:

> . . . the Negro is a sort of seventh son, born with a veil and gifted with second sight in this American world—a world which yields him no true self-consciousness, but only lets him see himself through the revelation of the other world. It is a peculiar sensation, this double-consciousness, this sense of always looking at one's self through the eyes of others, of measuring one's soul by the tape of a world that looks on in amused contempt and pity. One ever feels his twoness,—an American, a Negro; two souls, two thoughts, two unreconciled strivings; two warring ideals in one dark body, whose dogged strength alone keeps it from being torn asunder.[3]

Du Bois fought with the dilemmas imposed by racist structures and tried to change America. He was unsuccessful, though, and so disappointed by his inability to make America an equal nation with justice for all that he left the country, never to return. Yet, he is tied to this history of racial equality. Many people do not know the sad irony that August 28, 1963—the day blacks and whites, Jews and gentiles, women and men marched in Washington, D.C.—was the day that W.E.B Du Bois died. He did not die in this country, but rather as a lonely, broken man in Ghana, where he went to try to achieve the American dream. Roy Wilkins, who was one of the announcers at the march in Washington that day, announced it was Du Bois's voice calling people together. On that day, we had lost Du Bois, but we had Dr. King, who took us forward.

So many who talk about Dr. King and the progress we have made only listened to the second half of his speech. We go home cheering the great dream of equality, of character, of other values, of a true American dream and we always remember King for that speech, but what we forget is that what

---

3 Du Bois 7.

King said in 1963 is still relevant today. Almost 50 years ago, he said: "We cannot be satisfied as long as the Negro in Mississippi cannot vote and a Negro in New York believes he has nothing for which to vote."[4] That is what King said in 1963, yet the dilemma is as real today as it was then.[5]

The challenge to achieving racial equality and racial justice in the 21st century requires us to take a serious look at the criminal justice system. With as much progress as we have made in the last decade, we recognize that today there are still more black men in jails and prisons than enrolled in colleges in America, and incarceration rates of African Americans continue to increase disproportionately to the rates of incarceration for the majority population. Indeed, although African Americans only represent 13 percent of the population, they nevertheless represent 38 percent of today's prison population.[6]

The numbers are simply staggering and it is a crisis that must be addressed. Beyond the numbers, we see also the disproportionally harsh treatment of minorities in the juvenile justice system, which is so destructive to black communities. Black children are disproportionally targeted for arrests, drug offenses, and non-drug related offenses.[7] Black youth are more likely to be arrested, charged, prosecuted as adults, and sentenced to confinement than their white counterparts. As of April 2000, the Youth Law Center and the National Center for Crime and Delinquency's Building Blocks for Youth initiative reported that three out of every four youths committed to adult prisons are minorities, even though the majority of arrests involve white youths.[8] Despite the fact that drug use rates among blacks and whites are substantially similar, blacks are arrested substantially more, prosecuted substantially more, and receive sentences that are substantially longer.[9] And while incarceration rates are highest for black males, black women's rates of contact with the criminal justice system are skyrocketing. African Americans are now subjected to more racial profiling and racially disparate outcomes than any other group.[10]

Racial disparities in the criminal justice system, and racial profiling in

---

[4] Martin Luther King, *I Have a Dream* (New York: Scholastic Inc., 1963, 2007), 18.

[5] Charles J. Ogletree, *All Deliberate Speed: Reflections on the First Half-Century of Brown v. Board of Education* (New York: W.W. Norton and Co., 2004).

[6] The Sentencing Project, *Reducing Racial Disparity in the Criminal Justice System*, 2nd ed. (Washington, D.C., 2008). See also Michelle Alexander, *The New Jim Crow: Mass Incarceration in the Age of Colorblindness* (New York: The New Press, 2010) and Bruce Western, *Punishment and Inequality in America* (New York: Russell Sage, 2006).

[7] Eileen Poe-Yamagata and Michael A. Jones, *And Justice for Some* (Washington, DC: National Center for Crime and Delinquency, 2000).

[8] See Youth Law Center reports online at the YLC website: http://www.ylc.org/resources.php.

[9] Alexander op cit.

[10] Charles J. Ogletree, *The Presumption of Guilt: The Arrest of Henry Louis Gates, Jr. and Race, Class and Crime in America* (New York: Palgrave MacMillan, 2010).

particular, are difficult issues to address. My students will often respond, saying, "What you are telling us is that the criminal justice system is racist and that it treats people unfairly because of their race." I say, "That's not right. We have to look at this intellectually, empirically, and we have to use the data properly. We cannot simply conclude that race is what causes people to be profiled." And I tell them, "Every one of these examples is based on a true case. Customs officials do not stop people because they are black or brown. It has nothing to do with their race. After all, the courts have told us—in case after case, circuit after circuit, and state after state—it has nothing to do with race. They are stopped because, when they bought a ticket, they used cash or a check or a credit card. It has nothing to do with race. In fact, the reason they are arrested is because they are traveling with absolutely no luggage, or a lot of luggage, or a small amount of luggage that isn't noticed. It has nothing to do with race." I tell my students, "People are stopped, not because of race, but because they are the first off the plane, or the last off the plane, or somewhere in the middle of the plane so as to not be detected. It has nothing to do with race. People are flagged, not because they are flying, but because they are flying from a drug infested city, or to a drug infested city, or over a drug infested city." These are completely neutral factors, right?

David Cole has written a book filled with examples of racial profiling cases involving black suspects.[11] In each case, authorities argued that the stops were justified because people arrived late at night, arrived early in the morning, arrived in the afternoon, made reservations on short notice, purchased a ticket at the airport, bought a first class ticket, bought a coach ticket, used a one-way ticket, or used a round-trip ticket. The prosecutions were legitimate, we are told, because these black or brown individuals traveled alone, traveled with a companion, acted too nervous, acted too calm, made eye contact with the police officer, avoided making eye contact with the police officer, wore expensive clothing and jewelry, dressed casually, went to the restroom after deplaning, avoided the restroom after deplaning, walked quickly through the airport, walked slowly through the airport, walked aimlessly through the airport, and left the airport by a taxi cab, or limousine, or a private car, or a hotel courtesy van. So clearly it is not about race.

Ultimately we see that these issues of criminality are tainted by race, racial bias and prejudice; race becomes quite powerful and its impacts, prevalent. How, then, do we pursue a remedy that will allow us to truly achieve racial equality and racial justice in the new millennium? Do we pursue a course of being color blind, color conscious, or is there a third alternative? There are a number of people who have thought about it. Randall Kennedy suggested one proposal, which is instructive, though I ultimately disagree

---

11 David Cole, *No Equal Justice: Race and Class in the American Criminal Justice System* (New York: The New Press, 1999).

with him. Kennedy's view is that we must have a racially blind society in order to achieve racial justice, and one of the prime examples in our criminal justice system is capital punishment. Like many Americans, Kennedy does not believe that capital punishment is wrong in theory. But, he argues that it is acceptable only when it is enforced in a color-blind manner. He characterizes his view as a *victim-centered approach*, which shifts attention from African American criminals towards African American victims who suffer as a result of crime.[12] Accordingly to Kennedy, *McCleskey v. Kemp*,[13] which was one of the major cases on race and the death penalty, was wrongly decided not because it failed to value the life of the black criminal, Warren McCleskey, but because it failed to value the lives of black victims. Kennedy's color-blind argument is that more black murderers should receive the death penalty.

This line of thought colors Kennedy's discussion of the appropriate response to crack cocaine as well. He contends with equal force that the courts may be doing the black community a favor, and certainly not doing anything unconstitutional, by punishing African Americans more severely than whites based on the differential in sentencing for crack and powdered cocaine. He suggested the harsher punishment empowers the black community and advocates that more punishment will lead to more equality. I reject this notion because it exacerbates the harm while not solving the problem.[14]

Others have picked up on Kennedy's arguments and take them a step further. Dinesh D'Souza, for example, does not believe that policing in the African American community should be free from racial bias. Instead, he argues that the racial stereotypes used by police may be justified because they are rational or efficient. He argues, and is quoted as saying, that since policemen know from experience that blacks, especially young African American males, are more likely to commit street crimes than whites, they may practice a kind of "rational discrimination."[15] This does not mean that they should arrest young blacks simply for being black, but rather, they are more predisposed to see young blacks as potential criminals and thus show some bias in the way they pursue some criminals and not others. It is precisely this intellectual arrogance and hypocrisy that leads many police officers to engage in practices that become a self-fulfilling prophecy: the more blacks they arrest, the more blacks they think they should arrest because they begin to see black people as more criminally inclined, so they arrest more blacks which further

---

[12] Randall Kennedy, *Race, Crime, and the Law* (New York: Vintage Books, 1997).

[13] *McCleskey v. Kemp*, 481 U.S. 279 (1987).

[14] Charles J. Ogletree and Austin Sarat, *From Lynch Mobs to the Killing State: Race and the Death Penalty in America* (New York: New York University Press, 2006); *see also* Ogletree, *The Presumption of Guilt: The Arrest of Henry Louis Gates, Jr. and Race, Class and Crime in America* (New York: Palgrave Macmillan, 2010).

[15] Dinesh D'Souza, *The End of Racism* (New York: Free Press, 1995).

reinforces their belief in black criminality, and so on.[16]

In contrast to Kennedy and D'Souza, who argue for color-blindness or for explicit, "rational" bias, Paul Butler promotes a race conscious criminal justice system. He argues that the abuse of discretion along racial lines in the criminal justice system should be fought by what he calls *black power*; that is, that the black community should engage in self-help strategies to exert whatever influence it may have to balance the scales of justice. He suggests that criminal conduct among African Americans is often a predictable reaction to oppression. Sometimes, black crime is a symptom of internalized white supremacy. Other times, it is a reasonable response to the racial and economic subordination African Americans face every day. Punishing black people for the fruits of racism is wrong, he argues, yet this is the effect of punishment premised on a theory of just desserts. Instead, Butler argues for a new race conscious paradigm as follows:

> For pragmatic and political reasons, the black community is better off when some nonviolent law breakers remain in the community than go to prison. The decision of what kind of conduct by African Americans ought to be punished is better made by African Americans themselves based on the costs and benefits to their community.

He continues, stating:

> Legally, the doctrine of jury nullification gives the power to African American jurors to make this kind of decision when they sit in judgment of African American defendants. Considering the cost of law enforcement to the black community and the failure of white law makers to devise significant non-incarcerative responses to black anti-social conduct, it is the moral responsibility of black jurors to emancipate some guilty black outlaws.

Thus, he concludes, in order to make the system work and eliminate biases, blacks should acquit other blacks on the basis of race.[17]

Both Kennedy and Butler, in my view, overstate the significance of remedies. We cannot be completely color blind, and we cannot be completely color conscious. In both instances, the black community suffers. A community that suffers from increased criminalization suffers fundamental problems and those need to be addressed. And yet, the black community should not have to choose between its interest in security, in making sure it is free of violence and crime, and its interest in liberty, in making sure the community is not the subject of police profiling and police brutality. We should be treated like any

---

[16] Ogletree, *The Presumption of Guilt* (2010).

[17] Paul Butler, "Racially Based Jury Nullifications: Black Power in the Criminal Justice System," *Yale Law Journal* 105: 677 (1995), 679.

other members of the community: equally and justly under the law. We also have to think of remedies that emanate from our homes and communities.

When we think of the racial divide in the 21st century, we must develop constructive and meaningful solutions. We have to engage in serious self-diagnosis: what are our own individual and personal biases that prevent us from seeing the fact that we have societal problems that each of us must contribute to solving? We must make sure that we do not see criminality or drugs as a matter of race, but as a matter of crime, and that we do not label people because of their neighborhood or because of their address, or because of their ethnicity or race. We should identify examples of where people have come together and dealt with issues of race constructively and seriously, whether in South Africa with the Truth and Reconciliation Commissions, or in other parts of the world where people have been willing to accept differences in order to create stronger communities.

We also have to teach our children that they, too, are an integral part of this society. We must avoid or resolve problems that we were warned about 50 years ago. For example, when Thurgood Marshall and Charles Hamilton Houston went into the courts around the country trying to end racial segregation, they were confronted with the system after Jim Crow laws, where the schools were segregated on the basis of race and it was a perfectly legal system. Across the country, many of the same schools that were integrated in the 1940s, 1950s, and 1960s are more segregated in the 21st century than they were 50 years ago.

But we can achieve a solution to this problem of racial injustice in the new millennium if we do some important things. For instance, we have to stop the abandonment of our urban public schools. Lack of resources in our public schools results in white flight to the suburbs, and in white parents withdrawing their children from public schools. But equally pernicious and confounding, the black middle class is also leaving those same urban centers, draining those schools not only of their children's talent, but also of the resources from their pocketbooks. In this we have all collectively failed our children—failed to see that the public school system is one of our ways for redemption and renewal. We can and must reverse this trend.

Each of us plays an individual and collective role in supporting racial diversity in the new millennium. We have to go back to Emma Lazarus' 1883 statement, now inscribed in the base of Lady Liberty: "Give me your tired, your poor, your huddle masses yearning to be free." That statement is a symbol of what America is supposed to be—a welcoming, nurturing, opened-arms country, committed to democracy and equity for all. Even today, when we look at our immigration policy, we see it is racially charged. The public outcry in 2000 over the return of Cuban born Elián Gonzales might lead one to believe that the United States in the 21st century had realized the aspirations it had for immigration in the 20th century, but that is not true. Elián

Gonzales was an illegal immigrant, but we have a policy that allows Cubans who come to this country to stay if they reach land. At the same time, we also have a policy that forces Haitians who come to this country to be deported upon reaching land. That policy is based on race—it is not based on reason and it cannot be rational to have such a policy in the 21st century.

We should look skeptically at those who talk about economic policies being racially neutral when, at the same time, millions of black and brown people cannot find work. From the federal to local governments, we have to change our attitude towards race and make sure that we open our doors to those who are in need of shelter, those yearning to be free, and that we critically address the disparate impacts of seemingly racially-neutral language and policy.

It will be an enormous challenge to achieve racial diversity in the 21st century. However, unlike Derrick Bell, I do not think that racism is permanent.[18] I think it is serious. It is a disease, but it can be cured by people saying that, collectively and individually, we will do everything we can to ensure that justice in American does not mean *just-us*, but that it means justice for all of us.

I hope that our grandchildren and their children will be able to stand up and say: *My country 'tis of thee, sweet land of liberty, of thee I sing.* I hope they will sing these words and not know that sense of two-ness that Du Bois wrote of; that they will sing these words of freedom, of sweetness and inclusion and feel their truth down to their core. I hope they will be able to say that we are one people, one nation under God. I hope they will be able to say that we believe that we will be judged, not by the color of our skin, or the ethnic nature of our language, but by the character of our content. I hope they will be judged, not by who we think they are, but by whom they prove themselves to be. Ultimately, I hope they will be judged not from where they are, but from where they started and by how far they have come. We as a nation can achieve true racial diversity by making sure that each and every one of us makes that commitment. It is a dream in this land that if we survive for one, we must survive for all. More than a century ago, Frederick Douglass said: "If there is no struggle, there is no progress."[19] If, like Douglass said, we want crops, we have to plow up the ground; if we want rain, we have to accept that there will be thunder and the lightning; if we want the ocean, we must be willing to hear the roar of its many waters. And if we want to achieve racial justice in the 21st century, we have to do the work.

---

[18] Derrick Bell, *Race, Racism and American Law* (6th ed.) (New York: Little, Brown and Co., 2008), and see his *Faces at the Bottom of the Well: The Permanence of Racism* (New York: Basic Books, 1992).

[19] Frederick Douglass, "West India Emancipation: Speech delivered at Canandaigua, New York, August 3, 1857," *Frederick Douglass: Selected Speeches and Writings—The Library of Black America Series,* ed. P. S. Foner & Y. Taylor (Chicago: Lawrence Hill Books, 2000), 367.

2

Brown v. Board After 50:
Still Contested, Still Right

Jack Greenberg

Jack Greenberg is professor of law at Columbia University Law School. He served as assistant counsel to Thurgood Marshall at the NAACP Legal Defense and Educational Fund and later as its director-counsel. He has briefed and argued 40 cases in the U.S. Supreme Court, including Brown v. Board of Education. *Greenberg is a Fellow of the American Academy of Arts and Sciences and a recipient of the Presidential Citizens Medal.*

Brown v. Board of Education[1] has been a success story. This case made history when it overturned the doctrine of separate but equal, ushering in a new era of school desegregation. *Brown* celebrated its fiftieth anniversary in 2004 and we—justifiably—sang its praises, then and now. But like most successes, it has been incomplete. Seizing on what it has failed to accomplish, as well as imaginary shortcomings, the inevitable historical revisionists have emerged. They have been proclaiming a catalog of failures, which have sometimes attracted more attention than *Brown*'s achievements. In this essay I will address what *Brown* contributed to the national good, the claims that it has fallen short, and what history might have been if *Plessy v. Ferguson*[2] and its legitimization of segregation had been reaffirmed. I will also speculate a bit about the future.

Fiftieth Anniversary Acclaim

2004 was a year of popular acclaim for *Brown*. Even President Bush, never before noted as a fan of school desegregation, marked its fiftieth anniversary in Topeka at the school that was the subject of one of the cases grouped into the *Brown* litigation. It seems that every educational institution in the country, from elementary schools upward, churches, politicians, judges, entertainers, and almost all public voices praised the decision. I spoke at elementary and high schools, colleges, law schools, courthouses, judicial conferences, museums and elsewhere. My talks were an infinitesimally small fraction of all the attention lavished on the case. And with good reason. Although there was no such consensus fifty years ago, there surely is consensus now as to the rightness of *Brown* (with the few possible outliers who continue to hold to

---

[1] *Brown v. Board of Education of Topeka*, 347 U.S. 483 (1954).

[2] *Plessy v. Ferguson*, 163 U.S. 537 (1896).

racist ideals of separation). Nevertheless, despite this modern consensus, there is also what I call *a sour obbligato of disapproval.* Some have argued that *Brown* made no difference and that *Brown* made race relations worse. And there are those few who claim that the country would have been better off with a reaffirmation of *Plessy v. Ferguson,* the jurisprudential charter of separate-but-equal.

There are, of course, many commentators who have changed sides over the course of time and political evolutions. Take the Southern press, which at first virulently denounced the decision. Over the last fifty years, news media in the Southern states have done a 180-degree turnaround. *The Jackson Daily News* (Mississippi) had editorialized in 1954 that "Mississippi will never consent to placing White and Negro children in the same public schools."[3] But its successor, *The Clarion-Ledger,* wrote in 2004, "[I]nclusive, diverse schools [are] not just an ideal, but a necessity for a healthy society."[4] In 1954 the editor of the *Richmond News Leader,* James J. Kilpatrick, wrote of *Brown*: "[W]e do not accept it willingly, or cheerfully or philosophically."[5] But leaping forward to 2004 this newspaper proudly described it as a sign of the long national road that the nation had travelled in the past 50 years. Again, in 1954 the *Birmingham News* wrote: "States' rights which underlay the superseded [*Plessy v. Ferguson*] decision of 1896 still apply." But in 2004 it wrote: "Fifty years after separate was ruled unequal ... [W]hat has changed? To the shame of this great nation and this great state, too little." Other major Southern newspapers echoed these turnarounds.

The Future as Seen from 1954

When *Brown* was decided, Thurgood Marshall observed that there were 200 counties in Georgia and he speculated that we would have to file a school desegregation suit in each. He did not expect quick acquiescence, but thought that over time, perhaps over a long period of time, there would be compliance in the South. He and those around him, including myself, were not even contemplating *Brown*'s application in the North. But we had seriously underestimated the vehemence of the reaction to *Brown* in the South.

Marshall hadn't imagined, as no one could, that there would be a Congressional Manifesto in which all but three Southern members of the House and Senate denounced the Supreme Court. Nor did he expect Declarations of Interposition and Nullification, which echoed Southern defiance back on the eve of the Civil War. He did not anticipate State Sovereignty Commissions, well-funded state agencies that devoted their resources to fighting desegrega-

---

3 Fred Sullens, Editorial, *The Jackson Daily News,* May 18, 1954.

4 *The Clarion-Ledger,* Editorial, May 16, 2004, p. G4.

5 For more on Kilpatrick's writings against *Brown,* see Raymond Wolters, *Race and Education* (Columbia, MO: University of Missouri Press, 2008).

tion in all imaginable ways. There were laws requiring that schools be closed if a Black student were admitted; campaigns to impeach Earl Warren; pupil assignment laws that placed administrative obstacles in the way of Black children changing schools; and governmental efforts to put the NAACP and the Legal Defense Fund out of business along with lawsuits and criminal prosecutions that prohibited or punished civil rights activities. There were also state legislative investigations that harassed civil rights proponents and disbarment proceedings against lawyers and the like.

Nor did we anticipate interminable litigation in each individual case. Nor had we expected that federal judges, with a handful of exceptions, would, for all practical purposes, be far from avid in their pursuit of justice. Some were lukewarm in this endeavor, while others were outright defiant of the Supreme Court's and appellate-court decisions. Against this opposition, almost no desegregation took place for a decade and a half. In response to all this opposition, *Brown* and Southern resistance fighters helped to create a Civil Rights Movement that developed and flourished. The Freedom Rides were an embodied manifestation of *Brown*. The first Freedom Ride was scheduled to reach its destination in New Orleans on May 17, the anniversary of the case. Martin Luther King Jr. held prayer pilgrimages every May 17 and regularly extolled the virtues of the Supreme Court's decision. Many of the sit-in demonstrators said *Brown* inspired them. The Montgomery bus boycott was precipitated by activist Rosa Parks, a NAACP official who was steeped in *Brown*. The Supreme Court invalidated the Montgomery segregation ordinance in a *per curium* opinion that relied solely on *Brown*.

Nevertheless, the Southern states defended segregation fiercely on grounds such as federalism, separation of powers, legal history, Black pathology, disease, crime and so forth. They never once admitted that it was morally right. Finally, in an effort to establish that might makes right, segregationists put up physical resistance, which was crushed at Little Rock, the University of Mississippi and several dozen lesser venues. It became clear that opponents could not succeed in a physical war against the rule of law.

This history was the predicate for enacting the Civil Rights Acts of 1964. While one cannot claim that the Civil Rights Act never would have been enacted without *Brown*, it certainly would not have occurred as soon as it did without *Brown* as a legal and moral guidepost. *Brown*, of course, was a school case on its face, but it was more than that: it was a factor in reshaping society. By 1969 it had began to make a difference in the schools. That year the Supreme Court decided in *Alexander v. Holmes County*[6] that schools must desegregate immediately, and to a considerable extent they did. Not long after *Alexander,* perhaps half the Black school population began attending integrated schools, following which there was an immediate jump in the conven-

---

[6] *Alexander v. Holmes County Board of Education,* 396 U.S. 19 (1969).

tional measures of academic achievement among these students. The evidence was beginning to accumulate that Black children do better academically in integrated settings, and also in negotiating their way through society. After *Brown* and desegregation, a higher percentage of Black students went to college and otherwise achieved success. This is sometimes disparaged as a claim that a Black child is said to learn more by sitting alongside a White child. Rather, it is a function of disadvantaged children benefiting from association with others who have had better opportunities. They shared some of their experience with their classmates.

Despite progress over the past few decades, school desegregation has gone into sharp decline. The Black and Hispanic urban populations have grown larger and have become concentrated in urban centers. Whites have moved increasingly into the suburbs. You cannot do a lot of desegregation when there are no Whites with whom to integrate. And at the same time, legal doctrine has evolved in ways that have made desegregation less and less possible. The Supreme Court has failed to push integration. In the first Detroit school case, *Milliken v. Bradley*,[7] the Supreme Court prohibited crossing the city-suburb line as a means of integration. Then in the Oklahoma City school case, *Dowell v. Oklahoma City Board of Education*,[8] the Court held that once a system has been successfully desegregated, the injunction that ordered desegregation may be dissolved. This means, for all practical purposes, that a district may slip back into segregation and nothing can be done about it in the courts, absent new litigation.[9]

The Legacy of *Brown*

It was only recently that I came to understand that *Brown* was not primarily a school segregation case. It had to be more than that. How could *Brown*, by itself, have desegregated schools in the era of the Congressional Manifesto and associated depredations? The political environment had to be changed. *Brown* was a critical factor in that change. And change has indeed occurred. We now have 40 Black members of Congress.[10] Every large city and many small cities have had a Black mayor. The CEOs of American Express, Citigroup, Merrill Lynch, Time Warner, Xerox and other major corporations are or have been Black. When I began practicing law, there were some states with only a single Black lawyer. Now there are close to 10,000 Black law students

---

[7] *Milliken v. Bradley*, 418 U.S. 717 (1974).

[8] *Board of Education of Oklahoma City Public Schools v. Dowell*, 498 U.S. 237 (1991).

[9] See also *Parents Involved in Community Schools v. Seattle School District No. 1*, 551 U.S. 701 (2007) (incorporating the decision for *Meredith v. Jefferson County Board of Education* (2007)). In this split decision, the Supreme Court struck down desegregation efforts in both Seattle and in Jefferson County, Kentucky.

[10] As of 2012, there were 44 African American members of Congress, all of them in the House of Representatives, along with the country's first Black president, Barack Obama.

throughout the country.[11] Universities across the country, including the South, are integrated to a considerable extent by affirmative action. Constance Baker Motley was recently at the University of Mississippi, where she had litigated the *Meredith*[12] case. After her visit she described it as the most well integrated school in the country.

Brown's effects went beyond race as well. The notion of equality grew to accommodate claims for equality without regard to gender, ethnicity, sexual preference, disability, age, and so on. I have likened the situation in the United States before *Brown* to a frozen sea. Southern members of Congress controlled the committees of the House and Senate. Their hegemony depended on keeping Blacks from voting. They exploited what they called their *tradition* of White supremacy to stay in control. *Brown* was like an icebreaker ship, breaking a pathway through that frozen sea. When I suggested this metaphor to a friend who is a scholar of Kafka, he told me that Supreme Court Justice Robert H. Jackson used a similar metaphor in describing the path-breaking role of the Nuremberg trials. Jackson told his staff that they had to produce "an ice pick to break up the frozen sea within us."[13]

The picture we see today is mixed: Big advances coexist with Black unemployment that is double of the rate for Whites.[14] A quarter of all Blacks and 30% of Black children live in poverty.[15] Black male longevity in Harlem is less than that in Bangladesh.[16] Half the prisoners in America are Black.[17] And other indicia of subordinate status abound. Opening that path through the frozen sea made possible massive gains in human rights in America. But, ironically, schools gained least. Urban residential segregation increased as Whites moved to the suburbs. The Supreme Court held that courts could not require integration between city and suburb. School integration declined. Other court decisions allowed school systems to dissolve earlier court-ordered integration programs, which further reduced integration. Most integration

---

[11] For updated enrollment statistics, see The American Bar Association website, at: http://www.abanet.org/legaled/statistics/charts/stats%20-%2013.pdf.

[12] *Meredith v. Fair*, 298 F.2d 696 (5th Cir. 1962).

[13] For discussion, see Thomas Lambert, "Recalling the War Crimes Trials of World War II," *Military Law Review,* vol. 149:15 (1995). Jackson may have found the metaphor in Kafka who wrote in a letter to Oskar Pollack on January 27, 1904 that "a book must be the axe for the frozen sea within us."

[14] United States Bureau of Labor Statistics, *Labor Force Characteristics by Race and Ethnicity,* United States Department of Labor, Office of Employment and Unemployment Statistics, Division of Labor Force Statistics (Washington, D.C., 2009), at http://www.bls.gov/cps/cpsrace2009.pdf.

[15] National Poverty Center, 2011, at http://www.npc.umich.edu/poverty/#4.

[16] L. R. Jacobs and J. A. Morone, "Health and Wealth: Our Appalling Health Inequality Reflects and Reinforces Society's Other Gaps," *The American Prospect,* June 2004, at A20.

[17] Michelle Alexander, *The New Jim Crow: Mass Incarceration in the Age of Colorblindness* (New York: The New Press, 2010).

exists in small towns and rural areas. *Brown* has not integrated schools in large minority urban areas. Moreover, those schools are often woefully inadequate.

The failure to achieve full integration and equal opportunity for minority students in the wake of *Brown* has enabled critics to subordinate the great gains that this case did achieve. These critics focus on what remains to be done. Some have dismissed the decision as useless, and even harmful. Some argue that equalization, not integration, should have been the remedy. Much of the dissatisfaction has been expressed from within the legal academy. This is not as strange as it might seem. Few scholars attract notice, acclaim or tenure by embracing Supreme Court opinions. One does much better by pointing out what was wrong, not what was right. That means that the reflexive academic response is to look for what was wrong. Even those who approve the outcome are not likely to write unless they can demonstrate what they think is a better way to arrive at the same result: *man bites dog* gets more attention than *dog bites man*. Nevertheless, the nay-sayers have attracted what I believe is disproportionate attention.

The most influential critic of *Brown* wrote soon after the case was decided. His influence has extended beyond the academy as far as the world of politics. I am referring to Herbert Wechsler's "Towards Neutral Principles of Constitutional Law," one of the most famous law review articles of all time. Wechsler, a towering scholar, professor of Law at Columbia, director of the American Law Institute, chief reporter of the Model Penal Code, one of the pre-eminent figures in constitutional law, was personally opposed to racial segregation. This added to the hubbub created by the article he wrote questioning the legitimacy of *Brown* because it required Whites, over their objection, to attend school with Blacks. To him, the central issue was one of freedom of association. He wrote:

> Where the state must practically choose between denying the association to those individuals who wish it or imposing it on those who would avoid it, is there a basis in neutral principles for holding that the Constitution demands that the claims for association should prevail? I should like to think there is, but I confess that I have not yet written the opinion. To write it is for me the challenge of the school-segregation cases.[18]

The article was taken by many to confer legitimacy on massive resistance, although Wechsler denounced such opposition.

Charles Black wrote a powerful response to Wechsler, "The Lawfulness of the Segregation Decisions," which was informed by his upbringing as a Southerner who had seen how Blacks were treated under segregation: "If a

---

[18] Herbert Wechsler, "Towards Neutral Principles of Constitutional Law," *Harvard Law Review* 73:1 (1959), 34.

whole race of people finds itself confined within a system which is set up and continued for the very purpose of keeping it in an inferior station and if the question is then solemnly propounded whether such a race is being treated 'equally,' I think we ought to exercise one of the sovereign prerogatives of philosophers–that of laughter."[19]

While Black's article is well known, it created nothing like the éclat of Wechsler's *Neutral Principles*. Nevertheless, within the next ten years, Wechsler had effectively accepted Black's argument, though he never stated that Black's article was the reason. Wechsler found *Brown* to be more acceptable when seen as a decision against segregation prescribed by law. His later thinking on this topic, however, is virtually unknown. Again we see that *Man bites dog* sells more papers than *dog bites man*.

A half-century later, we still find within the academy a core of disapproval of *Brown*. One group argues, as Wechsler did, that the opinion was poorly reasoned and did not justify its conclusion that segregation is unconstitutional. Another strain does not believe that the decision contributed to improving the status of Blacks. These critics say that anything positive that followed *Brown* would have happened anyway. Yet, another argument has been that the decision made Blacks worse off, by stirring up massive resistance. One opinion has been that separate-but-really equal would have been a better ruling. Another group published a volume entitled, *What Brown v. Board of Education Should Have Said.*[20] These authors agree that school segregation was unconstitutional, but claim that they could have written a better opinion than Earl Warren's. Most of these second-opinion writers would have overruled *Plessy* explicitly, rather than implicitly, as *Brown* did. In *Brown*, the Supreme Court did not overrule *Plessy* in so many words, although within a week of the decision, it indicated that *Brown* did have that effect. The reason the justices did not overrule it outright in their initial opinion probably had to do with obtaining unanimity on the Court.[21] Another *Brown* author wannabe would have written that the Fourteenth Amendment originally was intended to prohibit school segregation, as revealed in its legislative history. This is nothing new—the *Brown* plaintiffs argued this because the Court had inquired about legislative history. The opinion did not develop this point because the Court had decided that the historical evidence

---

[19] Charles L. Black, "The Lawfulness of the Segregation Decisions," *Yale Law Journal* 69: 421 (1960), 424.

[20] Jack M. Balkin, ed., *What Brown v. Board of Education Should Have Said: The Nation's Top Legal Experts Rewrite America's Landmark Civil Rights Decision* (New York: New York University Press, 2002).

[21] One revised opinion invoked the privileges and immunities clause; *Brown* did not because the plaintiffs had not argued it, or at least did not argue it energetically. The Supreme Court had pretty much eviscerated the privileges and immunities clause in the *Slaughterhouse Cases* (83 U.S. 36 (1873)). The plaintiffs would have been arguing against that precedent, while they had good equal protection precedent upon which they could rely.

was inconclusive, as indeed it was.

One of the most frequent objections to *Brown* was to the Court's use of social science materials. This criticism is unfair. The Court did not rely on plaintiffs' social-science evidence, but merely referred to it. Why? Because *Plessy* (the case that had allowed segregation) had made assertions within the realm of the social sciences: *Plessy* stated that plaintiffs claimed that segregation had stamped them with a badge of inferiority, to which the Court replied that if that were so, it was "because the colored race chooses to put that construction upon it." In *Brown* the Court used social science to refute that empirical claim. Social science by 1954 had demonstrated that indeed segregation imposed a badge of inferiority. But, in legal terms, the Court did not find this as a fact. It merely observed that *Plessy's* unsubstantiated assertion was in conflict with contemporary evidence.

Nevertheless, a small band among the *Brown* rejectionists has persisted in a *sour obbligato* of disapproval. One argument among them is that *Brown* made no difference. Another group in the rejection front claims that *Brown* made things worse by stirring up massive resistance. They say historical forces would have ended segregation. Other rejectionists, principally Derrick Bell, would have dissented from the judgment in *Brown*. Bell argues that while segregation is despicable, *Brown* should not have required school desegregation. Separate but equal should have remained in place, but it should have been enforced strictly, with Black citizens playing a role in school governance and on committees in charge of equalization. According to Bell, there should have been a three-year time limit for reaching equality. This would have made segregation so expensive that school boards would have decided to integrate voluntarily. In the meantime, Black children would have received the benefit of equal, though separate, education. He does not say what would have followed if the cost of separate but equal education, strictly enforced, did not lead to integration.[22] Presumably courts would then have required integration. But then they would have been back to where they had started. Or, perhaps, they would have slogged away at attempting to enforce equalization.

Brown endorsers, among whom I stand, argue that *Brown* made a huge difference to the benefit of African Americans. Rejecting segregation and *Plessy* was integral to its message. If the Court had told the world that segregation is acceptable, that message would not have carried the moral force that inspired the sit-in demonstrators or the freedom riders. *Brown's* "all deliberate speed" implementation decision carried a sense of accepting segregation temporarily and was denounced, rightly, for that reason. In contrast, Bell's

---

[22] Derrick A. Bell, "Dissenting," in *What Brown v. Board of Education Should Have Said: The Nation's Top Legal Experts Rewrite America's Landmark Civil Rights Decision*, ed. Jack M. Balkin (New York: New York University Press, 2002): 185-206.

separate-but-equal solution not only embraces segregation, but allows it to serve as a platform for rejecting the central thesis of *Brown*.

But what if the opportunity that *Brown* presented had been lost? Or if separate but equal had been reaffirmed? What then? A lot of supposition must enter any such assessment. The rejectionists assume that civil rights would have been realized. But in my vision, history would have unfolded differently. The nay-sayers and I start from a common base. We agree that World War II, the Holocaust, the Universal Declaration of Human Rights, the massive North-South migration of Blacks, the role of Black voters in electing Truman, the recommendation of Truman's Committee on Civil Rights that segregation be prohibited, the Cold War, anti-colonialism—all contributed to the atmosphere in which the Court decided *Brown*. Legal doctrine had evolved in graduate and professional school cases to become a platform for *Brown*.

But the critics and I then go in different directions. They assume segregation would have withered and died. I disagree. Since one counterfactual history deserves another, here is mine. In this imagined counterfactual history, I will start with an imaginary opinion by Justice Reed ruling in favor of segregation. (He would have been the most likely dissenter in the actual decision.) First, his treatment of precedent: He would have cited *Plessy v Ferguson* as the legal grounds for upholding segregation. He would have then cited the Supreme Court's decision in *Gong Lum v. Rice*,[23] where the Court unanimously decided that the separate-but-equal principle applied to schools (thus barring the Chinese plaintiff from attending the local White-only school). On the Court at that time sat Justices Holmes, Brandeis and Stone, three of the greatest jurists the country has known. Later cases required graduate and professional schools to admit "colored" people because alternative "colored schools" were inferior, but they never held segregation unconstitutional. I imagine that Reed would have cited these precedents to reaffirm segregation.

While in the real world under *Brown*, plaintiffs' expert witnesses testified that segregation harms Black children by impairing their ability to learn, in the imaginary opinion, the Court would have held that social scientific studies are not a reliable basis for interpreting or applying the Constitution. The Court would have reasoned that it would be absurd to decide in one case that segregation is unconstitutional, but not in another, where different witnesses might testify using different studies.

As to constitutional history and the issue of whether segregation would have withered on its own in due time, there is little supportive evidence. The debates and documents of the era in which the Fourteenth Amendment was written and adopted, apart from isolated comments, demonstrate that Con-

---

[23] *Gong Lum v. Rice*, 275 U.S. 78 (1927).

gress did not intend to prohibit school segregation. Recall that Congress, in the face of the 14th Amendment, continued to fund segregated schools in the District of Columbia through 1954. Many Northern states that ratified the Amendment also maintained segregated schools. State courts, applying state constitutional provisions that resemble the Fourteenth Amendment, upheld racial segregation. It is inconceivable that Congress and those states would have voted to prohibit what they themselves were doing absent being pushed in this direction by *Brown*. Absent Congressional action, it was the courts that held the reins of change.

If, in our fictional account, the Court had upheld segregation, where could civil rights groups have turned? Not to politics—in the South most Blacks could not vote. An anti-lynching bill could not pass Congress. I imagine that Thurgood Marshall, a pragmatist, having no alternative, would have pursued a school-equalization strategy, hoping to achieve better education and economic pressure through investments in Black schools to desegregate all of public education. In this imaginary history, he would have filed equalization suits in United States District Courts in Macon, Georgia; Montgomery, Alabama; and Austin, Texas in 1954. In this imaginary litigation, years of procedural wrangling, hearings and appeals would follow in front of state boards of education, up and down the state judicial systems, in federal trial and appellate courts, and topped by a Supreme Court refusal to hear appeals.

Now let's imagine what would have happened when some lower courts sided with the desegregation argument and found for the plaintiff Black school children while the U.S. Supreme Court refused to intervene. For example, imagine the eventual outcome of an actual struggle provoked by a 1960 case in which one federal trial court, following a six-week trial, found for the plaintiffs and required Georgia to equalize Black and White schools in Macon, Georgia. The U.S. Court of Appeals in the region agrees, but the Supreme Court refuses to hear the appeal. To comply, the all-White Georgia state legislature would have had to levy taxes and appropriate funds. State legislators, we can be certain, would have refused and protested against federal interference in state affairs. The legislature might even have adopted a Resolution of Interposition and Nullification, like those promulgated at the beginning of the Civil War. Other Southern states would have done the same. Southern Congressmen and senators would have joined in a Southern Manifesto denouncing the federal judiciary. The Georgia legislature would have postponed action on funding equalization for a year. Year after year, the legislature would have done nothing. Marshall would have kept returning to the Court, but it would only have issued and re-issued earlier orders. It would not have held the legislators in contempt. That is where matters would have stood. This state of affairs would have caused the Black protest movement to take a new turn.

Martin Luther King, Jr. warned that if segregation persisted, "[M]illions of Negroes will, out of frustration and despair, seek solace and security in Black-nationalists' ideologies—a development that would inevitably lead to a frightening racial nightmare"[24] Following the Supreme Court's imaginary 1953 embrace of *Plessy* in our faux version of *Brown*, Martin Luther King's "frightening racial nightmare" would have continued. In reality, the Montgomery bus boycott ended with a Supreme Court decision citing *Brown*.

In the fictional embrace of *Plessy*, sit-in demonstrators and Freedom Riders would have been jailed for violating segregation laws. Blacks would have been jailed, constitutionally, for sitting at White lunch counters or riding in the front of the bus. Black Panthers, Black Muslims and SNCC (which had expelled White members) would have captured the Movement. They would have formed alliances with Weathermen, anti-Vietnam and campus activists. Militants carrying rifles would have invaded state legislatures, campus centers and courtrooms. They would have held up banks and Brinks trucks. The general public, police and the FBI would have reacted and overreacted. The NAACP, SCLC and CORE (once an integrated organization) and civil liberties organizations would have lost power to influence events.

The Soviet Union in those days was a formidable enemy that opposed the United States across the globe. We know that in South Africa, it had supported the African National Congress and other self-proclaimed liberation movements. We know that it had funneled support to the Communist Party in the United States. We know it sent aid to the Irish Republican Army. So we can expect that in the 1960s it would have sent funds surreptitiously to Black militants. Even as it was in real life, police and FBI cracked down, trampling civil liberties. But let's imagine an escalation of what actually happened, with armed Panthers disrupting the California legislature, as armed Black students did actually seize a student center at Cornell. Imagine that Robert Williams had formed a Black rifle club and self-defense force in North Carolina, or if Blacks in Louisiana had formed Deacons for Defense and Malcolm X had advocated violent resistance.[25] Imagine if the situation had gotten so out of hand that activists had disrupted a California trial, kidnapping and killing a judge and were themselves killed. As it was, there were race riots and violence, but it could have been much worse.

In this fictional account of *Brown* gone wrong, what would have happened on the international scene? Greece's anti-communist government and its allegiance to the West hung by a thread, threatening the Western alliance. The Soviets would have secured a General Assembly resolution denouncing United States' racial practices. African and Asian nations would have readily joined in. The Red Brigades in Italy, the Baader-Meinhof Gang in Germany

---

24 Martin Luther King, Jr., *Letter from a Birmingham Jail*, April 16, 1963, in "The Nationalization of Civil Liberties and Civil Rights," *Texas Quarterly* 12: 10 (1969).

25 Robert F. Williams, *Negroes with Guns* (New York: Marzani and Munsell, 1962).

and leftist parties in Chile, Nicaragua, El Salvador, Argentina, Bolivia and Honduras would have denounced us. In time, the country would have regained its senses. But race relations would have been frayed badly. In a generation or two, the Court would have had to return to the issue and decide a case with similar effect of the real *Brown v. Board of Education.*

Happily we did get *Brown* when we did, and the eventual overturning of separate-but-equal. As a result we have a vastly more integrated nation than in 1954, though we should not minimize how much we have fallen short. But neither should we minimize the advances that have been achieved. Those who are dissatisfied tell us that without *Brown* the country would have been the same, or better, or that the route of separate-but-equal would have been preferable. But there is no reason to think that their imaginary history is more plausible than mine. Indeed, I think that mine is more realistic, drawing as it has on real events that never fully matured.

I have not yet written of the nostalgia for the separate-but-equal that never was, which has been touted by Professor Bell. His is one of the negative responses to *Brown* that argues that strict enforcement of separate but equal would have been better. He says that the continuation of legal segregation would not have provoked massive resistance, would have made segregation too expensive to maintain, and would have brought about a transition to integration willingly and peacefully. But this argument does not require a response from imaginary history. We have relevant real history, ancient and modern.

The rule of law from 1896 to 1954 arose out of *Plessy* and required separate but equal public accommodations. But the equality side of the *Plessy* formula never was achieved. In 1930, a report for the NAACP, the Margold Report, considered but rejected the idea of filing equalization lawsuits. The NAACP decided against these suits because they had never worked. Even if a case were successful, inequality would return. In 1935, the dean of the Howard University School of Education reported that there had been 113 equalization suits, but that equalization never had been achieved. A Virginia case illustrates the impossible odds. Before filing the Virginia school integration case, Black students asked attorney-activist Spottswood W. Robinson to bring an equalization suit. For two and a half years he attempted to get the courts to equalize the schools. The court's equalization orders were not obeyed. Contempt did not produce the desired results. Having no alternative, he filed one of the cases that became *Brown v. Board of Education.*

We also have more recent history demonstrating that separate but equal would never work. Equal funding cases today have universally failed. For over three decades there has been a vigorous effort in state courts to enforce separate-but-equal. These are called school-finance equalization cases, although recently plaintiffs have lowered their demands to ask, not for equality, but for adequacy. While these are not racial discrimination cases, most of them amount to the same thing. The poor districts that seek equal or adequate funding almost always are Black and Hispanic districts.

The first such state case, *Serrano v. Priest*,[26] was filed over thirty years ago. The California courts ordered equalization. It still has not occurred. Indeed, because of taxpayer revolts, education in California is now worse for Blacks and Whites alike. Over a score of state courts have ordered that funding for poor school districts be raised to an adequate level or to a level equal to that of rich districts. But not once has such a case ended in equalization. Michael Heise, a scholar who has followed this litigation closely, has written: "Even successful challenges have not led to equal funding, nor have any of the suits done much to alter the basic structure of school finance schemes."[27]

Conclusion

Courts do not levy taxes or appropriate money. That is for the legislature. But legislatures have their own priorities and have refused to make large court-ordered allocations in their budgets. Voters defeat legislators who vote to spend money according to standards that voters disapprove. For example, James Florio was defeated as governor of New Jersey because he raised taxes. Some of the cases have resulted in larger appropriations for poor districts— not a small achievement—but no one would claim that equality has resulted. In New Jersey, it took thirty years to obtain higher appropriations for children in the lower grades, a result that might be called equal. In New York, the Court of Appeals in 2003 ordered that the New York City schools be funded on an adequate basis.[28] A committee was appointed that recommended appropriating over five billion dollars to the city's schools over a period of four years for operating expenses and over nine billion dollars for capital expenses, but the state legislature did nothing.[29]

Of course all school children deserve funding that is equal to the best that public schools offer any child. But, there is another problem when separate-but-equal funding is the sole remedy: it still would not repair the deficiencies that are the consequence of segregation. In several cases where courts have declined to order integration, they have required compensatory funding instead. In Kansas City, for example, court-ordered compensatory

---

[26] *Serrano v. Priest*, 5 Cal.3d 584 (1971) (Serrano I); *Serrano v. Priest*, 18 Cal.3d 728 (1976) (Serrano II); *Serrano v. Priest*, 20 Cal.3d 25 (1977) (Serrano III).

[27] Michael Heise, "Litigated Learning and the Limits of the Law: Symposium," *Vanderbilt Law Review*, 57: 2417 (2004), 2438.

[28] *Campaign for Fiscal Equity, Inc. v. State of New York* (I), Slip Op. 15615 (2003); see also *Campaign for Fiscal Equity, Inc. v. State of New York*, Slip Op. 08630 (2006).

[29] See *Campaign for Fiscal Equity, Inc. v. State of New York*, Slip Op. 08630 (2006). For current information on the *CFE* litigation, see the Campaign for Fiscal Equity's website at http://www.cfequity.org/.

funding amounted to two billion dollars.[30] In Detroit, additional funding was in the hundreds of millions of dollars, yet segregation did not disappear and school performance did not improve.

It takes more than money to improve schooling for disadvantaged minority students. Money is essential to complete relief, but it is not complete in itself. That is not to say that all-Black schools are incapable of providing education of the highest quality. There are a few such schools that perform excellently. But that is rare and rarely duplicated. Overall, integrated education is a far more reliable preparation for life in our increasingly diverse society.

So where are we? *Brown* wrought immense changes in America. To recapitulate the positive side: great numbers of African Americans are in the best universities; we have a Black president and Black cabinet members in the administration of both parties; we have more than forty Black members of Congress and Black CEOs of major corporations. But on the negative side, we still have racially disparate rates of unemployment, income, wealth, and longevity. Imprisonment of Black men is up. And unhappiest of all—since *Brown* was, after all, a school case—school segregation persists, particularly in large urban areas. Should we give up on school integration? Surely not. Integration exists in small towns and rural areas. There is hope in voluntary integration programs, some of which are highly successful. The voluntary METCO program in which Boston city children go to suburban schools has been going on for a generation. Black graduates have been highly successful and mothers who graduated from the program register their children in it as soon as they are born. Desegregation by means of magnet schools that attract urban and suburban students has also facilitated integration. The Connecticut state case *Sheff v. O'Neill*[31] has created integrated schools that work successfully. Programs like these should increase. The workplace increasingly is integrated. Affirmative action has promoted integration at the college and university level. We had thought that public schools would have been the leading edge of integration. Instead, *Brown* made it possible for other parts of society to move upward first, and hopefully, to take our schools with them.

---

[30] See, e.g., *Jenkins v. Missouri*, 959 F. Supp. 1151 (W.D. Mo. 1997).

[31] *Sheff v. O'Neill*, 238 Conn. 1, 678 A.2d 1267 (Conn. 1996).

3

Native American Rights in the 21st Century

John E. Echohawk

John Echohawk co-founded the Native American Rights Fund in 1970 and has been its Executive Director since 1977. He serves on many national boards and has received numerous awards for his leadership in the Indian law field. In 1992, Mr. Echohawk served on the Clinton-Gore transition team for the Department of the Interior and, in 2008, he served on the Obama-Biden transition team for the Department of the Interior.

Native histories are the histories of this land and considerations of justice, past and present, are at best fractured if they neglect issues of Native American rights. Yet Native American legal and political history is not generally taught in the public schools, and as a result, most Americans are largely unfamiliar with the legal and political status of Indian tribes. The histories of Native peoples are varied and began thousands of years prior to European contact. For the sake of brevity, though, this analysis will begin at what has come to be known as "first contact," in 1492. After this first contact, European powers debated whether Native people were human beings and, after reaching tentative conclusions on that issue, later debated whether they were nations. They had to conclude that there were Indian nations, if for no other reason than because the Indian nations had the power to make war, a power which they understood and recognized as linked to the power of nation-states.

Conflicts between tribes and settlers were often resolved through treaties, which are documents negotiated between sovereign nations. It was this practice of treaty-making that made its way into the Constitution of the United States. Article I, Section 8 says that Congress has the power to deal with other sovereigns—foreign nations, the several states and the Indian tribes. The United States made treaties with Indian tribes until the practice was stopped in 1871, when the House of Representatives became involved. In our system, the Senate ratifies the treaties and the House has no role in the process. However, in the case of Indian tribes and treaties, the House wanted to become involved, and as a result, the relationships with tribes began to be made through agreements negotiated, and then approved, by both branches of Congress—the Senate and the House.

Beginning with the Indian Allotment Act of 1887, Congress sought to break up the Indian nations and force assimilation of Indian people into the larger society. It did this by dividing up many of the tribal lands, which were held in common by the tribes. Individual Indians were allotted part of the tribal lands in an effort to make them individual land-owners and promote assimilation. What resulted was the loss of nearly two-thirds of Indian lands, since land soon found its way out of Indian ownership, and the Indians were worse off than before. The situation was so bad that Congress stopped the allotment process in the 1934 Indian Reorganization Act and began encouraging tribal self-government once again. By the 1950s, however, Congress changed Indian policies again and began terminating tribal governments and tribal lands, usually without the consent of the Indian people involved.

It was this federal Indian policy of termination that Native Americans confronted during the civil rights movement of the 1960s. The civil rights movement was mainly about enforcing existing American laws about equality in this country, but tribal people were primarily interested in getting America to enforce another set of existing laws that recognized tribal sovereignty and self-determination—the Indian treaties and the federal laws enacted to carry them out. Native Americans were faced with a termination policy that threatened their legal and political status as tribes under previously signed treaties that were now being abandoned or abrogated without consent of the tribes. Indian leaders pushed hard for a new policy of self-determination during the 1960s and officially succeeded in 1970, when President Nixon's Indian policy embraced Indian self-determination and rejected termination. Every President since then has also supported self-determination.

1970 was also the year that I graduated from law school at the University of New Mexico, under a government scholarship program designed to increase the number of Native American lawyers across the country. Since most tribes were poor at that time, very few tribes had attorneys. The only other legal representation available to Indians then was through the legal services programs being started by the federal government, some of which served Indian reservations. We needed lawyers to represent our people on the most important Indian rights cases, just like the civil rights lawyers had represented African Americans in important cases in the civil rights movement. Using this model, a group of tribal leaders and lawyers came together, and with the assistance of the Ford Foundation, started the Native American Rights Fund (NARF) to provide legal representation on important Indian rights cases across the country. I was fortunate to be one of those lawyers who helped organize the NARF, and have been with the organization ever since.

Together with Indian legal services programs and the growing number of private attorneys representing tribes, NARF helped to start a litigation explosion in Indian country, such that we saw more legal activity than ever before in tribal history. Issues addressed included the assertion of tribal sovereignty, the protection of our tribal natural resources, and the promotion of Native American human rights to our religions and cultures. The new Indian self-determination policy was largely implemented through these Indian advocacy efforts, which enforced and developed Indian rights based on the treaties and laws that have been part of our history in this country. As many issues that had been suppressed for so long started to move forward, an inordinate number of these Indian cases in litigation reached the United States Supreme Court. Despite earlier legal setbacks and problematic case law developed during the early part of the 20th century, the Supreme Court upheld the tribal positions in most cases during this new period of legal advocacy, sustaining the momentum of the Indian self-determination policy and making history. Unfortunately today, in the 21st century, the Supreme Court can no longer be counted on to continue this legacy supporting Native American rights.

The hostility of the Supreme Court is one of the greatest challenges confronting the tribes today. The Court has ruled against tribal interests in almost every case over the past dozen years or so. These adverse decisions have increased as the makeup of the Supreme Court has changed and it has become more conservative. Many of these bad Supreme Court cases have diminished the tribes' most precious asset—their sovereignty. This trend reached crisis proportions in 2001 when the Supreme Court issued two anti-tribal sovereignty decisions—*Atkinson Trading Company v. Shirley*[1] and *Nevada v. Hicks*.[2] *Atkinson Trading* held that the Navajo Nation had no sovereign authority to tax non-Indians on non-Indian land within the boundaries of the Navajo Nation, even though the tribal government was providing police and fire protection services to the non-Indians. *Nevada v. Hicks* held that tribal courts had no jurisdiction over a state official who had violated the civil rights of a tribal member and damaged Indian property, even though the state official had entered Indian land on the reservation. Taken together, these cases mean that tribes have little or no sovereign authority over non-Indians within Indian reservations, even on Indian land.

Tribal leaders were so concerned about these decisions that they met and formed the Tribal Sovereignty Protection Initiative in 2001. Alarmed by prospects of a tribal future that would have little or no authority to control the activities of non-Indians within tribal communities, tribal leaders decided to seek Congressional legislation that would overturn these Supreme Court decisions. I was asked to co-chair the legislative drafting committee. We drafted legislation for Congressional consideration that would affirm inherent tribal sovereign authority over non-Indians within Indian country, unless that sovereignty had been ceded by a tribe in a treaty or had been taken away from them by a specific act of Congress.[3] In response to concerns that tribal courts might not be fair to non-Indians who came before them, tribal leaders reluctantly agreed to limited federal court review of tribal court decisions involving

---

[1] *Atkinson Trading v. Shirley*, 532 U.S. 645 (2001).

[2] *Nevada v. Hicks*, 533 U.S. 353 (2001).

[3] See Draft Legislation entitled "Tribal Sovereignty and Economic Enhancement Act" of 2002/2003.

non-Indians. Since not all tribes want to exercise full civil and misdemeanor criminal jurisdiction over non-Indians, each tribe would be given the option of deciding how much of this inherent sovereign authority it wants to exercise, and thus the extent to which it will open tribal judicial decisions to federal court review. Intergovernmental agreements would still be recognized as a legitimate mechanism for tribes to use in implementing this inherent sovereign authority with affected states and local governments.

Another part of the Tribal Sovereignty Protection Initiative formed by tribal leaders was the Tribal Supreme Court Project, which I was also asked to co-chair. This Project was designed to more carefully coordinate tribal advocacy efforts before the Supreme Court in order to increase our success rate in the Supreme Court. It was modeled after a state project that was formed to assist with state cases before the Supreme Court. We believe that project has proven successful for the states and want to replicate that model for the tribes.

The Tribal Supreme Court Project was busy in the 2002-2003 term, as the Supreme Court took up three Indian cases for review. The first two, *United States v. White Mountain Apache Tribe*[4] and *United States v. Navajo Nation*,[5] were both from Arizona. These two cases involved tribal breach-of-trust of claims that were won in the lower courts against the United States. The *White Mountain Apache* case involved the historic Fort Apache, which is now held in trust for the Tribe by the government. The government had been using the property for a school, but was trying to turn the property back over to the Tribe in a state of disrepair.

The *Navajo Nation* case involved a coal mine on land that was held in trust for the Navajos. The Tribe was renegotiating a higher royalty rate with a coal company, but it had to be approved by the government as trustee. When government approval of the higher rate stalled, the Tribe renegotiated for a lower rate. Later, the Tribe found out that the higher rate was not approved because the coal company had been meeting with the Secretary of the Interior about it without the Tribe's knowledge.

The third tribal case that the Supreme Court decided to review in the 2002-2003 term was *Inyo County v. Bishop Paiute Tribe*.[6] County officials in California were investigating three tribal members for welfare fraud and sought tribal employment records. When the Tribe refused to turn the records over, county officials broke into the tribal records office with bolt cutters and took the records. The court of appeals held that the Tribe was not required to comply with state search warrants because of its tribal sovereign immunity.

---

[4] *United States v. White Mountain Apache Tribe*, 537 U.S. 465 (2003).

[5] *United States v. Navajo Nation (I)*, 537 U.S. 488 (2003).

[6] *Inyo County v. Paiute-Shoshone Indians of Bishop Community of Bishop Colony*, 538 U.S. 701 (2003).

Because of the Supreme Court's track record in Indian cases, tribes were very concerned about how the Court would rule in these three cases. Ultimately only one of the cases, *United States v. White Mountain Apache Tribe*, would be decided in the Tribe's favor.[7] Nevertheless, the legal battles to protect Native communities, lands, self-determination and sovereignty continued on.

In addition to protecting tribal sovereign rights in the 21st century, Native people are also determined to preserve their rights as beneficiaries of the federal government's trust responsibilities to Indians. Most tribal and individual Indian land on reservations is held in trust for the Indians by the federal government. As trustee, the government must approve any leases of Indian trust land, collect the money due under the leases, keep it in accounts for the Indian owners, and disperse it to the Indians as requested. Historically, the government has not done a very good job as trustee. Complaints of malfeasance and efforts to correct the government's performance of its trust duties have been around for decades, but nothing has ever changed. The latest Indian effort led Congress to enact the Indian Trust Reform Act of 1994. However, the Administration did not request any funds to implement the Act, and Congress did not force any funds on them.

Recognizing that Indian trust reform would never be accomplished by the political branches of government, Elouise Cobell and others brought a lawsuit against the Interior and Treasury Departments in 1996. This class action lawsuit was filed on behalf of 500,000 Indian account holders and charged the federal government with breach of trust. With representation by the Native American Rights Fund and private co-counsel, the case was filed in the United States District Court for the District of Columbia.[8] In 1999, the Federal District Court held that the federal government was in breach of trust for mismanagement of the individual Indian trust accounts and ordered an accounting. In 2001, the United States Court of Appeals for the District of Columbia Circuit affirmed the ruling and no review of that decision was sought by the Bush Administration in the Supreme Court.

In 2002, then Interior Secretary Gale Norton was held in contempt of court for violating court orders in the case, just as her predecessor, Interior Secretary Bruce Babbitt, had been in 1998. The government was ordered to file plans for trust reform and for an accounting. The *Cobell* plaintiffs asserted that some $13 billion should have gone through these accounts since they were established in 1887, and that the government could not account for it all. The accounts, they argued, should be restated to reflect that amount. Adding

---

[7] The Navajo Nation case returned to the Supreme Court in the 2008-2009 term, and once again the Court ruled against tribal interests. For more information on Supreme Court and other federal court cases relevant to Native American tribes, see the NARF archive at http://www.narf.org/nill/bulletins/ilb.htm.

[8] For the most current case related to the *Cobell* litigation, see *Cobell v. Salazar* (Cobell XXII), 573 F.3d 808 (D.C. Cir. 2009).

interest over that long period of time would bring the amount up to $137 billion. Moreover, the plaintiffs contended that this restitution should be made by readjusting Treasury accounts and not by Congressional appropriations. In 2009, after several more years of litigation over the accounting and restitution, the parties reached a settlement in the *Cobell* class action litigation. The settlement totaled $3.4 billion dollars, far less than the amount sought.[9]

The Indian trust fund mismanagement scandal is, unfortunately, just another example of federal neglect of Native people. Not only has the trust management system been neglected, but Indians have the lowest educational levels, the worst health, the highest unemployment rates, the worst housing, and the highest crime rates of any group of Americans. The United States needs to meet its legal and moral obligations to Native American people.

Native American rights in the 21st century should also include the final resolution of the remaining land and water rights claims that Indian people have pending in this country. These cases usually pit the tribes and the federal government as trustee against the states and private parties. In lieu of decades of litigation, settlements are often possible among the parties if everyone contributes their fair share to the solution. Unfortunately, the federal government is usually the party that is unable to come up with its fair share of the settlement. The Native American Rights Fund has worked with tribes, states and private parties in past years to create a favorable settlement policy in Washington. Many Indian water rights settlements and several land settlements have been achieved over the years, but more need to follow.

In conclusion, I want to reflect on achieving justice and protecting the rights of Native Americans in the 21st century. I want to do that by ending this chapter with a quote from the first ever State of Indian Nations address given by Tex Hall, President of the National Congress of American Indians, on January 31, 2003, just a few days after President Bush gave the State of the Union address. President Hall said this in concluding his address on behalf of Indian nations:

> Mr. President, members of Congress, and neighbors ... as you make decisions that will have a direct impact on the self-determination and future survival of Indian Nations, please consider what we have given up for this nation—in land, in labor, in lives. We do not exist today in a void—our past and our future span out from us in this moment, telling the true story of who we were and what we can be. If you do not remember the past—painful and sometimes shameful as it may be—you cannot rightly lead us into the future. What will be our legacy seven generations from today? Will this generation finally end the poverty that has plagued Indian nations throughout

---

[9] For more information on the settlement terms, see also the NARF website, at http://www.narf.org/cases/iim.html.

the 20th century? Will this generation choose to close the gaps in education and opportunity for Indian people? Can this generation carry our traditions, our languages, and our lifeways safely into a new era with strong, self-determining tribal governments? I believe it can. We look forward to a bright future for the seven generations to come and beyond, with roots in the past, flourishing in the future, if only we can work together today....[10]

---

[10] National Congress of American Indians, *2003 Annual Report,* 11, available at http://www. ncai.org/resources/ncai-publications/ncai-annual-reports/2003_NCAI_Annual_Report.pdf.

4

American Citizenship in the Post September 11, 2001 Era

Antonia Hernández

Antonia Hernández is nationally recognized for her commitment to underserved communities in Los Angeles and beyond. She has been president and chief executive officer of the California Community Foundation since 2004. She has served as president and general counsel of the Mexican American Legal Defense and Educational Fund (MALDEF) and is a member of the boards of directors of the American Constitution Society and the Local Initiatives Support Corporation (LISC).

As an immigrant, the child of a United States citizen father whose family was deported to Mexico during the Depression, and as an attorney who has for over twenty-five years sought to change our immigration laws, I have developed unique perspectives on citizenship and immigration. Those ideas and understandings grew and became even more nuanced through my work as President and General Counsel of MALDEF, the Mexican American Legal Defense and Educational Fund. These experiences have taught me that immigration and citizenship issues are of vital importance, hitting close to home while also implicating policies that reflect and shape our narratives about values, humanity, and exclusions. In this essay, I will focus on three main points: first, belonging and immigration policy; second, the need for immigration policies to provide pathways for inclusion; and third, the need for re-thinking our understandings of citizenship, boundaries and borders. Together these points reflect the interrelationship of citizenship and immigration. They speak to how we view ourselves as Americans.

Looking first at issues of belonging, there are many questions to address. First, can we reconcile our contradictory immigration and naturalization policy, which welcomes some people but not others? Can we begin to articulate a new definition of being an American that is more embracing and welcoming to all? As a country of immigrants, how can we have a liberal immigration and naturalization policy for some and emphatically exclusionary and discriminatory policies for others? And why, in a country whose people come from every corner of the world, is there no coherent institutional mechanism for integrating the new members into our nation?

Many people feel we have not needed such a policy in the past. But as our world gets smaller through technology and as demographic changes occur, we must rethink our current lack of a policy for integrating newly

47

arriving immigrants into our political, social and economic frameworks. We must reconcile recent global trends with developing international norms that apply to everyone. At the same time we must preserve our nation's autonomy, especially in light of the realities that the events of September 11 brought home to us.

It has been suggested that in today's new connected world, the concept of citizenship, of being attached to a specific political entity, is archaic or outmoded. Yet as we look around our world today, we find people embroiled in bitter conflicts involving political boundaries, often entailing ethnic or religious differences, all seeking to create new or preserve old boundaries, or to define who is in or who is out. We are left to ask, what then is the meaning of citizenship? Why do individuals fight and kill in the name of political entities for which they feel deep allegiances? And why does this matter in today's world?

Belonging to a clan has been a central human need from the beginning of time. Our first affiliation was to family. As families grew more important, they expanded to include a multitude of individuals, all connected by blood and/or marriage. From clans and other extended affiliations, civilizations evolved and the need grew to associate to a larger body for social, cultural, linguistic and political survival. Much has changed and we have made significant advances in human understanding, but the need to belong, to create clans around commonalities, is as strong today as it was in the beginning.

To understand the role of citizenship in the creation and preservation of nation states, one must keep in mind that the concept of citizenship is constantly evolving. Nationality is the legal and political connection between the individual and the nation state. Central to its success are reciprocal relationships, that is, each person within the entity having both rights and obligations. The individual expects protection and social and economic benefits. In return, the political entity imposes certain obligations on the individual. Citizenship is a tool used by the controlling majority to define rights and responsibilities and to exclude those not meeting the norms of the group. Citizenship is most often acquired at birth, the individual having no control over an accident of birth. The Romans called this *jus soli*, the right of a person to be a national of the country in which he was born. Others acquire citizenship by descent according to blood kinship, known as *jus sanguinis*, that is, nationality received from one's parents or by marriage or adoption. These concepts both remain important in citizenship law today.

A fundamental right of a nation state is to determine its nationality policy. This is considered an essential attribute of sovereignty. The classical concept of citizenship, as articulated in ancient Athens, was that privileged, educated males could be members of a small city-state. This narrow concept of citizenship has evolved into a complicated expansive, multifaceted contemporary understanding of the term. In most modern countries, citizenship can be acquired by naturalization based on laws that allow outsiders to become part of the political body.

Throughout history, nation states have been created and established flourishing civilizations, only to be destroyed by war, natural disasters, or internal rebellion and conflict. Alliances and allegiances may shift based on new political boundaries. Citizenship affiliations change for entire nations and groups when they are conquered, as was the case when the United States took the west from Mexico. Mass migration can bring forth a new nation, as was the case in the creation of the United States. On the other hand, evolutionary changes in any given nation may be slow and gradual, with the concept of nationality remaining seemingly unchanged.

In looking at the initial formation of the United States, one might contend there is nothing truly unique about its development as compared with the upheavals that created nations in other parts of the world. Native groups inhabited the territory for thousands of years. Different settler groups, unhappy with their governments, or their social, economic or religious circumstances, sought a new home in this land. As immigration grew and the settlers felt that England was not responsive to their needs, they revolted and created a new nation—the United States. The new European settlers did not seek to bring the native residents into their new country or to join the pre-existing sovereign nations of the native inhabitants. Instead, they superimposed their mother country's common values, language, religion and culture on this new land and on all of its peoples.

What was unique in human history was the American peoples' desire to create a new nation with strong democratic ideals of governance. Yet, even this noble desire had limitations. In some ways similar to ancient Athens, their desire to create a democracy was premised on a very limiting definition of who should benefit from these democratic ideals. The beneficiaries of democracy were defined as white, male, property owners. Women were not included and did not have the right to vote or participate in this new democratic nation/state. Slavery was legal, blacks had limited rights, and Native American populations were excluded. With such limitations, from the beginning, the United States accepted both the principles of *jus soli* and *jus sanguinis*.

Neither the Constitution nor federal law defined citizenship by birthright until after the Civil War. The legal basis for citizenship was laid down in the Fourteenth Amendment in 1868.[1] Yet the concept of citizenship as the birthright of the entire nation did not become well established until after World War I. Before then, notwithstanding widespread discrimination and excep-

---

[1] U.S. Const. Amend. XIV, § 1: "All persons born or naturalized in the United States, and subject to the jurisdiction therefore, are citizens of the United States and the State where they reside."

tions for certain groups, immigrants, particularly those from Europe, were welcomed as "the huddled masses yearning to breathe free." These immigrants faced relatively few obstacles in entering the United States and becoming citizens. Nevertheless, challenges remained. For many, these challenges were not in obtaining citizenship, but in acquiring the real rights and benefits of citizenship and political, social and economic acceptance. This was particularly pronounced for those immigrant groups facing heightened levels of discrimination.

At the inception of this country, the Constitution granted Congress the exclusive power to establish a "uniform Rule of Naturalization."[2] The first naturalization law was enacted in 1790. From the start, the naturalization laws incorporated then-prevailing views about race. For example, this first law limited naturalization to "any alien, being a free white person."[3] The law was amended after the Civil War to include persons of "African nativity ... and descent." The changes did not include Asians or others, and it was not until 1943 that Chinese were entitled to become citizens. Ironically, children born of Chinese immigrants were citizens by virtue of the Fourteenth Amendment, but Congress did not pass a race-neutral naturalization law until 1952.[4]

For those found acceptable, mainly Western European immigrants, the United States has had, and continues to have, a liberal but cumbersome naturalization process. But until recently, there were not many differences under the law between a citizen and a legal resident. The privileges restricted to citizens were few, such as the right to vote and run for President. American society can be, and has been, very welcoming to those chosen for admission. Unfortunately, the critical factors for many applicants in determining whether they were more or less likely to be admitted were based on race and a shared European origin.

As migration from Europe increased, the body politic of this country made allowances, making it easier for some to integrate into our society than others. Even today, people coming from Canada, England, France and certain other European countries are welcomed and perceived to fit the ideal of an American. People from other areas of the world frequently do not fit this stereotype. Thus, a constant complaint from immigrants is that Immigration and Customs Enforcement,[5] along with the general public, make assumptions about citizenship based on ethnic/racial features.

---

2 U.S. Const. art. I, § 8, cl. 4.

3 See Naturalization Act of 1790, ch. 3, § 1, 1 Stat. 103 (1790) (repealed 1795).

4 See Immigration and Nationality Act of 1952, ch. 2, § 311, 66 Stat. 163, 239 (1952).

5 As of 2003, the Immigration and Naturalization Service was split among U.S. Immigration and Customs Enforcement (ICE), U.S. Citizenship and Immigration Services (USCIS), and U.S. Customs and Border Protection (CBP), all of which fall under the authority of the Department of Homeland Security.

As one of those citizens whose citizenship status is sometimes in doubt, I can relate quite well to their frustrations. I am constantly asked, "Where do you come from?" When I respond that I am from Los Angeles, the reply too often is, "No, tell me really, where do you come from?" Granted, I was born in Mexico. But I came to the United States when I was eight years old and have been a citizen most of my life. Yet, I do not fit the stereotype of what an American should look like. My father, an American citizen who was born in Texas and deported by train to Mexico with his family during the Depression, still carries his birth certificate in his wallet because he is continually compelled to show that he belongs here. Although born in the United States, my father, by his appearance, is not perceived to belong. It is one of the Mexican American Legal Defense and Educational Fund's (MALDEF) missions to educate American society and help alter such perceptions of what it is to be an American.

Changes in American immigration laws in the 1960s and 1970s coincided with changes in the immigration flow into our country. People from countries that did not previously have large numbers of immigrants entering the United States began coming. The demographics and origins of the "sending countries" were different. Coupled with increased migration from Mexico, a new American was in the making.

Our troubled history with Mexico and the inflexible fact that we share a 2,000-mile border make the realities of migration flow from Mexico a difficult topic. The families of many Latinos, mainly Mexican Americans, have been here for centuries. Speak with anyone who comes from New Mexico and they will tell you that they can trace their ancestry back to times before the Mayflower. Those whose ancestors were here in the Southwest before 1850 will tell you that the political boundaries changed when the United States acquired new territories, but that the people did not move when the lines changed. Moreover, whatever laws were passed in the late nineteenth or early twentieth centuries to inhibit immigration coming into ports of entry on the Atlantic or Pacific coasts were not important to this population. The movement of people across the southern border remained uninterrupted. Until American laws and tightening of the southern border made crossing the border more difficult, people moved back and forth fairly easily between Mexico and the United States, and between Canada and the United States in the north.

Although the movement of people between the United States and Mexico had been relatively open over a great span of time, the phenomenon of mass migration from south of the border is recent. Some will argue that the policy of bringing in Mexican *Braceros* to work in the fields during the 1940s and 1950s created the precedent for the recent flows. But, prior to 1970, the migration flow was small. Another more recent development has been the flow of people from Central American countries, such as El Salvador and

Guatemala. Migration from these countries was practically non-existent until the political turmoil in those countries during the 1980s and 1990s.

But let me share a more graphic example. The Mexican American Legal Defense and Educational Fund, MALDEF, was created in 1968. At that time, 85 percent of the Mexican American stock was native born, with the remaining 15 percent being immigrants. By 2000, immigrants made up 38 percent of the Latino population in this country.[6] If you include the children of these immigrants, over 50 percent of the Latino community in the United States is of recent immigrant origin. Suffice it to say that to Latino communities, nationality and citizenship issues have become priority concerns. The 1990s witnessed the naturalization of more immigrants in the United States than ever before in our history. Of these new citizens, the percentage coming from Mexico, Central America and the Caribbean grew from 23 to 43 percent. Most importantly, Mexico is the country of origin of most of these new American citizens.[7]

It is against this demographic backdrop that the polarizing issues of citizenship and naturalization policies came into play. Even before September 11, the United States was moving on a path of policy changes that limited the rights of non-citizens, particularly those perceived as not looking or acting like traditional Americans. Beginning in the 1970s, states began passing laws limiting employment opportunities to United States citizens only. Some states wanted to limit the employment of police officers and teachers to citizens. Almost immediately, immigrant rights groups began challenging these laws. Our main legal argument was that states could not pass laws relating to immigration matters. We contended that only the federal government had the power to regulate these issues. Unfortunately, the United States Supreme Court allowed states to create these distinctions. A new period began in which, for the first time, legal differences between citizens and legal residents became much more pronounced.

During the 1970s and 1980s, efforts to create more distinctions between citizens and legal residents continued. But these were not the main priority of those seeking drastic changes in our immigration laws. This period is now recalled as the time in which the American public began a heated discussion about illegal migration. The primary concern was the illegal migration coming from south of the border, much of it from Mexico. The body politic, wanting more control of illegal migration and reduced migration flows across our

---

[6] See Pew Hispanic Center Fact Sheet, "U.S.-Born Hispanics Increasingly Drive Population Developments" (January 2002), at http://www.pewhispanic.org/files/factsheets/2.pdf.

[7] See Pew Research Center Publications, "Mexican Immigrants in the United States, 2008" (April 15, 2009), at http://pewresearch.org/pubs/1191/mexican-immigrants-in-america-largest-group. In 2008, 44% of new citizens came from North/Central America and the Caribbean; in 2009, the percentage dropped to 34%. See James Lee, *Naturalizations in the United States: 2009* (Washington DC: U.S.G.P.O., 2010).

southern border, prevailed when a major revision to our immigration laws passed in 1986. The major feature of this legislation, however, was a generous legalization program for those immigrants living illegally in this country.[8] To satisfy restrictionists, the legislation included sanctions for those who employed undocumented workers. For the first time in American history, employers were to be fined for hiring undocumented workers. As we know, the law did not deter illegal migration and the undocumented population is larger than it has ever been.

In 1994, a barrage of policy changes at every governmental level began limiting the rights of non-citizens.[9] In some states, like California, Arizona, and Texas, the migration from south of the border was clearly visible on an everyday basis. Many non-Latinos began to resent the demographic changes. To make matters worse, starting in the early 1990s, the nation was suffering a very difficult recession. California became fertile ground for anti-immigrant political mania. The recession was blamed on immigrants and all who looked like immigrants, phenomena we would see repeated again and again throughout the decades during economic downturns.

Immigrants, of course, were not the cause of the recession. Nevertheless, it was difficult to explain to the public that cutbacks in defense contracts, the savings and loans scandal, and other economic variables unrelated to migration had contributed to hard economic times. In fact, during this time, I gave a speech in which I pointed out that immigrants could not be responsible for job loss or economic upset: they could not work in most defense industry jobs, which required citizenship, and I did not know of any Latino immigrants who owned savings and loans. Nonetheless, it was difficult to convince a suspicious audience that Latinos were not in some way responsible for causing the recession.

During this time, the anti-immigrant fervor erupted in California. As with so many trends that sweep the nation, California led the way in showing its disfavor in reaction to changing demographics. In 1994, anti-immigrant forces put an initiative on the California ballot to deny most public benefits to undocumented residents. Proposition 187 targeted undocumented families for identification and deportation, denied children a public education, limited basic health benefits and required verification to receive any public benefits. California's Governor Pete Wilson made the passage of the proposition a central theme to his re-election. All Latinos became targets. MALDEF sought to

---

[8] 1986 Immigration Reform and Control Act, Pub. L. No. 99603, § 101, 100 Stat. 3359 (1986) (codified at 8 U.S.C. § 1324a).

[9] See, e.g., Lina Newton, *Illegal, Alien, or Immigrant: The Politics of Immigration Reform.* (New York: New York University Press, 2008), and JoAnne D. Spotts, "U.S. Immigration Policy on the Southwest Border From Reagan Through Clinton, 1981-2001," *Georgetown Immigration Law Journal* 16: 601 (2002).

educate the public about the grim legal, social and economic realities of the proposition and to defeat it. Unfortunately, it passed.[10]

It took the legal efforts of MALDEF, the ACLU and others to convince the federal courts to declare the law unconstitutional.[11] The separation of powers and supremacy clauses, which give exclusive jurisdiction to the federal government over the measures contained in Proposition 187, were the legal bases upon which the court invalidated Proposition 187.[12] Though the efforts by the State of California to enact immigration policy failed in the courts, they did not die in the public eye. This failed initiative was the beginning of a process in which many states and localities became more emboldened in their efforts to dictate and control immigration and naturalization policies through laws, regulations and practices. The counter-efforts to resist these measures continue.

Some good did come out of the anti-immigrant phobia of the 1990s. For years, activists in the Latino community had unsuccessfully led efforts to naturalize new immigrants. Mexican and Canadian legal residents had the lowest naturalization rates. Immigrants from those countries felt little need to become American citizens, mainly because the proximity to their home countries created a false sense of temporary residence in the United States and they felt that they could easily return home when necessary. But Proposition 187 jolted the Latino community. Latino American citizens, many of whom felt somewhat alienated from the recent immigrant community, quickly realized that non-Latinos did not make fine distinctions when it came to citizenship status and being Latino. Rather, the Latino community as a whole—citizen and immigrant alike—was painted with a broad brush.

Discrimination was widespread: if you looked like an immigrant, then you were an immigrant—and all of the negative stereotypes associated with immigrants attached just as easily to non-immigrant Latinos. Moreover, many Latino families consist of "mixed" legal relationships. For example, as of 2008, 73 percent of children living in families with unauthorized parents were U.S citizens by birth.[13] Little did the proponents of Proposition 187 and its progeny realize that it is not uncommon for citizens, legal residents and undocumented residents to be related and feel an affinity for each other's

---

[10] There are stark similarities between California's response to illegal immigration under Proposition 187 and more recent events in Arizona, where financial crisis and political focus on illegal immigration resulted in the hotly contested legislation known commonly as Senate Bill (SB) 1070 (passed in 2010).

[11] See *League of United Latin American Citizens v. Wilson*, 908 F. Supp. 755 (C.D. Cal. 1995).

[12] Notably, these same arguments regarding the federal government's exclusive right over immigration and naturalization formed the basis for successful challenges to Arizona's SB 1070.

[13] Jeffrey Passell and D'Vera Cohn, *A Portrait of Unauthorized Immigrants in the United States*, Pew Hispanic Center, April 2009, at http://www.pewhispanic.org/2009/04/14/a-portrait-of-unauthorized-immigrants-in-the-united-states.

legal status. Ironically, the majority's efforts to create greater distinctions between citizen and non-citizen frequently had the opposite effect for the Latino community. It brought us together in the realization that if one part of the community was at risk, then all of us were threatened.

An unexpected positive result from Proposition 187 was the dramatic increase in the number of immigrants wanting to become citizens. The efforts to create greater distinctions between citizens and legal residents provided a tremendous impetus for hundreds of thousands of Latinos to become citizens. In responding to a new political activism in Latino communities in California and throughout the United States, I entitled one of my speeches "Thank you Governor Wilson." Were it not for his ardent support of Proposition 187 and use of anti-immigrant themes propelling his 1994 re-election campaign, we would not have been able to galvanize our community to increase citizenship and expedite our political evolution.[14] For the Latino community—whether you live in Phoenix, Chicago, Atlanta, or Idaho—mention Proposition 187, and you get the same response: anger that loyal American Latinos, whether they served their country bravely or contributed in some other way to the making of America, still need to prove that they belong, that they are Americans.

In 1996 Congress once again passed federal legislation curtailing immigration and created more barriers to naturalization by increasing fees and erecting other hurdles under the Illegal Immigration Reform and Immigrant Responsibility Act (IIRIRA) and the Antiterrorism and Effective Death Penalty Act (AEDPA).[15] These laws imposed more restrictions on the public benefits legal residents could seek and receive. Interestingly, the end result was once again an increased incentive for legal residents to seek citizenship. Paradoxically, although legal permanent residents had the same obligations as citizens to pay taxes[16] and serve in the military when called,[17] under the new legislation, many of the benefits previously available to them were eliminated.[18] The IIRIRA and the AEDPA legislation significantly affected the civil rights of immigrants in this country by, for example, allowing Immigration and Naturalization Service (now Immigration and Customs Enforcement, or "ICE") officers to make many of the decisions related to the deportation of

---

[14] Kevin R. Johnson, "Race, the Immigration Laws, and Domestic Race Relations: A 'Magic Mirror' into the Heart of Darkness," *Indiana Law Journal* 73: 1111 (1998).

[15] See Antiterrorism and Effective Death Penalty Act (AEDPA), Pub. L. No. 104-132, 110 Stat. 1214 (1996); Illegal Immigration Reform and Immigrant Responsibility Act, Pub. L. No. 104-208, 110 Stat. 3009-546 (1996).

[16] 26 U.S.C. § 7701(b)(1)(A).

[17] 50 U.S.C. app. § 453; 50 U.S.C. § 455(a)(1)(3).

[18] See 8 U.S.C. § 1611 (restricting federal public benefits for aliens who are "not qualified"); 8 U.S.C. § 1612 (requiring legal permanent residents to work for 40 qualifying quarters in order to be eligible for benefits); 8 U.S.C. § 1631 (requiring federal "means-tested programs" to use the resources of the alien's sponsor to determine eligibility for benefits).

immigrants without judicial review.[19] As a result, families have been divided, with United States-born children in many instances forced to leave their country of birth because their parents were deported. For legal permanent residents, even minor criminal infractions can lead to deportation. And immigrants without documents can be detained indefinitely and deported without any review.

By making it more difficult to become a citizen and by creating greater divisions between citizens and legal residents, the 1996 changes adversely impacted the immigrant community and had negative consequences for society at large. While the United States over time has developed a complicated restrictive immigration/naturalization policy, we have never had a coherent immigrant policy. As we have become a much more diverse society and truly are a country in which people from throughout the world are well represented, the need for comprehensive immigration and immigrant integration policies has become more and more pressing. We seem to assume that immigrants will find their way no matter how many barriers we place before them. In the past, without a coherent immigrant policy, our approach has brought us, at best, mixed success. Most immigrants hailing from European countries or well-educated backgrounds who speak English seem to do well enough and are generally accepted by the body politic. But the vast majority of immigrants, particularly those coming from developing or underdeveloped countries and those who, by and large, come from different racial, ethnic, or religious backgrounds, have a much harder time integrating into American society. We do not offer much in the way of guidance or assistance, but then complain that they are not becoming American quickly enough.

As we grapple with the reality that we have become a nation of immigrants and that we have within our society people coming from every country, every ethnic group, every religion and every culture, we need to develop policies that provide the tools immigrants need to integrate into America society. We need to be clear as to what we expect from each individual and delineate what that individual will receive in return. We must seriously turn to the question of defining who is an American. This is, in essence, a second opportunity to create viable immigration and immigrant policies—to create a society in which membership is not premised on what you look like, but rests on the ideals embodied in our Constitution. We must make the promise of equality of opportunity and equal protection under the law a reality for all.

The events of September 11 have added a layer of complexity to an already complicated issue. Congress has now passed more restrictive laws distinguishing citizens from legal residents and further marginalizing undocumented persons. For example, post 9/11 federal law requires that baggage

---

[19] See 8 U.S.C. § 1252 (limiting judicial review over orders of removal).

screeners at airports be United States citizens.[20] One might ask, what is wrong with that? Ask the director of the San Francisco International Airport, who would be required to fire baggage screeners, 80 percent of whom are not citizens but legal permanent residents. In Los Angeles, the law mandates termination of 40 percent of the screeners. Who would be hurt by this? Well, for example, a baggage screener from El Salvador who served four years in the U.S. Army and whose husband and child are United States citizens. The irony is that this person and all legal residents can and do serve in our military, and can and do die protecting our liberties. Having borne arms for the United States, they are nevertheless deemed too dangerous to screen our luggage.

Our efforts to tighten citizenship and naturalization laws in this country are occurring at a time when other forces in the world are moving in the opposite direction. The need to create international rules that apply to everyone who comes to this country is becoming more evident as global markets define an increasingly interconnected world. As technology makes our world smaller and economic interests become more intertwined, nations are creating new rules and reluctantly conceding some of their national prerogatives. We already have international laws that govern how we treat the environment, conduct war, how we treat refugees and prisoners, as well as laws that ease the movement of goods, services and capital.[21]

Should we be moving in the direction of creating larger governmental bodies that pursue specific interests reaching beyond borders and redefining how boundary lines restrict us? Have advances in computer technology and travel made it necessary to create reconfigured political alliances that redefine how we view non-citizens? Developments in the European Union are an example of a new political unit that includes many countries that have chosen to give up some of their national prerogatives.[22] At the same time, however, in the area of migration, change has not come to Europe. Instead, the individual EU nations have tightened access to their territories from the outside in order to enjoy freedom of movement within the EU.[23] In essence, they have created a larger territory in which its residents could move more freely, while at the same time tightening the doors to those on the outside. Sooner or later, the

---

[20] See Aviation and Transportation Security Act, Pub. L. No. 107-71, 115 Stat. 597 (2001).

[21] See Arctic Environmental Protection Strategy, June 14, 1991, 30 I.L.M. 1624; Geneva Convention Relative to the Treatment of Prisoners of War, Aug. 12, 1949, 6 U.S.T. 3316, 75 U.N.T.S. 135; United Nations Protocol Relating to the Status of Refugees, Jan. 3, 1967, 19 U.S.T. 6223, 606 U.N.T.S. 267; United Nations Convention on Contracts for the International Sale of Goods, Apr. 10, 1980, 19 I.L.M. 668.

[22] As of 2012, there were 27 member nations of the European Union, each having representation in EU legislative and judiciary bodies. For more information, see the official EU website at http://europa.eu.

[23] Theodora Kostakopoulou, "'Integrating' Non-EU Migrants in the European Union: Ambivalent Legacies and Mutating Paradigms," *Columbia Journal of European Law,* 8(2): 1 (2002).

EU and other countries employing restrictive immigrant policies will be required by economic and social realities to come to grips with such seemingly contradictory policies.

Worldwide, the migration of individuals seeking economic opportunity or fleeing oppression or war has increased dramatically.[24] Television and other recent technologies have opened eyes and made more people mobile. It is inevitable that the movement of people will continue and increase. Thus, at a time when we are trying to provide stronger security, we must also continue to question efforts to create greater distinctions between citizens and residents. As we move forward, we will likely see a greater interest in redefining citizenship. We are now witnessing a growing trend toward dual citizenship. Efforts to provide limited voting rights to legal residents are also a subject of discussion. In the United States, legal residents must wait five years before they can apply for citizenship, with a further waiting period post application that can exceed two years. Some have proposed that legal residents be allowed to vote in local elections, such as school board and city governance. The idea is that persons who are affected by the decisions of political entities should have the opportunity to vote in the elections of those officials who will make decisions. To some this may sound like an election out of the "Wild West." Others would respond this is exactly how things were run a hundred years ago out West—and we did not come out so badly after all.

In conclusion, consider the following questions: Is citizenship as we know it still relevant? Are our current laws and views of American citizenship as applicable as past laws, in light of the recent strides we have made in technology, trade and travel? Should the events of September 11th impede our efforts to remove artificial and outmoded views about citizenship?

The ethnic composition of the United States will continue to change. That train has left the station. The United States population includes more than 48 million Latinos and 13 million Asians and the number of immigrants coming from the Middle East and Africa is also increasing.[25] In a country of over 300 million people, the percentage of citizens from non-European countries is increasing and that trend will continue. What policies will we implement to take these rapid and significant demographic changes into account?

Our definition of who is an American must change along with our immigration policies. We must develop an immigrant policy that serves the future

---

24 United Nations High Commission on Refugees (UNHCR), "Statistics and Operational Data," at http://www.unhcr.org/pages/49c3646c4d6.html.

25 Pew Hispanic Center, *Statistical Portrait of Hispanics in the United States, 2009*, Table 1, February, 2011, at http://pewhispanic.org/files/factsheets/hispanics2009/Table%201.pdf; and see Aaron Terrazas, "Middle Eastern and North African Immigrants in the United States," *Migration Information Source*, March 2011, at http://www.migrationinformation.org/USfocus/display.cfm?id=830.

needs of the 21st century, not one based on our past perceptions. But to have an effective immigrant policy we must be clear about our perceptions of ourselves. Many would like to think that change only happens one way, and that the immigrant is the one who must change. The reality is that both our people and our country have changed. That change has kept this country vibrant, and the cutting edge of change is our fluidity and our willingness to engage in that process. As a country of immigrants, we have become more cosmopolitan, more worldly. Our tastes in music, dance, art and how we live have expanded. As a result, we are a more tolerant and open people. We now need an immigrant policy that is compatible and consistent with our changing worldview.

In closing, I return to the question of how we should define American citizenship at this juncture in our history. The experiences and perspectives of immigrants offer insights into how we might frame such a definition. As an immigrant, I do not claim to represent all immigrants. But, in working with and living among immigrants, I do have a good feel for why many risk their lives to come to America. Most immigrants come seeking better economic opportunities. We all want the American dream. We seek a place in which our talents and contributions will be valued and measured by what we produce and not by how we look or speak; where we will be allowed to practice our religious beliefs without interference from the government; where the government will protect our right to worship or not worship at all; where we are free to read and speak our mind; where we can assemble and be free to associate with whomever we wish; and where collectively we can decide how we want to be governed. In return, we must respect differences, support the values enunciated in the Constitution and the Bill of Rights, uphold our laws, support through our taxes the communal amenities which sustain and improve our quality of life, and participate in the governance of our country. That is why my parents brought me to this country.

Being an immigrant, I have at times yearned for deeper roots. I have often told people that I never felt more Mexican than when I was in the United States, and never felt more American than when I was in Mexico. On September 11th, when the terrorists attacked, I was on a plane in the middle of the Atlantic returning from a meeting in Italy. The flight was ordered to return and I spent the next five days madly trying to get home. I wanted nothing more than to be home in America. I can think of no better tribute an immigrant can give to this country than to feel at peace in my adopted home.

5

Guarding Our Freedoms

Anthony Lewis

Anthony Lewis held the James Madison Visiting Professorship at Columbia University from 1983 through 2008 and was a columnist for The New York Times *from 1969 to December 2001. He has twice won the Pulitzer Prize, first in 1955 for a series of articles in* The Washington Daily News *on the dismissal of a Navy employee as a security risk, and again in 1963 for his coverage of the Supreme Court. In 2001, Mr. Lewis was awarded the Presidential Citizens Medal.*

How do we guard our American freedoms in a time of fear? While the contexts and circumstances may differ, it is an issue that confronts every generation. Most recently, fear of terrorism provided the context through which the (George W.) Bush Administration could brush aside, abruptly, rights protected by the Constitution and by international law. Because of fear and our willingness to cast aside long held Constitutional and civil-rights values, ideas foreign to American beliefs, such as detention without trial, denial of access to lawyers, and years of interrogation in isolation are now American practices.

Fear and its repressive consequences are not something new in our history. At the very beginning of the republic, in 1798, Congress passed and President Adams signed into law a Sedition Act that made it a crime to criticize the President. The stated reason for the act was the threat of French Jacobin terror coming to the United States. The then-dominant Federalist Party used the statute to prosecute, fine and imprison members of the emerging Jeffersonian opposition: editors, publishers, even a Jeffersonian member of Congress. Again and again in our history politicians have used fear as a weapon. "The paranoid style in American politics," the late Richard Hofstadter called it.[1] Woodrow Wilson's Justice Department sent people to prison for long terms for criticizing the draft during World War I, and for criticizing Wilson. His Attorney General, A. Mitchell Palmer, rounded up thousands of aliens in a night and deported them as menaces. Fifty years ago we had Senator Joe McCarthy, playing on the fear of communism.

If the United States has been especially susceptible to the politics of fear, it is not only an American phenomenon. Lord Steyn, one of the law lords who make up Britain's highest court, said recently: "It is a recurring theme in

---

[1] Richard Hofstadter, "The Paranoid Style in American Politics," *Harpers Magazine* (Nov. 1964): 77-86.

history that in times of war, armed conflict or perceived national danger, even liberal democracies adopt measures infringing human rights in ways that are wholly disproportionate to the crisis."[2] Lord Steyn gave some British examples of what he called disproportionate infringement of civil liberties in wartime, notably the detention of aliens during World War II—among them German Jews who had found refuge in Britain from Hitler—without any proper hearing. But the main target of his remarks was the Bush Administration's handling of prisoners it was keeping in Guantánamo Bay, Cuba.

As of 2004 there were roughly 660 of those prisoners, men and boys, including a 13-year-old and two other teenagers imprisoned for a year.[3] From what we know, which is not much, the prisoners are held in stringent conditions, in solitary confinement, and subject to frequent interrogation. We have the impression that almost all were captured in the war in Afghanistan, as fighters there for the Taliban or al Qaeda. But that impression, it now seems, is wrong. A substantial number were arrested by governments as remote from Afghanistan as Gambia, in West Africa, turned over to American authorities and then taken to Guantánamo.

My first insight into the fact that many of the Guantánamo prisoners were apparently not fighting in Afghanistan came from a brief filed in the United States Supreme Court in January of 2004 by members of the British parliament. The brief describes what is known about 10 British subjects, and two others with British connections, who are held in Guantánamo. One is Martin Mubanga, the son of a former government official in Zambia, in southern Africa. His father moved to London thirty years ago. Martin was arrested while visiting Zambia. He was turned over to U.S. agents, for reasons never explained, and taken to Guantánamo. Three of the British subjects, all of Pakistani descent, were friends who lived in Tipton, in the British Midlands. One was Asif Iqbal. In July 2001 his parents went to Pakistan to find a bride for him. Asif, who was 20 years old, followed in September. The marriage was arranged, and Asif told his parents he was going to Karachi to meet friends. He telephoned from there and the next thing they knew, he was in Guantánamo. Asif's two friends had followed him to Pakistan. There, the brief says, the three were apparently seized and turned over to Northern Alliance forces in Afghanistan. They, in turn, handed the three over to American

---

[2] Lord Johan Steyn, "Guantánamo Bay: The Legal Black Hole," 27th F. A. Mann Lecture, British Institute of International and Comparative Law, November 24, 2003, at http://www.statewatch.org/news/2003/nov/Guantánamo.pdf. See also Clare Dyer, "Law Lord Castigates US Justice: Guantánamo Bay Detainees Facing Trial by Kangaroo Court." *The Guardian*, November 26, 2003, at http://www.guardian.co.uk/politics/2003/nov/26/uk.lords.

[3] As of the publication of this essay, Guantánamo Bay remains open, though the prisoner population has been significantly reduced, with plans by the Obama administration to close the facility pending relocation of prisoners to Supermax prison facilities and/or acceptance of prisoners into willing host countries.

forces, which were offering rewards for possible terrorists. Of course those men and the other British prisoners may have given a false picture of their activities and may in fact have terrorist connections. But there has been no real opportunity to test the truth: no hearing, no means of exoneration if they were in fact innocent.

The Third Geneva Convention, which the United States signed and ratified, provides that when there is a dispute about a prisoner's status—whether he is a regular prisoner of war, for example, or something unlawful like a spy or a terrorist—the issue is to be decided by an independent "competent tribunal." But the Bush Administration declined to follow the Convention. It declared unilaterally that everyone in Guantánamo was an "unlawful combatant." An Administration brief put before the Supreme Court stated the matter quite bluntly. "The President," it said, "in his capacity as commander in chief, has conclusively determined that the Guantánamo detainees ... are not entitled to prisoner-of-war status under the Geneva Convention."

Parents and relatives of some of the Guantánamo prisoners challenged President Bush's unilateral determination that they were unlawful combatants by filing petitions for *habeas corpus*, the writ used to test the legality of an imprisonment.[4] The Bush Administration took the position that United States courts could not consider the cases because Guantánamo is outside the area of American sovereignty. Though the United States has total control of the area under a perpetual treaty with Cuba, the United States Court of Appeals for the District of Columbia Circuit agreed with the government's argument. When the plaintiffs sought review in the Supreme Court, the Justice Department warned that this was not the Court's business, but a matter committed to the President for decision as commander in chief. The Supreme Court, however, agreed to hear the cases, holding that "United States courts have jurisdiction to consider challenges to the legality of the detention of foreign nationals captured abroad in connection with hostilities and incarcerated at Guantánamo Bay."[5] It also bears noting that while the cases have generated significant controversies here at home, the Guantánamo detentions have aroused strong and widespread criticism abroad, particularly in Britain, given the strong alliance between the U.S. and Britain in the so called "war on terror." Take, for example, the British brief filed in the Guantánamo litigation mentioned above. It was quite a remarkable document, signed by 175 members of the House of Commons and the House of Lords. Among them are a former Conservative Lord Chancellor, Lord Mackay, and a greatly-respected law lord, now retired, Lord Browne-Wilkinson. Moreover, Prime Minister

---

4 See, e.g., *Rasul v. Bush*, 542 U.S. 466 (2004); *Hamdi v. Rumsfeld*, 542 U.S. 507 (2004).

5 *Rasul v. Bush*, 542 U.S. 466 (2004) (321 F.3d 1134, reversed and remanded). For additional Supreme Court decisions related to Guantánamo Bay, see *Hamdi v. Rumsfeld*, 542 U.S. 507 (2004); *Hamdan v. Rumsfeld*, 548 U.S. 557 (2006); *Boumediene v. Bush*, 553 U.S. 723 (2008); and *Kiyemba v. Obama*, 559 U.S. 131 (2010) (per curiam).

Tony Blair[6] and his government were pressed to seek changes in the American policy—an embarrassment for Blair, given his strong support of George Bush's wars in Afghanistan and Iraq.

Moreover, it was Guantánamo that led Lord Steyn to speak out about wartime civil liberties in a lecture in the fall of 2003. It was an extraordinary speech from a sitting judge, passionate in its condemnation of the U.S. policy. "The Guantánamo prisoners," Lord Steyn said, are in "a legal black hole.... As matters stand at present, United States courts would refuse to hear a prisoner at Guantánamo Bay who produces credible medical evidence that he has been and is being tortured. They would refuse to hear prisoners who assert that they were not combatants at all...." Lord Steyn concluded, "as a lawyer brought up to admire the ideals of American democracy and justice, I would have to say that I regard this as a monstrous failure of justice."[7] And this failure has real implications for the lives of detainees. While initially we believed that Guantánamo prisoners had not been physically tortured, subsequent disclosures about Guantánamo and the Abu Ghraib prison in Iraq showed that U.S. personnel had engaged in waterboarding of prisoners, beating and other actions hitherto regarded by the United States as prohibited by the International Convention Against Torture. And for those who were not physically tortured, endless interrogation, isolation and harsh conditions of confinement still took a heavy psychological toll. Thus it is perhaps not surprising that as of 2004, thirty-two of the Guantánamo Bay prisoners had attempted suicide.[8]

Shortly after the terrorist attacks of September 11, 2001, President Bush issued an order calling for military tribunals to try any non-Americans who supported terrorism or harbored terrorists. The Defense Department has indicated several times that some of the Guantánamo prisoners may be charged before such tribunals, but it was not until 2006 that Congress passed the Military Commissions Act (the "MCA"), creating military tribunals for Guantánamo Bay detainees. Congress subsequently amended the MCA via the Military Commissions Act of 2009. Even today, use of the MCA remains contested due to the lack of procedural protections, questions of fairness, and Supreme Court rulings related to the right of detainees to seek hearings

---

[6] Tony Blair resigned his position as Prime Minister on June 27, 2007.

[7] Steyn op cit.

[8] The numbers of attempted and successful suicides by prisoners at Guantánamo Bay are unclear, with some reports referencing all acts of self-harm, others attempted suicides, and still others deaths attributed to suicide or natural causes. Alex Eichler reports in *The Atlantic Wire* that at least six suicide attempts by prisoners at Guantánamo Bay have resulted in the prisoner's death ("Afghan Prisoner at Guantánamo Dies in Apparent Suicide," May 19, 2011, http://www.theatlanticwire.com/politics/2011/05/afghan-prisoner-guantanamo-dies-apparent-suicide/37905/; see also "Guantánamo Suicides 'Acts of War,'" *BBC News* June 11, 2006, http://news.bbc.co.uk/2/hi/5068606.stm).

within the civilian federal court system regarding the legality of their detentions.

Difficult legal questions were inevitable. What law would a defendant be charged with violating? Would a criminal law of the United States be said to apply to, say, an Afghan citizen who fought against American forces on behalf of the Taliban, whose government then controlled almost all of Afghanistan? Would al Qaeda terrorists be charged under international human rights laws of the kind applied by the International Criminal Tribunal for the Former Yugoslavia or the law to be applied by the new International Criminal Court against suspected perpetrators of genocide and war crimes—the court so fiercely opposed by the Bush Administration? The Pentagon had already designated some military lawyers to act as defense counsel before the tribunals. But five of the uniformed officers who were selected filed a brief in the Supreme Court arguing that the system created by President Bush was flawed by its failure to provide for ultimate appeal from the military tribunals to a civilian court.

Another area of harsh policy on the part of the Bush Administration was its treatment of aliens inside the United States. In the weeks after 9/11, Attorney General Ashcroft ran a program of mass detention of aliens, targeting mainly Muslims and Arabs, on suspicion that they had a connection to terrorism. At first the Justice Department issued a weekly running total of detainees, but it stopped this practice on November 5, 2001, when the figure reached 1,182. The total number detained in this and other Ashcroft programs is probably around 5,000. Many of those arrested were held for weeks or months in jail. In the words of *New York Times* legal writer, Adam Liptak, their treatment "inverted the foundation principles of the American legal system."[9] They were arrested essentially at random, without probable cause to believe they were supporters of terror. They were held for long periods without charges. They were treated as guilty until proven innocent—detained, that is, until a lengthy F.B.I. process concluded that they "posed no danger to the United States." Eventually nearly all were charged with violations of immigration law, such as overstaying visas or a visiting student failing to inform the government of a change of courses. Many were held for months after judges ordered them released, or after they agreed to leave the country.

What was done to those detainees in prison is hard for an American—this one, anyways—to believe. They were beaten, humiliated, kept in solitary confinement with fluorescent lights on 24 hours a day. At the Metropolitan Detention Center in Brooklyn, New York, guards allowed prisoners to try to telephone a lawyer once a week. Guards informed them it was time to make

---

9 Adam Liptak, "Threats and Responses: Assessment—For Jailed Immigrants, a Presumption of Guilt," *The New York Times*, June 3, 2003, at http://www.nytimes.com/2003/06/03/us/threats-and-responses-assessment-for-jailed-immigrants-a-presumption-of-guilt.html.

that call by asking a prisoner, "Are you okay?" That was supposedly shorthand for, "Do you want to telephone a lawyer?" The Justice Department's Inspector General, Glenn A. Fine, described such mistreatment of detainees in a scathing report issued in 2003.[10] This report was especially critical of the Brooklyn Center. But the report concluded that the whole alien detention program was problematic, with F.B.I. agents making little effort to distinguish real terrorist suspects from people picked up by chance, and detainees held without access to lawyers or family members. In fact, it was hard for families to find the detainees. Their names were kept secret so that if they were arrested away from home, their families were left thinking they had just disappeared. Places of detention were also kept secret, and deportation hearings were closed. The whole program was blanketed in secrecy, a hallmark of tyranny.

When the Inspector General published his report, Attorney General Ashcroft brushed off the criticism. His spokesperson, Barbara Comstock, said, "We make no apologies for finding every legal way possible to protect the American public from further terrorist attacks."[11] The Inspector General's description of lawless behavior by prison guards was confirmed, six months later, when videotapes taken at the Brooklyn prison that were supposedly thrown away turned up.

The two areas just described, the Guantánamo Bay prison and the mass detentions after 9/11, both involve non-Americans. American citizens may feel they are safe from the methods used against aliens, but they are not. The Bush Administration used similar methods against citizens, and its lawyers argued that citizens have no greater protection of their freedom.

As of 2004, two Americans, Yaser Esam Hamdi and José Padilla, had been imprisoned for more than 20 months, without charges, without the right to see a lawyer, without trial. They were in solitary confinement, subject to endless interrogation. Under the legal theory of the Bush Administration, applied unilaterally to these two men, they could remain in isolated imprisonment without a trial for the rest of their lives.

The first of these two American detainees, Yaser Esam Hamdi, was seized in Afghanistan during the war there. President Bush declared him to be an "enemy combatant" and ordered him held without charge. When Hamdi's father sought his release on a writ of *habeas corpus*, the United States Court of Appeals for the Fourth Circuit held that the President had the power to detain a citizen when he was found, like Hamdi, on or near a foreign battle-

---

[10] Glenn A. Fine, *The September 11 Detainees: A Review of the Treatment of Aliens Held on Immigration Charges in Connection with the Investigation of the September 11 Attacks*, Office of the Inspector General, June, 2003, at http://www.justice.gov/oig/special/0306/analysis.pdf.

[11] Statement of Barbara Comstock, Director of Public Affairs, Regarding the IG's Report on 9/11 Detainees, Department of Justice, June 2, 2003, at http://www.justice.gov/opa/pr/2003/June/03_opa_324.htm.

field. The court said it was not deciding what the President could do with someone arrested inside this country on suspicion of a terrorist connection. [12] Ultimately, Hamdi's father asked the Supreme Court to hear his case. The Bush Administration strongly opposed review, but the Court granted the Hamdi petition. [13]

The other American citizen detainee, José Padilla, was born in Brooklyn. He was a gang member, served several prison terms, and while in prison, converted to Islam. In May 2002 he flew into O'Hare Airport in Chicago from abroad. Federal agents arrested him there and took him to New York, serving him with an order to be a material witness before a grand jury looking into the terrorist attack on the World Trade Center. A judge appointed a lawyer, Donna Newman, to represent Padilla and set a hearing for June 11, 2002. But on June 10th, Ms. Newman got a telephone call saying she need not come to court the next day. There would be no hearing, because her client had been taken away to a Navy brig in South Carolina and detained as an enemy combatant.

On that same day, Attorney General Ashcroft told the world about the case. He happened to be in Moscow, but he made a statement on television. "We have captured a known terrorist," he said. "While in Afghanistan and Pakistan, [Padilla] trained with the enemy.... In apprehending him, we have disrupted an unfolding terrorist plot to attack the United States by exploding a radioactive 'dirty bomb.'"[14] What Ashcroft said sounded frightening, but of course at the time of his statement, there had been no process to test the truth of his dramatic claims. I had always thought that legal ethics barred a prosecutor from pronouncing a prisoner guilty before a trial, but perhaps that is an old-fashioned view. Nevertheless, in Padilla's *habeas corpus* proceeding before the United States District Court in New York, the judge found that the government merely had to show "some evidence" for its description of Padilla as an enemy combatant. The evidence produced by the government was a statement by a Pentagon official, not subject to cross-examination and without any first-hand witnesses. The judge said that was enough to justify Padilla's detention. But he did say that Padilla should be allowed to talk to his lawyers, for the limited purpose of informing them of any facts inconsistent with his designation as a terrorist.

The judge's call for a limited right to counsel was strongly disputed by

---

[12] The District Court ruling was later reversed by the Supreme Court, which found that although the United States government could detain unlawful combatants, U.S. citizen detainees had a right to a hearing on that detention before an impartial civilian court judge. See *Hamdi v. Rumsfeld*, 542 U.S. 507 (2004), *reversing* 316 F.3d 450 (4th Cir. 2003).

[13] *Hamdi v. Rumsfeld*, 542 U.S. 507 (2004).

[14] "Ashcroft Statement on 'Dirty Bomb' Suspect," *CNN U.S.*, June 10, 2002, at http://articles.cnn.com/2002-06-10/us/ashcroft.announcement_1_dirty-bomb-abdullah-al-muhajir-al-qaeda-officials?_s=PM:US.

the Bush Administration. It said any visit by a lawyer to Padilla might damage his interrogation by destroying the necessary "atmosphere of dependency and trust between the subject and interrogator." That seemed to me a bit of inadvertent candor—an implicit acknowledgement that the interrogators want to overbear Padilla's will. In the criminal law, after all, the *Miranda* rule assures the right to counsel at the start of any questioning precisely because a prisoner alone in the hands of his or her jailers may be overborne in interrogation. The Padilla case went to the United States Court of Appeals for the Second Circuit. By a vote of two to one, a panel of that court rejected President Bush's claim to power to detain Americans without trial. Even the dissenting judge said that Padilla should be allowed to consult counsel. The Justice Department sought review of the Padilla decision and I believe the outcome of this case, as well as the Hamdi appeal, will have large import for American freedom.[15]

While President Bush and his administration had been much criticized for unilateralism in foreign policy—acting without consulting allies out of disregard for their views—the Hamdi and Padilla cases show a striking unilateralism at home. In both, the President claimed a right to determine not only the law, but also the facts, all on his own. He asserted the novel legal power to detain American citizens indefinitely, without trial or counsel, in the absence of specific authorization by Congress. And his lawyers argued for *habeas corpus* proceedings so narrow that the detainees would have no real ability to contest the facts underlying their designation as enemy combatants. As we saw in the Guantánamo cases, President Bush decided "conclusively" that the prisoners were unlawful combatants, as his lawyers put it, notwithstanding the terms of the Geneva Convention. Moreover, he claimed that his determination was beyond review in any court.

This attempt to prevent any meaningful access to the courts is especially alarming. Judges are the last line of defense for citizens against abuse of official power. The British parliamentarians' brief in the Guantánamo case makes the point well. The United Kingdom and the United States share an unshakeable commitment to the rule of law, the brief says.

> Recourse to an independent and impartial tribunal is required by the rule of law, especially when the justification for detention is contested or uncertain.... [We] respectfully submit that this Court should preserve the judiciary's vital role to insure that executive ac-

---

[15] Padilla's case was eventually heard by the Supreme Court (*Rumsfeld v. Padilla*, 542 U.S. 426 (2004)). However, the Court did not decide the substantive issues of the case. Instead, the Court found that the lower court petitions had been improperly filed in the wrong jurisdiction and against the wrong defendant due to Padilla's move from a state-run jail in New York to a South Carolina military detention facility. The case was sent back to the lower court for dismissal without prejudice. The government later filed charges against Padilla in criminal court, where he was convicted for conspiracy to commit terrorism. He has since appealed his conviction.

tions violate neither the Constitution of the United States nor the international rule of law and human rights.[16]

British interest in the Guantánamo situation raises a question: Why are we less concerned about the role of our judiciary than they are? If someone tried to file a similar brief in the Supreme Court on behalf of members of the United States Congress, he would have little chance of finding 175 Senators and Representatives willing to sign it. There was not much public outcry about the Bush Administration's disregard for civil liberties, and the press has only latterly begun to pay serious attention.

The basic reason for the lack of American public concern must be fear. The attacks of September 11 were traumatic, arguably making us feel more vulnerable than we have in living memory. The repression of civil liberty accompanying the present fear is especially dangerous, I think, because it has no time limit. Wars are usually over in a few years. After them, Americans have tended to regret abuses done in the name of security. We eventually apologized to the Japanese-Americans who were moved during World War II internment from their homes on the West Coast to confinement in desert camps. But it is hard to imagine or even define an end to the war on terror. The terrorists are not going to surrender. The endless prospect of perceived national danger is cause to be on our guard more than ever before against loss of liberty in the name of security. If we let down our guard, if we allow our freedom to be eaten away, the terrorists will have won. The idea of a political system based on law has been the great American contribution to political theory—a government of laws, not men, as John Adams put it. We rely on the law to protect our system and ourselves. We abandon that faith in the law at our peril.

I conclude with the words of Justice Aharon Barak, the much-respected judge president of the Israeli Supreme Court, who so memorably addressed the question of terror and the law when he noted:

> Terrorism does not justify the neglect of legal norms. This is how we distinguish ourselves from the terrorists themselves. They act against the law, by violating and trampling it, while in its war against terrorism, a democratic state acts within the framework of the law.... It is, therefore, not merely a war of the State against its enemies; it is a war of the Law against its enemies.[17]

---

16 Brief of 175 Members of Both Houses of the Parliament of the United Kingdom of Great Britain and Northern Ireland as Amici Curiae in Support of Petitioners in the Case of *Rasul et al v. Bush et al.*, January 14, 2004, 12, at http://www.appellate.net/guantanamo_bay/AmiciCuriae_175_Members_Parliament_United_Kingdom_Northern_Ireland.pdf.

17 Aharon Barak, "The Supreme Court and the Problem of Terrorism," in *Judgments of the Israel Supreme Court: Fighting Terrorism Within the Law*, January 2, 2005, at http://www.jewishvirtuallibrary.org/jsource/Politics/sctterror.html.

6

Perilous Times: Civil Liberties in Wartime

Geoffrey R. Stone

Geoffrey Stone is Edward H. Levi Distinguished Service Professor of Law at the University of Chicago, where he has served as dean of the law school and provost of the University. He is a Fellow of the American Academy of Arts and Sciences, a member of the National Board of Directors of the American Constitution Society, the National Advisory Council of the American Civil Liberties Union, and the American Law Institute.

War excites great passions. Thousands, perhaps millions, of lives may be at risk. The nation itself may be at peril. Emotions run high. Spies, saboteurs, and terrorists are thought to lurk around every corner. Fear and patriotism become the order of the day. If ever there is a time to pull out all the stops, it is surely in wartime. In war, the government may conscript soldiers, commandeer property, control prices, ration food, raises taxes, and freeze wages. May it also limit civil liberties?

The United States has a long and unfortunate history of overreacting to the perceived dangers of wartime. Time and again, Americans have allowed fear and fury to get the better of them. Time and again, Americans have suppressed dissent, imprisoned and deported persons thought to be disloyal, and then later regretted their actions. In the discussion that follows, I will briefly explore these issues in seven episodes in American history: the "Half War" with France in 1798, the Civil War, World War I, World War II, the Cold War, the Vietnam War, and the War on Terrorism.

As we shall see, there are important lessons to be learned from this history. One lesson is that the pressures existing in a wartime environment naturally cause citizens to demand protection from enemies—both real and imagined—indeed to demand that their government protect them. Another lesson is that government officials often act too quickly to acquiesce to those demands, even if they know that the demands are unnecessary and unreasonable, because they are unwilling to explain to their constituents that their demands are unwarranted. A third lesson is that political leaders, or would-be political leaders, often exploit the fears and anxieties of wartime for partisan political advantage. And fourth, judges, whom we normally look to to preserve our most fundamental freedoms, often fail in these circumstances, because judges often share the same fears and anxieties of the public and, in any event, question whether they have the expertise to second-guess legislative and executive branch claims about what the national security requires. They therefore too often defer to governmental demands and reach decisions we later come to regret. But let us turn now to the history itself.

The Sedition Act of 1798

The period from 1789 to 1801 was a critical era in American history. In a climate of fear, suspicion and intrigue, America's new Constitution was put to a test of its very survival. At the time, the nation's first two political parties were engaged in a bitter political struggle. The Federalists, led by Alexander Hamilton and John Adams, were concerned primarily with strengthening the nation economically, preserving social stability, enhancing federal power, and ensuring the nation's national security. They were deeply distrustful of the common man and believed that the nation's economic elite should hold the reins of governance. In contrast, the Republicans, led by Thomas Jefferson and James Madison, were distrustful of a strong federal government and were less concerned about social stability and security than with individual liberty.

These two groups eyed each other with great suspicion and animosity. The Federalists had essentially controlled the nation from the beginning, but in the election of 1796 John Adams had defeated Thomas Jefferson by a scant 3 electoral votes (71 to 68). There was thus great uncertainty and anxiety as people looked ahead to the election of 1800. The Republicans did not trust the Federalists, and the Federalists did not trust the Republicans. Each thought that the other would take the nation in dangerous and destructive directions.

Against this background, in 1798 the United States found itself embroiled in a European war that then raged between France and England. A harsh political debate divided the Federalists, who favored the English, and the Republicans, who favored the French. The Federalists were then in power and the administration of President John Adams initiated a series of defense measures that brought the United States into a state of undeclared war with France. The Republicans fiercely opposed these measures, leading the Federalists to accuse them of disloyalty. President Adams, for example, declared that the Republicans "would sink the glory of our country and prostrate her liberties at the feet of France."[1]

In this environment, and over the strong objections of the Republicans, the Federalists enacted the Sedition Acts of 1798, which prohibited the publication of "any false, scandalous, and malicious writing" against the government of the United States, the Congress, or the President, with intent to defame them or bring them into "contempt or disrepute."[2] This was a stun-

---

[1] Citations from historical documents in this essay may be found in Geoffrey R. Stone, *Perilous Times: Free Speech in Wartime from the Sedition Act of 1798 to the War on Terrorism* (New York: W.W. Norton, 2004). See also Stone's *War and Liberty: An American Dilemma* (New York: W.W. Norton, 2007), and *Top Secret: When Our Government Keeps Us in the Dark* (Lanham, MD: Rowman & Littlefield, 2007).

[2] Sec. 2, The Alien and Sedition Acts of July 14, 1798.

ning development, given that only eight years earlier the nation had adopted an amendment to the Constitution that forbade Congress to make any "law abridging the freedom of speech." The Federalists argued, however, that every government necessarily had the authority to "preserve and defend itself against injuries and outrages which endanger its existence," and that in time of war the nation could not afford to tolerate the same degree of disagreement and dissent as it could in a time of peace. They insisted that—faced with an external threat—the people must be unified. Criticism of the government would alienate the people from their leaders, demoralize citizens, and strengthen the resolve of the enemy.[3]

The Republican James Madison responded that the Sedition Act violated the First Amendment because it undermined "the responsibility of public servants and public measures to the people" and embraced the "exploded doctrine 'that the administrators of the Government are the masters, and not the servants, of the people.'" The Republicans maintained that, even in time of war, free and open debate is essential to self-government. But the Federalists had the votes.

The Republicans also understood that the real reason for the Sedition Act of 1798 had less to do with the prospective war with France—which never materialized—than with the election of 1800. Indeed, the Federalist enforcement strategy was aimed directly at that election. Its objective was to silence every leading Republican newspaper and critic as the contest between Adams and Jefferson drew near.

The Federalists used the Act ruthlessly, but only against members or supporters of the Republican Party. One Republican congressman, Matthew Lyon, was prosecuted and convicted for declaring that under President Adams "every consideration of the public welfare" was "swallowed up in a continual grasp for power." Another Republican, James Callender, was convicted for accusing Adams of contriving "a French war, an American navy, a large standing army, an additional load of taxes, and all the other symptoms and consequences of debt and despotism." Despite these efforts to stifle criticism of the Adams administration in the guise of protecting the national security, the Federalists' plan backfired. As it turned out, the American people were outraged by the Sedition Act, and Jefferson handily defeated Adams in the pivotal presidential election of 1800.

Although the Supreme Court did not have occasion at the time to rule on the constitutionality of the Sedition Act, President Jefferson, who defeated Adams in the election of 1800, pardoned all those who had been convicted under the Act, and in 1840 Congress repaid all the fines, noting that the Act had been passed under a "mistaken exercise" of power and was "null and

---

[3] Lucas A. Powe, Jr., *The Fourth Estate and the Constitution: Freedom of the Press in America* (Berkeley, CA: University of California Press, 1991), 57.

void." The Supreme Court has never missed an opportunity in the years since to remind us that the Sedition Act of 1798 has been judged unconstitutional in the "court of history."[4]

The Civil War: Lincoln's Suspensions of *Habeas Corpus*

During the Civil War, the United States faced perhaps its most severe challenge. There were sharply divided loyalties, fluid military and political boundaries, easy opportunities for espionage and sabotage, and more than 600,000 combat fatalities. In such circumstances, and in the face of widespread and often bitter opposition to the war, military conscription, and the Emancipation Proclamation, President Abraham Lincoln had to balance the conflicting interests of military necessity and individual liberty. At the core of this conflict was the writ of *habeas corpus*, which has historically guaranteed a detained individual the right to a prompt judicial determination of whether his detention by government is lawful. The writ is a bulwark of Anglo-American law, for it protects the individual against the excesses of executive overreaching.

The writ of *habeas corpus* works as follows: If government officers seize an individual, the writ gives that individual (or his representative) a right to go to a court of law to ask the court to determine whether the detention is lawful. If the court finds that detention is not lawful, it will issue the writ and order the individual's release. The writ of *habeas corpus* prevents the executive from unjustifiably seizing people, tossing them in a lock up, and throwing away the key, by enabling an *independent* branch of the government—the judiciary—to determine whether government detentions are lawful. The writ is therefore a fundamental element of American freedom.

Nonetheless, the Constitution authorizes suspension of the writ of *habeas corpus* in cases of rebellion or invasion when the civil peace requires it. At the very outset of the War, Lincoln found himself in a dire situation. After the attack on Fort Sumter, the nation's Capitol was vulnerable to Confederate attack. Washington, D.C. is tucked between two border states: Maryland and Virginia. Virginia had already seceded and Maryland had not yet decided whether it would stay in the Union or secede. As Union troops tried to make their way down from the North in order to protect the Capitol, pro-secessionist mobs in Baltimore attacked the soldiers, dismantled railroad lines, and effectively blocked the soldiers' access to Washington. The local police were unable (or unwilling) to manage the situation, thus posing the question whether Lincoln could declare martial law and suspend the writ of *habeas corpus*. He agonized over the matter, but finally decided that it was

---

4 See *New York Times Co. v. Sullivan*, 376 U.S. 254, 276 (1964); *Watts v. United States*, 394 U.S. 705 (1969).

necessary and therefore appropriate for him to do so. As a consequence of his decision, the troops were able to reach Washington.

The problem for Lincoln was that the Constitution grants the power to suspend the writ of *habeas corpus*, not to the President, but to Congress. By suspending the writ in these circumstances, without congressional authorization, Lincoln arguably acted unconstitutionally. Complicating the situation even further, Congress was not in session at the time and in those days there was no way for Congress to reconvene quickly. In such circumstances, most historians and legal scholars agree that Lincoln's suspension of the writ at this point in the War, although technically unconstitutional, was both necessary and appropriate.

During the course of the Civil War, however, Lincoln suspended the writ of *habeas corpus* on eight separate occasions. Over time, the suspensions grew ever more aggressive. His most extreme suspension order, in September 1862, was applicable *nationwide* and declared that "all persons ... guilty of any disloyal practice ... shall be subject to court martial." It is unknown exactly how many civilians were arrested by military authorities during the Civil War. Estimates range from 13,000 to 38,000. In some instances, civilians were taken into military custody merely for criticizing the war. The most prominent example of this was former Ohio congressman Clement Vallandigham, who was arrested by military authorities and later exiled by Lincoln because of a speech he delivered in 1863 in which he described the war as "wicked, cruel and unnecessary" and as a "war for the freedom of blacks and the enslavement of whites."

In 1866, a year after the war ended, the Supreme Court held in *Ex parte Milligan*[5] that in at least some of these instances Lincoln had exceeded his constitutional authority as commander-in-chief. The Court ruled that the president was not constitutionally empowered to suspend the writ of *habeas corpus*, even in time of war, if the ordinary civil courts were open and functioning. The Court declared that the Constitution governs "equally in war and in peace," and proclaimed that "no doctrine involving more pernicious consequences was ever invented by ... man than that [the Constitution itself] can be suspended" in time of national emergency.

World War I: The Espionage Act of 1917

The story of civil liberties during World War I is, in many ways, even more disturbing. When the United States entered the war in April 1917, there was strong opposition to both the war and the draft. Many citizens argued that the war raging in Europe did not threaten any vital interests of the United States and that the nation's real goal in entering the war was not to "make the world safe for democracy," as President Woodrow Wilson proclaimed, but to protect

---

5 *Ex parte Milligan*, 71 U.S. (4 Wall.) 2 (1886).

the investments of munitions dealers and armaments manufacturers and others who made millions off the War. President Wilson had little patience for such dissent. He warned that disloyalty "must be crushed out" of existence and that disloyalty "was ... not a subject on which there was room for ... debate." Disloyal individuals, he explained, "had sacrificed their right to civil liberties."

After declaring war, Congress quickly enacted the Espionage Act of 1917, which made it a crime for any person to "cause or attempt to cause insubordination, disloyalty, or refusal of duty in the military forces of the United States" or to "obstruct the recruiting or enlistment service of the United States." Although the Espionage Act was not intended to suppress dissent generally, aggressive federal prosecutors and compliant federal judges soon transformed it into a full-scale prohibition of seditious utterance. The administration's intent in this regard was made evident in November 1917 when Attorney General Charles Gregory, referring to war dissenters, declared: "May God have mercy on them, for they need expect none from an outraged people and an avenging government."

The Department of Justice prosecuted more than 2,000 individuals for allegedly disloyal or seditious expression, and in an atmosphere of fear, hysteria and clamor, most judges were quick to mete out severe punishment— often 10 to 20 years in prison—to those deemed disloyal. The result was the suppression of virtually all genuine debate about the merits, morality and progress of the war.

At this point, I should make an important observation about the nature of free speech. When individuals decide to sign a petition, attend a lecture, or participate in a protest march, they know that their individual participation, in and of itself, is not likely to have any appreciable impact on national policy. Thus, if people know that by signing a petition, marching in a demonstration, or attending a lecture they might land in jail for 5, 10 or 20 years, they will probably say, "You know, I think I will skip that protest today, because going there is not going to make any difference, and I don't want to be the one they pick out to go to jail." This is what we mean by the *chilling effect*. The very nature of free speech is such that an individual's own speech usually does not benefit that individual very much, so he is easily intimidated by the government into remaining silent. It may be that one person's decision to forego free speech is no big deal, but when many people each make the same individual decision, the result can be a complete distortion of public discourse and government decision-making.

And where was the Supreme Court in all this? In a series of decisions in 1919 and 1920, the Court consistently upheld the convictions of individuals who had agitated against the war and the draft—individuals as obscure as Mollie Steimer, a Russian-Jewish émigré who had distributed anti-war leaflets in Yiddish on the lower East Side of New York, and as prominent as

Eugene V. Debs, who had received almost a million votes as the Socialist Party candidate for President in 1916.[6]

Between 1919 and 1923, after the War had ended, the federal government released from prison every individual who had been convicted under the Espionage Act. A decade later, President Franklin Roosevelt granted amnesty to all of these individuals, restoring their full political and civil rights. And over the next half-century, the Supreme Court overruled every one of its World War I decisions, holding in effect that every one of the individuals who had been imprisoned or deported in this era for his or her political dissent had been punished for speech that should have been protected by the First Amendment.

World War II: Internment Camps

On December 7, 1941, Japan attacked Pearl Harbor. Two months later, on February 19, 1942, President Roosevelt signed Executive Order 9066, which authorized the Army to "designate military areas" from which "any persons may be excluded." Although the words "Japanese" or "Japanese American" never appeared in the Order, it was understood to apply only to persons of Japanese ancestry.

Over the next eight months, more than 110,000 individuals of Japanese descent were forced to leave their homes in California, Washington, Oregon and Arizona. Two-thirds of these individuals were American citizens, representing almost 90% of all Japanese-Americans. No charges were brought against these individuals and there were no hearings. They did not know where they were going, how long they would be detained, what conditions they would face, or what fate would await them. They were told to bring only what they could carry. Many families lost everything. On the orders of military police, these individuals were transported to one of ten permanent internment camps, which were located in isolated areas in wind-swept deserts or vast swamplands. Men, women and children were placed in overcrowded rooms with no furniture other than cots. They found themselves surrounded by barbed wire and military police, and there they remained for some three years.

Why did this happen? Certainly, the days following Pearl Harbor were dark days for the American spirit. Fear of possible Japanese sabotage and espionage was rampant, and an outraged public felt an understandable instinct to lash out at those who had attacked us. But this act was also very much an extension of more than a century of poisonous racial prejudice against the "yellow peril." Ultimately, the decision to intern all men, women

---

[6] See *Schenck v. United States,* 249 U.S. 47 (1919); *Frohwerk v. United States,* 249 U.S. 204 (1919); *Debs v. United States,* 249 U.S. 204 (1919); and *Abrams v. United States,* 250 U.S. 616 (1919).

and children of Japanese ancestry was made by the President, as commander-in-chief. The decision was opposed by the Attorney General, the Director of the FBI, and the Secretary of War. Although FDR explained the Order in terms of military necessity, there is little doubt that domestic politics played a role in his thinking: 1942 was an election year. The incarceration of 110,000 individuals of Japanese ancestry was, in part, a way to strengthen his party's chances in the upcoming election.

In *Korematsu v. United States*,[7] decided in 1944, the Supreme Court, in a six-to-three decision, upheld the constitutionality of the President's action in a decision that has since come to be regarded as one of the darkest moments in the Court's history. The Court offered the following explanation:

> We are not unmindful of the hardships imposed upon a large group of American citizens. But hardships are part of war, and war is an aggregation of hardships. Korematsu was not excluded from the West Coast because of hostility to his race, but because the military authorities decided that the urgency of the situation demanded that all citizens of Japanese ancestry be segregated from the area. We cannot—by availing ourselves of the calm perspective of hindsight—say that these actions were unjustified.

The Supreme Court has never cited its decision in *Korematsu* with approval. It is regarded as a stain on the Court, just as the internment is regarded as a stain on the United States itself. Indeed, in 1980 a congressional commission concluded that Executive Order 9066 had violated the rights of Japanese Americans. Eight years later, President Ronald Reagan signed the Civil Liberties Restoration Act of 1988, which offered an official Presidential apology and reparations to each of the Japanese-American internees who had suffered discrimination, loss of liberty, loss of property and personal humiliation because of the actions of the United States government.

The Cold War: The Era of McCarthyism

As World War II drew to a close, the nation moved almost seamlessly into what came to be known as the Cold War. The Berlin blockade, the fall of China, the Soviet atomic bomb, the Korean War, and the Cuban missile crisis were not a string of independent events, but a slow-motion hot war, conducted on the periphery of rival empires. During this era, the nation demonized members of the Communist Party. Joseph McCarthy, Richard Nixon, J. Edgar Hoover, the American Legion and a host of political opportunists all fed—and fed upon—the image of the domestic Communist as less than a full citizen of the United States.

The long shadow of the House Committee on Un-American Activities fell across our campuses and our culture. In hearings before HUAC, such promi-

---

[7] *Korematsu v. United States*, 323 U.S. 214 (1944).

nent actors as George Murphy and Ronald Reagan testified that the media had been infected with sly, un-American propaganda. Fear of ideological contamination swept the nation like a pestilence of the national soul. Hysteria over the Red Menace produced a wide-range of federal and state restrictions on free expression and association. These included extensive loyalty programs; emergency detention plans for alleged subversives; pervasive webs of federal, state and local undercover informers to infiltrate dissident organizations; legislative investigations designed to harass dissenters and to expose to the public their private political beliefs and associations; and direct prosecution of the leaders and members of the Communist Party of the United States.

A good example was the federal loyalty program enacted during the Truman administration. This program defined as "disloyal" any sympathetic association with any organization "designated by the Attorney General as Communist, or subversive." The implications were clear. The Attorney General's list initially encompassed seventy-eight organizations, but it quickly swelled to more than 250, including, for example, the International Workers Order, a fraternal benefit society that specialized in low-cost insurance, and the Joint Anti-Fascist Refugee Committee, which provided relief for refugees of the Spanish Civil War. Inclusion of an organization on the Attorney General's list was tantamount to public branding. Contributions dried up, membership dwindled, meeting places disappeared. The greatest impact of the list, however, was on the freedom of American citizens. Because the criteria for listing were vague and undisclosed, because organizations had no right to contest their listing, and because new groups were constantly being added to the list, individuals had to be wary of joining *any* organization. The only "safe" course was to join nothing.

Because of the elusiveness of the concept of "disloyalty," no federal employee or prospective federal employee could ever consider herself exempt from the perils of investigation. Was it disloyal to advocate disarmament, to argue that the Communist Party should be legal, to subscribe to the Communist Party newspaper, to read books by "Communist" authors? Any slip of the tongue, any unguarded statement, any criticism of government policy, could lead to one's undoing. The anonymity of informers left every individual open to fools, schemers, paid informers, scandalmongers, and personal enemies. The only sane approach was to keep one's head down, and never look up. As one government employee tellingly remarked, "If Communists like apple pie and I do, I see no reason why I should stop eating it. But I would."

The key Supreme Court decision in this era was *Dennis v. United States*,[8] in which the Court upheld the convictions of the leaders of the American Communist Party for allegedly conspiring to advocate the violent overthrow

---

[8] *Dennis v. United States*, 391 U.S. 494 (1951).

of the government. Over the next several years, the Court clearly put its stamp of approval on an array of actions we today look back on as exemplars of McCarthyism.

Eventually, however, the Court began to take a more critical look. Over the next decade, the Court constrained the power of legislative committees to investigate political beliefs, invalidated restrictions on the mailing of Communist political propaganda, limited the circumstances in which an individual could constitutionally be denied public employment because of her political beliefs or associations, and restricted the authority of a state to deny membership in the bar to individuals because of their past Communist affiliations. Although the Court proceeded in fits and starts during this decade, in the end it played an important role in helping bring this sorrowful era to a close.

The Vietnam War: COINTELPRO and the Pentagon Papers

In the Vietnam War, as in the Civil War and World War I, there was substantial and often bitter opposition both to the war and the draft. Over the course of the war, the United States suffered through a period of intense and often violent struggle. After President Nixon announced the American "incursion" into Cambodia, for example, student strikes closed a hundred campuses. Governor Ronald Reagan, asked about campus militants, replied: "If it takes a bloodbath, let's get it over with." On May 4, 1970, National Guardsmen at Kent State University responded to taunts and rocks by firing their M-1 rifles into a crowd of students, killing four. Protests and strikes exploded at more than twelve hundred of the nation's colleges and universities. As Henry Kissinger put it later, "The very fabric of government was falling apart."

Despite all this, there was no systematic effort during the Vietnam War to prosecute individuals for their opposition to the war. The courts, and especially the Supreme Court, played a key role in achieving this result. In 1969 the Court, in *Brandenburg v. Ohio*, effectively overruled *Dennis* and held that even advocacy of unlawful conduct cannot be punished unless it is intended to incite and is likely to incite "imminent lawless action." The Court had come a long way in the fifty years since World War I.

This is not to say that the government did not find other ways to impede dissent, however. The most significant of these was the FBI's extensive effort to infiltrate and to "expose, disrupt and otherwise neutralize" allegedly "subversive" organizations, ranging from civil rights groups to the various factions of the anti-war movement. In this secret COINTELPRO (counter-intelligence program) operation, the FBI compiled political dossiers on more than half-a-million Americans. This program reflected a systematic effort to harass dissident organizations, sow dissension within their ranks and inform public and private employers of the political beliefs and activities of dissenters. When these activities finally came to light, they were sharply condemned by Congress and, in 1976, Attorney General Edward Levi declared that such practices were incompatible with our national values and instituted a series of guidelines designed sharply to restrict FBI surveillance of political organizations and activities.

Another major issue during the Vietnam War involved the publication of the Pentagon Papers. In 1967, Secretary of Defense Robert McNamara commissioned a top-secret study of the Vietnam War. That study, which filled forty-seven volumes, reviewed in great detail the formulation of United States policy toward Indochina, including military operations and secret diplomatic negotiations. In the spring of 1970, Daniel Ellsberg, a former Defense Department official, gave a copy of the Pentagon Papers to the *New York Times*. After the *Times* began publishing excerpts from the papers, the United States filed a complaint for injunction. The matter quickly worked its way to the Supreme Court, which held in *New York Times v. United States*[9] that the government could not constitutionally enjoin the *Times* from publishing the information. Having learned important lessons from the long history of controversies over government efforts to restrict dissent in wartime, the Court held that the publication of even classified information cannot constitutionally be restrained unless the government can prove that the disclosure would "surely result in direct, immediate, and irreparable damage to our Nation."

The War on Terror: Government Secrecy

The terrorist attacks of September 11, 2001 shocked the American people. Images of the collapsing towers of the World Trade Center left the nation in a profound state of fear, fury, grief, and uncertainty. Anxious that September 11 may have been but the first wave of attacks, Americans expected and, indeed, demanded that their government take immediate and decisive steps to protect them.

Not surprisingly, in the wake of September 11, President George W. Bush, like Lincoln and Roosevelt before him, claimed far-reaching powers to address the crisis. Many of his measures were deeply problematic, including secret detentions of non-citizens; closing deportation proceedings from public view; secret detentions of American citizens based solely on executive branch determinations that they might be "enemy combatants"; warrantless interception of telephone calls and email communications; examination of individuals' financial, medical, educational, and library records with no showing of even reasonable suspicion that anything unlawful was afoot; and denial of hearings and access to *habeas corpus* to "enemy combatants" detained at Guantánamo Bay. Perhaps the most dangerous policy of the Bush Administration, however, was its attempt to hide its decisions from the American public. In an effort to evade the constraints of separation of powers, judicial review, checks-and-balances, and democratic accountability, the Bush Ad-

---

9 *New York Times v. United States*, 403 U.S. 712 (1971).

ministration systematically promulgated its policies in secret, denied information to Congress, abused the classification process, narrowly interpreted the Freedom of Information Act, redacted vast quantities of information from government websites, punished government whistleblowers, jailed journalists for refusing to disclose their confidential sources, threatened to prosecute the press for revealing the administration's secret programs, and broadly invoked executive immunity and the state secrets doctrine to prevent both Congress and the courts from evaluating the lawfulness of its programs.

By shielding its decisions from legal, congressional, and public scrutiny, the Bush Administration undermined the single most central premise of a self-governing society: it is the *citizens* who must evaluate the judgments, policies, and programs of their representatives. As James Madison observed, "A popular Government, without popular information, or the means of acquiring it, is but a Prologue to a Farce or a Tragedy; or perhaps both." For the government to hide its actions from the American people, except in the most compelling of circumstances, undermines the very essence of American self-governance.

Conclusion

What can we learn from this history? I would like to offer five observations.

First, the United States has a long and unfortunate history of overreacting to the perceived dangers of wartime. In each instance, we allowed our fears to get the better of us.

Second, it is often argued that in light of the sacrifices we ask citizens (especially soldiers) to make in time of war, it is small price to ask others to surrender some of their peacetime freedoms to help the war effort. As the Supreme Court argued in *Korematsu*, "hardships are part of war, and war is an aggregation of hardships." This is a seductive but dangerous argument. To fight a war successfully, it is necessary for soldiers to risk their lives. But it is not necessarily "necessary" for others to surrender their freedoms. That necessity must be convincingly demonstrated, not merely presumed. And this is especially true when, as is usually the case, the individuals whose rights are sacrificed are not those who make the laws, but minorities, dissidents and non-citizens. In those circumstances, "we" are making a decision to sacrifice "their" rights—not a very prudent way to balance the competing interests.

Third, it is often said that the Supreme Court will not decide a case against the government on an issue of military security during a period of national emergency. The decisions most often cited in support of this proposition are the World War I cases on free speech, *Korematsu*, and *Dennis*. In fact, however, there are many counter-examples. During the Korean War, the Court rejected President Truman's effort to seize the steel industry. During the Vietnam War, the Court repeatedly rejected national security claims by the Executive, including its effort to restrain the publication of the Pentagon

Papers. And in the years after 9/11, the Court consistently rebuffed the more extreme positions of the Bush Administration. So, although it is true that the Court tends to be wary not to "hinder" an ongoing war, it is also true that the Court has a significant record of fulfilling its constitutional responsibility to protect individual liberties—even in time of war.

Fourth, it is useful to note the circumstances that have tended to produce these abuses. They invariably arise out of the combination of a national perception of peril and a concerted campaign by government to promote a sense of national hysteria by exaggeration, manipulation, and distortion. The goal of the government in fostering such public anxiety may be either to make it easier for it to gain public acceptance of the measures it seeks to impose or to gain partisan political advantage, or, of course, both. Fifth, the central challenge is to figure out how to make use of the knowledge that we are likely to make bad and unjust decisions in times of fear and uncertainty. Even when we are aware of the tendency to over-react, we tend immediately to assume that the situation confronting us is different from earlier situations. So even though we know that people may have acted excessively in the past, our actions in the present seem reasonable.

I suggest that the single most important element in learning how to address this dilemma is to develop within the United States a *culture of civil liberties*, in which people understand their history, including the risks and tendencies that plague us as a democracy. In this culture of civil liberties, individuals would understand the importance of being skeptical about government claims of "necessity" and of political leaders who try to whip up a sense of hysteria. People must learn to approach demands to restrict civil liberties in wartime with a strong presumption against it. Restricting liberties should be a last, not a first, resort. We should demand that the government *prove* to us they have done everything reasonable to keep us safe before it starts locking people up because of their national origin, or detaining them without giving them access to a court, or punishing them because they have said things that anger the President. We must also insist on government transparency and we must learn to question government claims that "the people" shouldn't be allowed to know.

There is no easy prescription to protect against these dangers. To strike the right balance in wartime, a nation needs judges who will stand fast against the furies of the age; members of the press and the academy who will help citizens see the issues clearly; public officials with the wisdom to know excess when it exists and the courage to preserve liberty when it is imperiled; and most important of all, an informed and tolerant public who will value, not only their own liberties, but also the liberties of others.

7

"Hear the Other Side": *Miranda*, Guantánamo, and Public Rights to Fairness and Dignity[1]

Judith Resnik

Judith Resnik is the Arthur Liman Professor of Law at Yale Law School. She is a Managerial Trustee of the International Association of Women Judges. In 2001, Resnik was elected a fellow of the American Academy of Arts and Sciences, and in 2002, a member of the American Philosophical Society. In 2008, she received the Fellows of the American Bar Foundation Outstanding Scholar of the Year Award, and in 2012 her book Representing Justice: Invention, Controversy, and Rights in City-States and Democratic Courtrooms *(with Dennis Curtis, Yale University Press, 2011) won two PROSE awards from the American Publishers Association and the SCRIBES award from the American Society of Legal Writers.*

Obligations of Respect

Injunctions to judges to "hear the other side" date back centuries but the meaning of that imperative has changed. This essay sketches facets of the transformation of this ancient precept into a robust constitutional commitment to fair and dignified treatment, respectful of "the other side," as a central value in American political thought and legal practice.

The 1966 decision of *Miranda v. Arizona* exemplifies that ideal, applied to detained individuals suspected of crimes. Rather than leaving such persons isolated and unprotected, the Supreme Court insisted that "the dignity and integrity of its citizens" and "the inviolability of the human personality" required their custodian, the government, to accord them rights to consult lawyers and to remain silent.[2] The private encounter between an individual and the state became a matter of public record and oversight.

Yet by 2011, these precepts had weakened. The complex of buildings, ideas, laws, and practices for which the words "Guantánamo Bay" provide a shorthand had tested and undermined those commitments. State coercion

---

[1] All rights reserved, copyright © Judith Resnik, 2013. This essay builds from and therefore reproduces a few of the images in *Representing Justice: Invention, Controversy, and Rights in City-States and Democratic Courtrooms*, a book co-authored with Dennis Curtis (New Haven, CT: Yale University Press, 2011).

[2] *Miranda v. Arizona*, 384 U.S. 436, 460 (1966).

had gained many champions, arguing the necessity of bending obligations of fairness and dignity in the face of well-founded fears.

Guantánamo is often posited as a unique response to terrorism, and hence not much relevant to those focused on other issues. Yet the fact of detention laces the lives of millions of people, their families, and communities within the United States. As of 2010, more than two million people were incarcerated in jails and prisons as part of seven million under some form of supervision. Daily counts in "non-criminal" detention run by the federal Immigration and Customs Enforcement averaged about 31,000.

Further, while the scale of the challenges that the government faces when dealing with terrorism differs from that when responding to crime, efforts to stem the "war on terror" resemble those aimed at the "war on crime." Consider the key elements that form the predicate for post-9/11 detention: interrogation and the need to get information from people who may well be planning, or have done, terrible harm to others; holding some individuals for interrogation and creating incentives for them to provide information; sorting out people who are guilty from those who are innocent; deciding whom to detain, and dealing over long periods of time with people determined to be egregiously dangerous, even as they too are in need of safety or discipline while confined.

These challenges are not *sui generis* to 9/11 but are variations on the core problems of criminal law that the *Miranda* decision addressed in 1966. Further, although the procedures at Guantánamo are at odds with legal traditions of independent judges, defendants' rights to voluntary confessions, and public processes, the decisionmaking there is continuous with developments in various less high profile administrative contexts, where judges are less independent, individuals less protected, and the public less welcome.

Below, I outline the development of legal precepts that the state had to accord "fair" treatment to individuals, whether in criminal or civil disputes, and that, for those in detention, democratic (as contrasted with "despotic") norms governed. I then detail some of the practices undermining those obligations before turning to examine the reasons to reconstitute public and democratic practices of government obligations to respect all persons, including those detained at the state's behest.

Constituting a Legal Right to Fairness

The Latin maxim *"Audite et Alteram Partem"* ("Hear the Other Side") has been traced through biblical narratives and Greek and Roman law to St. Augustine of Hippo, a Roman Christian theologian of the fifth century.[3] During the Renaissance, that text was inscribed in various town halls around Europe. Shown below is one example (fig. 1), likely added in the late-

---

[3] See John M. Kelly, "Audi Alteram Partem," *Natural Law Forum* 9: 103 (1964).

seventeenth century to the entryway of the Gouda Town Hall.

Figure 1: Arch above the entrance to the Gouda Town Hall (Staudhius), Gouda, The Netherlands, 1459. Architect: Jan Keldermans. Inscription circa 1695.
Image reproduced with the permission of the Streekarchief Midden-Holland (Regional Archive Middle Holland), inv. nr 6668.

By the end of the eighteenth century, English judges had embraced the directive as a limitation on the exercise of government power. A 1799 English court explained *audi alteram partem* as "one of the first principles of justice,"[4] and especially relevant to criminal law: "every man ought to have an opportunity of being heard before he is condemned."[5] By the mid-twentieth century, "hear the other side" was also heralded as a feature of English civil administrative law: "That no man is to be judged unheard was a precept known to the Greeks, inscribed in ancient times upon images in places where justice was administered, proclaimed in Seneca's *Medea*, enshrined in the Scriptures, embodied in Germanic proverbs, ascribed in the Year Books to the law of nature, asserted by Coke to be a principle of divine justice, and traced by an eighteenth-century judge to the events in the Garden of Eden."[6]

Those ideas crossed the Atlantic. Figure 2 shows the phrase—Hear the Other Side—placed on the walls of the Supreme Court of Illinois, built in 1908. Yet the application of this precept entails a series of judgments about who has rights to be heard about what kinds of claims. Those issues have been a preoccupation of American constitutional law for the last century.

---

[4] See *The King v. G. Gaskin*, 101 Eng. Rep. 1349, 1350 (1799). Kelly (op cit., 107) cited the earlier decision of *Boswel's Case*, 77 Eng. Rep. 326, 331 (K.B. 1606), as the first in English law to refer to *audi alteram partem*.

[5] *The King v. G. Gaskin*, at 1350.

[6] de Smith 1955.

Figure 2: *Precedent, Justice, and Record*, Albert H. Krehbiel, 1909, Courtroom mural, Supreme Court Building, Springfield, Illinois.

Photograph reproduced with permission from the Administrative Office of the Illinois Courts and the Krehbiel Corporation.

Consider, as the United States Supreme Court did in 1958, the question of whether a prisoner had sufficient mental competency to be executed. The Court upheld a California statute permitting a prison warden to rely solely on reports from prison psychiatrists when making that determination. Justice Frankfurter dissented: *"Audi alteram partem*—hear the other side!—a demand made insistently through the centuries, is now a command, spoken with the voice of the Due Process Clause of the Fourteenth Amendment, against state governments" even when claims "may turn out not to be meritorious."[7]

Over time, Justice Frankfurter's view prevailed, as the Court assessed the qualities of procedures provided when the government determined liberty and property interests. During the second half of the twentieth century, judicial interpretations made "hear the other side" a constitutional obligation, as justices read the Due Process Clauses of the Fifth and Fourteenth Amendments of the United States Constitution to require that the government ensure an "opportunity to be heard" when individuals faced the loss of certain property or liberty interests.

The word "fairness" does not appear in state and federal constitutions written at the country's founding. Yet the term became, by the 1970s, a regular part of Supreme Court jurisprudence as the Court obliged the government to provide "fair" hearings when, for example, terminating statutory

---

[7] *Caritativo v. California*, 357 U.S. 549, 558 (1958).

entitlements to government benefits, jobs, or licenses.[8] Depending on the context, constitutionally fair decisionmaking requires independent judges, in-person hearings, specific allocations of burdens of proof, reasons for the decisions rendered, oversight of whether evidence supports a criminal verdict and of the quality of eyewitness identification, and review of the award of punitive damages. Furthermore, when interpreting the Fourth, Fifth, Sixth, Eighth, and Fourteenth Amendments, Supreme Court justices repeatedly invoked concerns about asymmetrical power relations between the state and individuals and at times specifically adverted to problems of equality, fairness, and dignity. The Court articulated rights of persons to be insulated from unreasonable searches and seizures, to be provided lawyers, if indigent, to remain silent while in custody, and to be held in jails and prisons whose conditions comport with minimal standards of decency.[9]

The Dignity of Fairness: *Miranda* and "Democratic" Detention

The 1966 decision of *Miranda v. Arizona* is an important pillar in that development. The decision stands for the idea that a person taken into custody by the government is in a dignified position vis-à-vis the state. That posture imposes an obligation on state actors to inform the detainee of rights of silence as well as rights of access to lawyers, assigned to equip that person in the encounter with the state.

The path to the 1966 *Miranda* decision included several instances in which justices compared American constitutional requirements of "democratic" detention to the "despotic" detention found elsewhere. For example, in 1943 in *McNabb v. United States*, the Supreme Court insisted that individuals detained by the police had rights to be brought before a neutral third party. Justice Frankfurter's majority opinion stressed the need for a prompt appearance because a "democratic society, in which respect for the dignity of all men is central, naturally guards against the misuse of the law enforcement process."[10] In 1944, in *Ashcraft v. Tennessee*, Justice Black reiterated that concern, as he distinguished the United States from "certain foreign nations," who would "wring from [detainees] confessions by physical and mental torture."[11]

---

[8] The doctrinal developments are analyzed in Resnik 2011b, and in Resnik and Curtis, ch. 13 (2011); Resnik 2008a.

[9] Judith Resnik and Julie C. Suk, "Adding Insult to Injury: Questioning the Role of Dignity in Conceptions of Sovereignty," *Stanford Law Review* 117 (2003): 1921-1962; Gerald Neuman, "Human Dignity in United States Constitutional Law," in Dieter Simon and Manfred Weiss, eds., *Zur Autonomie des Individuums, Liber Amicorum Spiros Simitis* (Baden-Baden: NomosVerlagsgesellschaf, 2000).

[10] *McNabb v. United States*, 318 U.S. 332, 342-343 (1943).

[11] *Ashcraft v. Tennessee*, 322 U.S. 143, 155 (1944) (concluding that the "Constitution of the United States stands as a bar against the conviction of any individual in an American court by means of a coerced confession").

The contrast between democratic and "despotic" criminal justice systems played a role in the 1951 decision of *United States v. Carignan*, in which a defendant had not been permitted to testify before a jury about the "involuntary character" of his confession. Although no evidence appeared "of violence, of persistent questioning, or of deprivation of food or rest," the defendant confessed only after he was assured by a court officer that no one had been hanged in the past twenty-seven years. In a concurring opinion, Justice William O. Douglas detailed the disturbing degree of power held by jailors:

> [T]he accused is under the exclusive control of the police, subject to their mercy, and beyond the reach of counsel or of friends. What happens behind doors that are opened and closed at the sole discretion of the police is a black chapter in every country—the free as well as the despotic, the modern as well as the ancient.... [W]e in this country ... early made the choice—that the dignity and privacy of the individual were worth more to society than an all-powerful police."[12]

The distinction between despotic and democratic regimes was invoked again in the briefing by John Frank on behalf of Ernesto Miranda. In addition to quoting Justice Douglas' *Carignan* opinion about the totalizing powers of the jailer, Frank insisted:

> We are not talking with some learned historicity about the *lettre de cachet* of pre-Revolutionary France or the secret prisons of a distant Russia. We are talking about conditions in the United States, in the Twentieth Century, and now.[13]

These arguments carried the day in the 1966 Supreme Court *Miranda* ruling, itself a constitutional icon. Chief Justice Earl Warren wrote the five-person majority decision that linked the constitutional prohibition against compelled self-incrimination to the history of "inquisitorial and manifestly unjust methods of interrogating" detainees.[14] Warren's opinion discussed police who "resorted to physical brutality—beatings, hanging, whipping—and to sustained and protracted questioning incommunicado in order to extort confessions." Further, he cited police manuals arguing the importance of "privacy" that purposefully isolated individuals to deprive them of "outside support." Because genuine individual privacy was the "hallmark of our democracy," "mental" like physical coercion was unacceptable ("the blood of the accused is not the only hallmark of an unconstitutional inquisition" that was "destructive of human dignity").

Further, and in contrast to the foreign practices providing negative ref-

---

[12] 342 U.S. 36, 40-42 (1951).

[13] Brief for Petitioner at 46-47, *Miranda v. Arizona*, 384 U.S. 436 (1966) (No. 759).

[14] *Miranda*, 384 U.S. at 442 (citing *Brown v. Walker*, 161 U.S. 591, 596-597 (1896)). The quotes that follow in the text are drawn from the majority opinion, 446-488.

erences evident from the *McNabb, Ashcraft,* and *Carignan* opinions and the *Miranda* brief, the majority turned to non-United States law as a positive exemplar. Chief Justice Warren reported on legal safeguards for interrogation provided in Scotland, India, and Ceylon, as well as by the FBI and the Uniform Code of Military Justice.

The rule that emerged from *Miranda* prohibited the use of defendants' statements as evidence in court if obtained through coercion. The Court imposed the burden on the prosecution to demonstrate protection of the "privilege against self-incrimination," and explained that the obligation attached for "custodial interrogations ... initiated by law enforcement officers after a person has been taken into custody or otherwise deprived" of his or her freedom of action in "any significant way."[15] The mechanism for enforcement of the privilege was (absent the fashioning of "other fully effective means") to inform the person of rights to remain silent and to be addressed in "the presence of an attorney, either retained or appointed."

This imposition of forms of what today would be called "transparency" and "accountability" hearkens back to Jeremy Bentham's nineteenth-century insistence on "publicity"—that judges (and others) had to be subjected to the public eye. Just as Frank urged that lawyers be present to witness police questioning, Bentham wanted ordinary observers to be able to take notes at trials, to serve as insurance for the good judge and as a corrective against "misrepresentations" made by "an unrighteous judge."[16] Thus, centuries apart, Bentham and Frank shaped and joined in movements that used third-party interventions to impose standards of conduct on government officials.

Guantánamo Bay: Torture Memos, Closed Procedures, and *Boumediene*

The holding in *Miranda* has provoked a vast debate about its legal bases, scope, and utility. Recent Supreme Court decisions have put more of an onus on detainees to invoke *Miranda* rights, have limited the circumstances in which such rights attach, and have permitted information obtained outside the parameters of *Miranda* to be used to impeach testimony.[17] Yet, until the last decade, *Miranda* remained as an indictment of coercion and also implicitly of torture. I use the word "implicitly" because, secure under the *Miranda*

---

[15] *Id.* at 444. In 2011, the Court held, 5-4, that a detainee's age (in that instance, a thirteen-year-old) was a factor to consider when determining whether a person was in custody for purposes of *Miranda* warnings. See *J.D.B. v. North Carolina,* 131 S. Ct. 2394 (2011).

[16] Bentham 1827, 351. See generally Resnik 2011a.

[17] See for example *Florida v. Powell,* 559 U.S. 50 (2010); *Berghuis v. Thompkins,* 130 S. Ct. 2250 (2010); *Missouri v. Seibert,* 542 U.S. 600 (2004); *Edwards v. Arizona,* 451 U.S. 477 (1981). Some argue these new interpretations constitute the "evisceration of *Miranda*" (Brooks 2010, 190, 197), while others believe that police practices coupled with the limited education of most suspects rendered warnings ineffective (Weisselberg 2008, 1519).

framework, torture garnered little attention. Until 9/11, the topic was a matter for legal historians rather than one prompting a battery of books and articles about whether (or not) torture is permissible and whether (or not) practices such as waterboarding constitute torture.[18]

The injustice of torture is reflected in a seventeenth-century print (fig. 3) after Pieter Bruegel, in which a diminished Justice stands in the midst of mayhem. She is blindfolded, which was unusual for that era, and crowned with a dunce-like or courtesan cap. Her covered eyes suggest that she was being shielded from seeing the injustice—the physical aggression all around her—going forth in her name.

Figure 3: *Justice*, etching attributed to Philip Galle, circa 1555–1559, after the 1539 drawing by Pieter Bruegel the Elder.
Rosenwald Collection. Image copyright 2005, Board of Trustees, National Gallery of Art, Washington, D.C.

This Bruegel image was once a relic of things long gone. The received wisdom was that torture had been abandoned during the early Enlightenment, not only because it was gruesome but also because it yielded unreliable information. Of course, covert and unlawful acts of torture took place thereafter. Examples included revelations (brought back by contemporary events) that in the early 1900s, American soldiers tortured Filipinos by using what was then called "water cure torture."[19] But that such acts were covert underscored their illegality and hence made plain the norm against torture.

---

[18] Fried and Fried 2010; Greenberg 2006; Levinson 2004.

[19] Kramer 2008; Rejali 2007.

Moreover, in the wake of World War II, the United States became part of a worldwide movement to ban torture. In 1988, the United States signed the United Nations Convention Against Torture (CAT) and, in conformance with its obligations, added to the federal criminal code prohibitions required under CAT. In 1996, Congress enacted the War Crimes Act, making "grave breaches" of the Geneva Conventions a federal crime.[20]

But, since 9/11, detainees have been subjected to coercive interrogations, to torture, and to decisionmakers (one ought not call them "judges") who have not been required to "hear the other side." At the outset, I offered an image (fig. 1) of the doorway of a Renaissance Town Hall (a multi-function civic space in which a variety of government services, adjudication included, were provided) and a photograph (fig. 2) of the interior of the 1908 Illinois Supreme Court building.

Images borrowed from the U.S. Department of Defense's website (fig. 4) enable glimpses of a new site of government decisionmaking, Guantánamo Bay, once known primarily as a United States Naval Base on the Island of Cuba. Guantánamo is now recognized worldwide as a detention camp, where several hundred people were held in the wake of 9/11, where some were confined in isolating conditions for years, and where the government has convened "military tribunals."

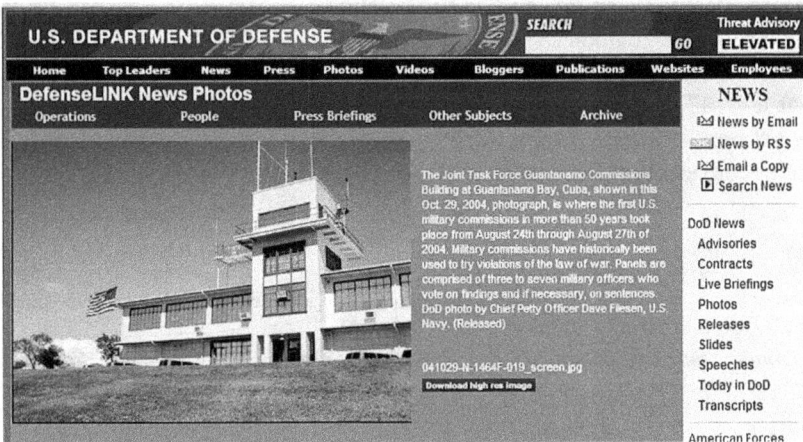

Figure 4: Joint Task Force Guantánamo Commissions Building at Guantánamo Bay, Cuba.
Photograph posted October 29, 2004, U.S. Department of Defense, website, DefenseLINK News Photos, at http://www.defenselink.mil/photos/newsphoto.aspx?newsphotoid=5763. Facsimile, Yale University Press.

---

[20] Convention Against Torture and Other Cruel, Inhuman or Degrading Treatment or Punishment, December 10, 1984, 1465 U.N.T.S. 85; Pub. L. No. 103-236, 108 Stat. 382, 463-64 (1994), 18 U.S.C. §§ 2340-2340A (2006) (amending the criminal code to reflect CAT obligations); Pub. L. No. 104-192, 110 Stat. 2104 (1996), 18 U.S.C. § 2441 (2006) (enacting the War Crimes Act to provide criminal penalties under U.S. law for certain war crimes).

Given the millions in state and federal jails and prisons, the relatively small number of people imprisoned have made a remarkable impression. Guantánamo (or "Gitmo") has become a bizarre icon in popular culture. For example, in 2008, the *New York Times* headline, "Guantánamo, Evil and Zany in Pop Culture," accompanied a story about a movie, "Harold and Kumar Escape from Guantánamo Bay," that joined a cache of books, plays, and songs depicting Guantánamo as "the gulag of our times."[21] In England, the play "Honor Bound to Defend Freedom" (the phrase used as a "call" and "response" on the base) offered somber details as it protested "U.S. abuses of human rights."[22] A stanza from a British singing group, The Divine Comedy, captured the social meaning of the naval base.

> They haven't departed.
> They haven't gone home.
> The trials haven't started.
> No evidence shown.
> They don't get no visits.
> They don't get no calls,
> and nobody tells them nothing at all.[23]

At Guantánamo, and contrary to the precepts of *Miranda v. Arizona*, the United States government permitted abusive interrogations, including violent shaking, waterboarding, and other methods of torture described by the euphemisms of "enhanced" or "harsh interrogation."[24] The authorization of these practices was not known to the public until the revelations in 2005 of what are called the "Torture Memos." This excerpt (fig. 5), from the set of Department of Justice memoranda, provides a visual counterpart to the seventeenth-century Bruegel print (fig. 3).

---

[21] Glaberson 2009. The term "gulag" was used in the Foreword of Amnesty International's Annual Report in 2005 (Amnesty International 2005).

[22] *Guantánamo: Honor Bound to Defend Freedom* by British journalist Victoria Brittain and novelist Gillian Slovo is a "docudrama" cataloguing the experiences of five British detainees, released from Guantánamo in February 2004. See http://www.tricycle.co.uk/about-the-tricycle-pages/about-us-tab-menu/archive/archived-theatre-production/Guantánamo-honor-bound-to-defend-freedom/.

[23] The Divine Comedy, *Guantánamo* (EMI Records 2006).

[24] "US Could Use Harsh Interrogations Again: White House," February 6, 2008, http://afp.google.com/article/ALeqM5h4U8FVhXOldAvFcCDWG2H2ku7pdA. One United States official explained in 2008 that as long as waterboarding "doesn't involve severe or physical pain and it doesn't last very long" and as long as "you would not expect that there would be prolonged mental harm," it's not torture. Justice Department's Office of Legal Counsel: Hearing Before the Subcomm. on the Constitution, Civil Rights, and Civil Liberties of the H. Comm. on the Judiciary, 110th Cong. 19 (Feb. 14, 2008) (testimony of Steven G. Bradbury, Principal Deputy Assistant Attorney General, Office of Legal Counsel, U.S. Department of Justice).

[logo enlarged]

Excerpts from the "Torture Memos"
(pages 1, 46)

U.S. Department of Justice

Office of Legal Counsel

Office of the Assistant Attorney General   Washington, DC 20530

August 1, 2002

Memorandum for Alberto R. Gonzales
Counsel to the President
Re: Standards of Conduct for Interrogation under 18 U.S.C § § 2340-2340A

You have asked for our Office's views regarding the standards of conduct under the Convention Against Torture and Other Cruel, Inhumane and Degrading Treatment or Punishment as implemented by Sections 2340-2340A of title 18 of the United States Code. As we understand it, this question has arisen in the context of the conduct of interrogations outside the United States. We conclude below that Section 2340A proscribes acts inflicting, and that are specifically intended to inflict, severe pain or suffering, whether mental or physical. Those acts must be of an extreme nature to rise to the level of torture within the meaning of Section 2340A and the Convention. We further conclude that certain acts may be cruel, inhuman, or degrading, but still not produce pain and suffering of the requisite intensity to fall within Section 2340A's proscription against torture. We conclude by examining possible defenses that would negate any claim that certain interrogation methods violate the statute.

. . . We conclude that torture as defined in and proscribed by Sections 2340-2340A, covers only extreme acts. Severe pain is generally of the kind difficult for the victim to endure. Where the pain is physical, it must be of an intensity akin to that which accompanies serious physical injury such as death or organ failure. Severe mental pain requires suffering not just at the moment of infliction but it also requires lasting psychological harm, such as seen in mental disorders like posttraumatic stress disorder. Additionally, such severe mental pain can arise only from the predicate acts listed in Section 2340. Because the acts inflicting torture are extreme, there is significant range of acts that though they might constitute cruel, inhuman, or degrading treatment or punishment fail to rise to the level of torture.

Figure 5: Excerpt of Memorandum for Alberto R. Gonzales, Counsel to the President, Re: Standards of Conduct for Interrogation under 18 U.S.C. §§ 2340-2340A.
Available at http://www.washingtonpost.com/wp-srv/nation/documents/dojinterrogationmemo20020801.pdf.

Lawyers advised the Attorney General of the United States that, under federal law, "for an act to constitute torture, [it required the infliction of] pain that is difficult to endure ... equivalent in intensity to the pain accompanying serious physical injury, such as organ failure, impairment of bodily function, or even death." Further, for "purely mental pain or suffering to amount to

torture ... it must result in significant psychological harm of significant duration ... lasting for months or even years."[25] The officialdom of that advice is
confirmed by the logo (expanded here for legibility) of the Justice Department,
whose eagle, like the blindfolded Justice at the center of Bruegel's image,
silently witnesses the injustice going forth under its wing.

After the disclosures, some government officials—current and former—
continued to defend techniques such as waterboarding, even as others decried
them as "wrong."[26] Thus, and to my utter amazement, the legal community
reached the point of debating not only the process to insulate detainees
against coercion (i.e., should *Miranda* warnings be given? and what are the
consequences of failures to do so?), but also what levels of stunning forms of
coercion are legally permissible.

Ariel Dorfman has written that torture is a crime "committed against the
imagination," as it "corrupts the whole social fabric because it ... obliges us to
be deaf and blind and mute."[27] (Bruegel's blindfolded *Justice* parallels Dorfman's description.) Yet, almost fifty years after *Miranda* seemed to insist on
torture's impermissibility, a rudimentary knowledge of "the law of torture"
has become necessary for law professors such as myself, teaching about
federal law. An extensive literature seeks to delineate distinctions among
torture and cruel, inhuman, and degrading treatment. My own efforts to stay
abreast are aided through a listserv called "Torture"—comprised of concerned
lawyers, law professors, and journalists producing often-daily messages under
a header that is at risk of being normalized.

By 2005, various sectors of the United States government rejected the
legal advice provided by the Torture Memos. Yet neither Congress nor the
courts have thus far imposed sanctions for the many acts of wrongdoing. In
December of 2005, Congress insisted through The Detainee Treatment Act of
2005 (DTA) that "[n]o individual in the custody or under the physical control
of the United States Government ... shall be subject to cruel, inhuman, or
degrading treatment or punishment."[28] But another facet of that statute permitted the use of information obtained through coercion as long as military

---

[25] Memorandum from Jay S. Bybee, Assistant Att'y Gen., Office of Legal Counsel, to Alberto
R. Gonzales, Counsel to the President, on Standards of Conduct for Interrogation Under 18
U.S.C. §§ 2340–40A (Aug. 1, 2002), at http://fl1.findlaw.com/news.findlaw.com/nytimes/
docs/doj/bybee80102mem.pdf.

[26] Compare Santora 2007 (citing Rudolph Giuliani, Mitt Romney and Fred Thompson as
supportive of torture) and Fried and Fried 2010.

[27] Dorfman 2004, 8–9.

[28] The Detainee Treatment Act of 2005, Pub. L. No. 109-148 [hereinafter DTA], § 1003 (a), 42
U.S.C. § 2000dd. The DTA amended 28 U.S.C. § 2241 in an effort to limit federal court
jurisdiction over habeas corpus petitions or other claims challenging any aspect of detention
at Guantánamo. The Supreme Court held that the DTA did not eliminate federal court jurisdiction over pending habeas claims by detainees held at Guantánamo. *Hamdan v. Rumsfeld*,
548 U.S. 557 (2006).

officials found that it had probative value. The statute also sought to limit detainees' access to courts. Further, the statute provided immunity for federal officials or their agents from liability, and several courts have rebuffed lawsuits seeking redress for injuries from such treatment.

In addition to the issue of torture, a second major breach of the fairness injunction can be seen by considering the process by which decisions on detention are made. Recall the injunction in *Miranda* that detainees not be left solely dependent on their custodians. In contrast, soon after 9/11, the Executive branch, under the leadership of George W. Bush, took the position that it alone had authority over detainees, and that the federal judiciary had no power to review its decisions. In November of 2001, the President decreed that the status of Guantánamo detainees was to be determined through an ad hoc process run by the Department of Defense (DOD). In compliance with the Executive Order, the Department of Defense issued "Military Commission Order No. 1," in March of 2002. The order outlined procedures for the Secretary of Defense, described throughout as the "Appointing Authority," to create special commissions to decide the fate of detainees.[29]

But the constitutional obligation of fair treatment persuaded the Supreme Court to intervene. In 2004, the Court ruled in *Hamdi v. Rumsfeld* that due process constrained the Government's treatment of at least citizen detainees and perhaps others.[30] In response, the Executive elaborated its proceedings for detainees. Below, I sketch a few of the details to illuminate how they depart from "hear the other side" values.

The DOD created a "Combatant Status Review Tribunal" ("C-SRT"), authorized to decide whether a detainee was an "enemy combatant" ("EC"), a term variously defined, including those who have been "a part of or supporting the Taliban or al Qaeda forces, or associated forces that are engaged in hostilities against the United States or its coalition partners" as well as "any person who has committed a belligerent act or has directly supported hostilities in aid of enemy armed forces,"[31] and those with connections to a long list of organizations and entities, set forth in an Executive Order. DOD reported that after more than 550 C-SRTs "between July 30, 2004 and June 15, 2007," 534 detainees were "properly classified" as enemy combatants and 38 detainees were "no longer classified" as such.[32]

---

[29] See Military Order of Nov. 13, 2001, Detention, Treatment, and Trial of Certain Non-Citizens in the War Against Terrorism, 66 F.R.D. 57833 (Nov. 16, 2001); U.S. Department of Defense Military Commission Order No. 1 (Mar. 21, 2002), http://www.defense.gov/news/Mar2002/d20020321ord.pdf [hereinafter Military Commission Order No. 1 (2002)].

[30] *Hamdi v. Rumsfeld*, 542 U.S. 507 (2004); *Rasul v. Bush*, 542 U.S. 466, 480 (2004).

[31] See Guantánamo Detainee Processes, updated Oct. 2, 2007, http://www.defenselink.mil/news/Sep2005/d20050908process.pdf; *Al-Bihani v. Obama*, 590 F.3d 866 (D.C. Cir. 2010), *cert. denied*, 131 S. Ct. 1814 (Apr. 4, 2011).

[32] U.S. Department of Defense Combatant Status Review Tribunal Summary, http://www.defenselink.mil/news/Nov2007/CSRTUpdate-Nov2-07.pdf.

But should such proceedings be called "hearings"? The rules let "neither the detainee" nor a personal representative "see evidence" deemed classified.[33] Detainee lawyers reported that virtually all the evidence relied upon was marked classified. Further information about process defects comes from an affidavit, submitted in June of 2007, to the United States Supreme Court in support of a request that the Court take a case challenging detainees' limited access to court. The affiant, Lieutenant Colonel Stephen Abraham, a long-time member of the reserves, was assigned after 9/11 to work at the Office for the Administrative Review of the Detention of Enemy Combatants, and he has served on a C-SRT. Abraham detailed the poverty of the information used for detention ("often outdated, often 'generic,' rarely specifically relating to the individual subjects of the CSRTs or to the circumstances related to those individuals' status"), the inability to verify whether exculpatory information existed, and the pressures to find a person an "enemy combatant" ("[w]hat were purported to be specific statements of fact lacked even the most fundamental earmarks of objectively credible evidence").[34]

In addition to its classification processes, the government proffered another procedure, termed a "Military Commission," through which formal charges would result in sentences, including the possibility of death. As a result, the question of whether individuals should be "tried"—and on what charges and through what procedures—outside the open and operating system of federal and military courts was (and remains) fiercely debated. The Bush Administration set forth regulations for and charged several individuals in Military Commissions. In the Military Commission Act of 2006, Congress charted a path for such proceedings and authorized the imposition of death, subject to review by the President or his designee.

After the Obama Administration came into office in 2008, the focus shifted. The President sought to close the detention facility at Guantánamo and to use regular federal courts. But congressional opposition to bringing detainees onshore was sufficiently fierce as to produce legislation blocking the use of funds for such purposes. Further, after the 2008 *Boumediene v. Bush* holding that Congress had unconstitutionally limited Guantánamo detainees' habeas corpus rights in the federal courts, Congress enacted another statute— the 2009 Military Commissions Act (MCA)—revising but again providing for the use of commissions.[35] In March of 2011, President Obama issued an Executive Order that commission proceedings would resume, even as he also

---

[33] Military Commission Order No. 1 (2005) at 6(B)(3).

[34] Declaration of Stephen Abraham, para. 8, and para. 22, Reply of Petitioners to Opposition to Petition for Rehearing at 6, *Al Odah v. United States*, 127 S. Ct. 3067 (2007) (No. 06-1196) [hereinafter Abraham Declaration].

[35] *Boumediene v. Bush*, 553 U.S. 723 (2008); Military Commissions Act of 2009, Pub. L. No. 111-84 §§ 1801-1807, 123 Stat. 2190, 2574-2614, 10 U.S.C. §§ 948a to 950t (Supp. III 2010) [hereinafter 2009 MCA].

expressed his commitment to using regular courts when possible.

What distinguishes C-SRTs and Military Commissions from pre-trial proceedings and criminal trials in the federal courts? Decisionmakers, procedure, and constitutional rights are the answers. Unlike federal courts, in which judges have life-tenure to protect their impartiality, the military decisionmakers work inside a chain of command under the Secretary of Defense. Further, unlike federal judges, who must state that they "will administer justice without respect to persons, and do equal right to the poor and to the rich, and ... will faithfully and impartially discharge and perform all the duties incumbent ... under the Constitution and laws of the United States," MCA commission members are not required to affirm commitments to the Constitution.[36] The lack of independence is not a matter of formal structure but also practice. After a few military personnel voiced public disagreements with the procedures, some lost their jobs.

Moreover, after the Supreme Court's decision in *Boumediene*, a Military Commission sitting in Guantánamo concluded that the Fifth Amendment did not govern proceedings there.[37] Thus, Congress could decide the scope of rights. In the 2009 MCA, Congress provided more procedural protections than had been available before. Indeed, the 2009 MCA pledged that the "opportunity to obtain witnesses and evidence shall be comparable to the opportunity available to a criminal defendant in a court of the United States under article III of the Constitution."[38] Yet, the statutory system's offer of "comparable" rights departs in various ways from the constitutional guarantees.

The role played by *Miranda* illustrates the distance. While the 2006 MCA had expressly recognized the permissibility of relying on evidence adduced through "harsh" measures (if other indices of reliability existed), the 2009 MCA imposed some limits, for no "statement obtained by the use of torture or by cruel, inhuman, or degrading treatment ... whether or not under color of law, shall be admissible."[39] But instead of the requirements of *Miranda*,

---

36 Compare 28 U.S.C. § 453 (2006) and M.M.C. 2010, Rule 807 (b)(2)(B), II-75-76. Each member was to swear that he or she would "faithfully and impartially perform according to your conscience and the laws applicable to trial by military commission, all the duties incumbent upon you as military judge of this military commission...." Members of the military would also have taken an oath under 10 U.S.C. § 502 (2006), affirming that they would "support and defend the Constitution of the United States against all enemies, foreign and domestic; ... bear true faith and allegiance to the same; and ... obey the orders of the President of the United States and the orders of the officers appointed over [him or her], according to regulations and the Uniform Code of Military Justice...."

37 See *United States v. Hamdan*, 1 M.C. Rept 121 (MC 2008). See also Doyle 2010.

38 2009 MCA, 10 U.S.C. § 949j(a)(1) (Supp. III 2010).

39 2009 MCA, 10 U.S.C. § 948r (Supp. III 2010). The caveat was that admissibility was permitted "against a person accused of torture." *Id.* The subsequent quote from the statute can be found at 2009 MCA, 10 U.S.C. § 949r(c) (Supp. III 2010).

admissibility turns on "the totality of the circumstances." Statements can be used if "reliable and possessing sufficient probative value," so long as the statements were made "incident to lawful [or during closely related] conduct during military operations" and "the interests of justices would best be served by admission," or the statement was made "voluntarily." The 2009 MCA also aimed to limit *Miranda* rights beyond Guántanamo; Congress insisted that no government official or employee "may read to a foreign national ... captured or detained outside the United States as an enemy belligerent" and under United States control "the statement required by *Miranda v. Arizona* ... or otherwise inform such an individual of any rights that the individual may or may not have to counsel or to remain silent consistent with *Miranda v. Arizona.*"[40]

Yet another departure from the constitutional parameters of federal courts is the role accorded the public in Guantánamo proceedings. The United States Constitution guarantees a "public and speedy trial" to criminal defendants; the interaction among the Due Process Clause, the First Amendment, and common law traditions ensures open courts in civil proceedings. Yet, according to both the Executive and Congress, rights of public access for Guantánamo detainees depend on the Executive Branch.

Until 2004, the military deemed its classification processes "administrative" and kept them closed. In August of 2005, the Department of Defense's Military Order No. 1 provided access to military commissions, dependent on the "discretion of the Appointing Authority."[41] Proceedings were to be "open to the maximum extent practicable." Yet, the Presiding Officer had the power to "close proceedings" to protect classified or "classifiable" information, for the safety of personnel, and for "other national security interests." Closure could come without hearing the other side or notification to outsiders. Further, the Presiding Officer could exclude the accused or "any other person" aside from the military defense counsel.

After the presidency changed, the policy shifted. Under the 2010 Manual for Military Commissions, public access appears to be the presumption ("military commissions shall be publicly held"). Yet upon "essential findings of fact appended" to a trial record, and in order to maintain "decorum ... or for other good cause," military judges can limit the "number of spectators in, and the means of access to, the courtroom, and exclude persons from the courtroom."[42]

Moreover, no reporter can get onto the base without permission (and a

---

[40] National Defense Authorization Act for Fiscal Year 2010, Pub. L. No. 111-84, div. A, title X, § 1040(a)(1), 123 Stat. 2190, 2454 (2009).

[41] Military Commission Order No. 1 (2005), at 6(B)(3). The quotes that follow are drawn from these provisions.

[42] M.M.C. 2010 at Rule 806(b)(1), II-73. Other provisions for closure are set forth in (b)(2).

passport). To qualify, under the Obama Administration's 2010 media "ground rules," reporters had to sign statements agreeing to abide by the rules as a "condition of access."[43] Reporters had to commit not to reveal "protected information" and to know that, while eleven seats were reserved for media (including a sketch artist), the military retained the right to close proceedings. Individuals found to have failed to comply could be permanently excluded, as could their "parent" news organizations.

The veil of secrecy and the insistence on control at Guantánamo not only represent a departure from the United States tradition of "open courts" but also stand in sharp contrast to the rules of other tribunals dealing with individuals alleged to have committed heinous acts. The International Criminal Tribunal for the former Territories of Yugoslavia (ICTY), for example, permits persons to watch from behind heavy glass walls that secure the courtroom; the court transmits its proceedings to the Balkans, where they are broadcast in English, French, and Bosnian/Serbian/Croatian.[44] Further, the accused has access to the court, personally, to register concerns directly and in public to the international judges. To deal with the need to protect information for security reasons (for example if an individual witness was at risk), the blinds are closed, shutting out the live audience, and the broadcast screen scrambled; voices are recalibrated to make them unidentifiable.

In short, as Eugene Fidell—the head of the National Institute of Military Justice—made plain, while "a few words of praise" were in order for the improvements in 2009, "even with the best of arrangements ... Guantánamo is a remote and inconvenient venue for the military commission proceedings. The administrative complexities of arranging air transportation as well as full-time minders for visitors cannot be overstated."[45]

"America Now": Beyond 9/11

While offshore, Guantánamo Bay is actually not out of sight. A 2007 photograph (fig. 6) made the point, offering a glimpse of the detention camp beyond a sign affixed to the barbed wire and proclaiming that "no photography" was authorized. Through such pictures, the government helped to shape demonic images of terrorists, as the government also sought to demonstrate its own abilities to keep them, literally and metaphorically, at bay.

---

43 Department of Defense, "Media Ground Rules for Guantánamo Bay, Cuba," Sept. 10, 2010, http://www.defense.gov/news/d20100910groundrules.pdf.

44 The ICTY provided that all proceedings other than deliberations "shall be held in public, unless otherwise provided." Rule 78 ("Open Sessions"), Rules of Procedure and Evidence, International Criminal Tribunal for the former Territories of Yugoslavia, IT/32/Rev.36, http://www1.umn.edu/humanrts/icty/ct-rules7.html; Regulations for the Establishment of a Complaints Procedure for Detainees, paras. 4, 7, International Criminal Tribunal for the Former Territories of Yugoslavia, IT/96, http://www.icty.org/x/file/Legal%20Library /Detention/IT96UNDU_complaints_en.pdf.

45 Fidell 2009.

Figure 6: The outer fence and guard tower at Camps 1 & 4 at Camp Delta at the U.S. Naval Station in Guantánamo Bay, Cuba, April 24, 2007.
Photograph copyright Paul J. Richards/AFP/Getty Images.

The symbolism of Guantánamo comes not only from its barbed wire perimeters, its tightly controlled procedures putting military personnel in charge, and its ground rules for the press and the public, but also from its appropriation of the terminology and iconography of courts. The room depicted in figure 7, for Military Commission hearings, is inside the Joint Task Force (JTF) building in an area denoted "Camp Justice," shown in this 2009 photograph (fig. 8) with flags flying. A close-up of the sign (fig. 9) displays the logo, which is a variation on the official seal of the Department of Defense that is, in turn, based on the Seal of the United States. In the "Camp Justice" version, the eagle, adorned with a red, white, and blue shield, has three arrows in its talons. Beneath is a circular crown of thirteen stars encircled by the Department's name. Superimposed are scales and a pentagon at the logo's center. The words "Freedom through Justice" and "Office of Military Commissions" complete the picture.

Figure 7: Interior of a hearing room, Guantánamo Bay, January 2006.
Photograph reproduced courtesy of Joint Task Force (JTF) Guantánamo Bay Public Affairs.

Figure 8: Camp Justice, Guantánamo Bay.
Photograph reproduced with the permission of the photographer, Travis Crum (November 2009).

Figure 9: Detail of logo, Camp Justice, Guantánamo Bay.
Photograph reproduced with the permission of the photographer, Travis Crum (November 2009).

Through the terminology of trials, the image of scales, and the name of justice, the government seeks to use Guantánamo Bay as a stage on which to demonstrate the legitimacy of its decisions, now entailing forms of prolonged detention without trial. "Camp Justice" thus bears a resemblance to Renaissance spectacles of executions, which Michael Foucault famously analyzed as serving the "double role" of demonstrating "the splendor of truth and of power ... the culmination of the ritual of investigation and the ceremony in which the sovereign triumphed."[46]

Guantánamo is often posited as a unique response to terrorism that is in many ways foreign to the system in which it sits. But as much as I would like the structure of decisionmaking at Guantánamo Bay to represent a radical and aberrational departure from American law, I cannot make that claim. Rather, the fact of detention laces the lives of millions within the United States. At the outset, I contrasted the numbers (a few hundred) at Guantánamo with the millions in jails and prisons. The case law emanating from Guantánamo is likewise dwarfed by the numbers of decisions relating to regular prisoners in state and federal prisons. From 2003 to 2009, when both the press and the academy focused on Supreme Court rulings in seven cases related to 9/11 detainees, the Court also dealt with eighty cases ruling on claims from other prisoners, also arguing unlawful detention, conviction, or conditions of confinement.[47] And the challenges of sorting the rightly detained from those who ought to be permitted liberty are likewise daunting.

Moreover, although Guantánamo is in tension with a tradition of independent judges, defendants' rights to voluntary confessions, and public processes, it is also continuous with developments in other less high profile contexts, where judges are less independent, defendants less protected, and the public less welcome. The criminal justice system offers sad parallels. Beginning in the 1970s inside the territorial United States, the federal government pioneered new prison designs, known as "supermax" and committed to profound isolation. Individuals may be locked up, indefinitely, in solitary confinement for 23 hours a day.

Yet, their procedural protections are—per the United States Supreme Court's 2005 ruling—minimal rather than exacting, if extant at all.[48] "Fairness," translated as giving opportunities for both sides to amass and present

---

[46] Foucault, 1979, 56; Puppi 1991.

[47] Resnik 2010, 619.

[48] *Wilkinson v. Austin*, 545 U.S. 209 (2005). See for example *Ajaj v. United States*, 293 F. App'x 575, 582-584 (10th Cir. 2008) (finding that elements at ADX [Florence Supermax] such as "lockdown 23 hours per day in extreme isolation," "indefinite confinement," and "limited ability to exercise outdoors" did not, individually or in concert, amount to an Eighth Amendment violation); *Georgacarakos v. Wiley*, No. 07-cv-01712-MSK-MEH, 2010 WL 1291833, at *12 (D. Colo. Mar. 30, 2010) (violations at ADX, though "undoubtedly extremely restrictive ... are not so extreme or inhumane that they could be deemed a significant departure from contemporary standards of decency, applied to the prison context").

evidence, has been put aside by judges, explaining that the fearsomeness of prisoners requires deference to decisions of prison officials to subject humans to indefinite solitary confinement. Furthermore, just as Congress reduced 9/11 detainees' access to regular courts through the MCA of 2006 and 2009, Congress has also limited prisoners' opportunities to obtain judicial review of claims of wrongful convictions or of intolerable conditions while detained.[49]

Turn from the criminal docket to the civil side and the administrative adjudication that I detailed earlier. Whether subject to Homeland Security or seeking veterans benefits, individuals who disagree with the United States government have limited opportunities for public accountings. Tens of thousands of decisions are reached in administrative agencies each year, but almost none are made in proceedings that are readily accessible to the public. In some instances, no rights of public access exist and in others, it is difficult to find the hearing rooms where decisions are made. No uniform system of publication permits web-based dissemination of the opinions rendered in the many adjudicating agencies. Moreover, administrative law judges deal with high caseloads, limited resources, and less judicial independence. As of 2008, for example, some 228 Department of Justice employees, called "immigration judges," were each assigned about 1,200 cases a year, as contrasted with life-tenured federal judges, then averaging about 380 cases yearly.

Thus, the procedures at Guantánamo are not utterly foreign from the procedural world of prisoners in the criminal system or from the outsourcing to administrative agencies that make dispute resolution processes invisible to the public. Indeed, the federal government understood as much, for when the Appointing Authority at Guantánamo first banned access, it relied on such precedents and denoted its processes "administrative" as an explanation for their closure.

Yet an important distinction exists between the procedures at Guantánamo and various administrative and "alternative dispute resolution" (ADR) procedures in other settings. The closure of ordinary administrative proceedings and the privacy of ADR are argued as benefiting the participants—for example, by shielding from public scrutiny individuals seeking the state's financial support. More generally (whether empirically supported or not), the movement toward ADR is justified as offering more than adjudication can—more access for claimants, less cost, and more congenial procedures. In contrast, the government's move to appoint itself the judge and create its own CSRT–Military Commission activities was claimed to benefit the government and the public, by giving the government unfettered control over detainees.

---

49 Antiterrorism and Effective Death Penalty Act of 1996 (AEDPA), Pub. L. No. 104-132, 110 Stat. 1214 (codified as amended in scattered sections of 18 U.S.C. (1996)); Prison Litigation Reform Act of 1995, Pub. L. No. 104-134, Title VIII, 110 Stat. 1321, 1321-66, 18 U.S.C. § 3601 nt. (1996).

No arguments were offered that the process improved the opportunities of detainees to be treated fairly.

Further, the procedures at Guantánamo attempted to cut off opportunities for comment from those other than representatives of the government or detainees. One could read government materials extolling Military Commissions as providing "a full and fair trial, while protecting national security and the safety of all [those] involved, including [the] accused."[50] Or one could learn of claims made by objectors—such as the Center for Constitutional Rights, the American Civil Liberties Union, some members of the press, the United Nations Special Rapporteur for the Independence of Judges and Lawyers, and the Rapporteur on Torture—condemning the processes as profoundly unfair and illegal. But closure and secrecy have dispossessed citizens of their capacity to evaluate these claims directly.

In contrast, when proceedings are readily accessible to an audience of third parties who are not themselves disputants, those "spectators and auditors" (to borrow Jeremy Bentham's terms) are able to put their descriptions and commentary into the public realm.[51] By providing the public a space through which to interpret, own, or disown what has occurred, public procedures thus teach that conflicts do not belong exclusively to the disputants or to the government.

The "open courts" required by constitutional law makes adjudication a democratic process in which the public can both monitor the power of the government and, after seeing the application of law to fact, participate in efforts to seek changes in underlying laws. Adjudication is democratic in another sense, in that it obliges litigants to treat each other as equals as they argue—in public—about alleged misbehavior and wrongdoing. Litigation forces dialogue upon the unwilling (including the government), and momentarily alters configurations of authority. Judges, as representatives of the state, must likewise participate, as they too are disciplined in how they are to act. This function of courts as potentially egalitarian political venues is why the federal government has tried to escape them. The government does not want to be seen as according the (alleged) "terrorists" the dignity obliged by public adjudication under democratic conditions.

Law's edicts—from criminal sanctions to the transfer of custody of a child or of money in a property dispute—do violence, as they intrude profoundly on individual autonomy. When the force of law is faced and engaged in open court processes, we—those outside the immediate dispute—responsibly exercise our roles in understanding, legitimating, delegitimating, and

---

[50] United States Department of Defense, Military Commissions, at www.dod.mil/pubs/foi/operation_and_plans/Detainee/death_investigation/ghost_detainees/Pages_1041-1057_from_Joint_Staff_Ghost_Detainee_part_44_of_45.pdf.

[51] Bentham 1827, 356.

interpreting what law means, what justice entails, how its practices occur, and what forms of state-sanctioned violence are intolerable.

John Frank understood this well. In 1944, he wrote an article praising an 1866 Supreme Court decision—*Ex Parte Milligan*—which had insisted that a United States citizen charged with treason could not be tried in a military commission when regular courts were "open."[52] Frank argued that *Milligan* had become fashionable to malign but that the critics were "wrong"—and moreover that the then-Attorney General was wrong in criticizing it.[53] Frank insisted that *Milligan* was a great case, and deeply correct. Open and ordinary courts that cabined judicial authority by hearing both sides, like insulation of individuals from the police, were essential to the constitutional order.

John Frank's admonitions are haunting now. Decades later, it has become popular to champion state coercion, explained as necessarily bending the dignity of fairness owed to all persons. The Torture Memos, even though subsequently withdrawn, have had an enormous legal and conceptual impact, transforming the boundaries of permissible discourse and practice. My anxiety is not only about the underlying activities (gruesome as they are) but also about the corruption of legal norms. Current entrants to the profession hear discussions about the legality of torture that are being normalized. Because waterboarding and other methods of "harsh" interrogations have gained toeholds as plausible within, instead of antithetical to, the fabric of American law, Frank's brief in *Miranda* has new currency, and hence, I conclude by quoting it again.

> We are not talking with some learned historicity about the *lettre de cachet* of pre-Revolutionary France or the secret prisons of a distant Russia. We are talking about conditions in the United States, in the Twentieth Century, and now.[54]

---

[52] Frank 1944.

[53] In that essay, Frank explained that he had worked at Interior when he wrote the article, and then by the time the article was published, he was at the Department of Justice, and hence, that his opening commentary turned out to be opining that his own boss was "wrong." Frank 2001, 7.

[54] Brief for Petitioner at 46-47, *Miranda v. Arizona*, 384 U.S. 436 (1966) (No. 759).

References

Amnesty International, 2005. *Amnesty International Report 2005: The State of the World's Human Rights.*

Bentham, Jeremy. 1827. "Rationale of Judicial Evidence" in John Bowring, ed. 1843, *The Works of Jeremy Bentham* (vol. 6). Edinburgh: William Tait.

Brooks, Peter. 2010. "Silence the Body" in Austin Sarat, ed., *Speech and Silence in American Law.* New York: Cambridge University Press.

de Smith, S. A. 1955. "The Right to a Hearing in English Administrative Law." *Harvard Law Review* 68: 569-599.

Dorfman, Ariel. 2004. "The Tyranny of Torture: Is Torture Inevitable in Our Century and Beyond." in Sanford Levinson, ed., *Torture: A Collection.* Oxford: Oxford University Press.

Doyle, Charles. 2010. *Terrorism,* Miranda, *and Related Matters,* Congressional Research Service: CRS 7-57000, R-41252. May 24.

Fidell, Eugene R. 2009. "Brig-adoon: Report from Guantánamo." National Institute of Military Justice, Reports from Guantánamo Bay, Vol. 2: 29-33, available at www.scribd.com/doc/60447800/GTMO2.

Foucault, Michel. 1979. *Discipline and Punish: The Birth of the Prison.* Alan Sheridan, trans. New York: Vintage Books.

Frank, John. 2001. *A Sort of Professional Autobiography.* Phoenix: Lewis & Roca, LLP.

Frank, John. 1944. "*Ex Parte Milligan* v. The Five Companies: Martial Law in Hawaii." *Columbia Law Review* 44: 639-668.

Fried, Charles, and Gregory Fried. 2010. *Because It Is Wrong: Torture, Privacy, and Presidential Power in the Age of Terror.* New York: W.W. Norton & Co.

Glaberson, William. 2009. "Guantánamo, Evil and Zany in Pop Culture." *New York Times,* February 18: A1, 11, available at http://www.nytimes.com/2008/02/18/us/18gitmo.html.

Greenberg, Karen J. 2006. *The Torture Debate in America.* New York: Cambridge University Press.

Kramer, Paul. 2008. "The Water Cure: Debating Torture and Counterinsurgency—A Century Ago." *New Yorker,* February 25.

Levinson, Sanford. 2004. *Torture: A Collection.* Oxford: Oxford University Press.

Puppi, Lonelle. 1991. *Torment in Art: Pain, Violence and Martyrdom.* New York: Rizzoli.

Reich, Charles. 1964. "The New Property." *Yale Law Journal* 73: 733-787.

Rejali, Darius M. 2007. *Torture and Democracy.* Princeton, NJ: Princeton University Press.

Resnik, Judith and Dennis Curtis. 2011. *Representing Justice: Invention, Controversy, and Rights in City-States and Democratic Courtrooms.* New Haven, CT: Yale University Press.

Resnik, Judith. 2011a. "Bring Back Bentham: 'Open Courts,' 'Terror Trials,' and Public Sphere(s)." *Law & Ethics of Human Rights* 5: 1-69.

Resnik, Judith. 2011b. "Fairness in Numbers: A Comment on *AT&T v. Concepcion, Wal-Mart v. Dukes,* and *Turner v. Rogers,*" *Harvard Law Review* 125: 78-170.

Resnik, Judith. 2010. "Detention, the War on Terror, and the Federal Courts." *Columbia Law Review* 110: 579-686.

Resnik, Judith. 2008a. "The Story of *Goldberg*: Why This Case Is Our Shorthand," in Kevin M. Clermont (ed.), *Civil Procedure Stories*. 2nd. New York: Foundation Press.

Santora, Marc. 2007. "3 Top Republican Candidates Take a Hard Line on the Interrogation of Detainees." *New York Times*, November 3: A17.

The Divine Comedy, *Guantánamo*. 2006. Lyrics available at http://www.lyricsty.com/divine-comedy-guantanamo-lyrics.html (last accessed on January 7, 2013).

Weisselberg, Charles. 2008. "Mourning *Miranda*." *California Law Review* 96: 1519-1602.

8

Security and Civil Rights in a Post 9/11 World

Janet Napolitano

Janet Napolitano was sworn in on January 21, 2009 as the third Secretary of the U.S. Department of Homeland Security. Prior to joining the Obama Administration, Secretary Napolitano served as Governor of the State of Arizona, Attorney General of Arizona, and U.S. Attorney for the District of Arizona. While Governor, she chaired the National Governors Association and the Western Governors Association.

The framework for our security must be different today than it was in times past because of the different kinds of threats against the United States that now exist. The Department of Homeland Security (DHS) was founded in the wake of the 9/11 terrorist attacks to help secure our country from a myriad of evolving threats. The reality is that threats evolve faster than before, and we must respond accordingly. Amid these threats, our duty to secure our nation as well as our privacy and civil rights requires an approach by executive agencies that seeks to protect these values from the outset.

DHS is constantly seeking ways to keep our borders and ports secure, to enforce our immigration laws, to make our cyber networks stronger and more resilient, and to prepare our nation for disasters or attacks of any kind. But above all, our first mission is to prevent terrorism and enhance security, and it is clear that securing the country from attacks requires a broad-based and collaborative effort. This mission puts a heavy emphasis on partnerships across different levels of government, the public and private sectors, and international borders. It is a mission that demands we evolve our security as quickly as the threats against us evolve. At the same time, though, we must maintain a focus on securing our national values—the rights and liberties of Americans that define us as a country—while we fight terrorism.

In a time of new and changing threats, we have to change our traditional paradigm of how we think about rights and security. As we move forward, we must create a better way of relating our national security to our national values, including personal privacy and the core civil rights and civil liberties set forth in the Constitution.

Too often, the effort to achieve the right balance is portrayed as a kind of ideological tug-of-war: You need to be either on one side or the other. This is a misleading—and potentially dangerous—way of thinking about this topic, especially in a world of rapidly moving and changing threats. Rather than two

111

competing sides in a zero-sum game, our national security and our national values are inextricably intertwined, and, in fact, mutually reinforcing.

In truth, not only is security interrelated with our core values, but security itself is also a fundamental value. The Universal Declaration of Human Rights, for example, places "security of person" alongside life and liberty as foundational rights. Within the Constitution itself, we find many of these values are interrelated. The Preamble states that we must "insure domestic tranquility" and "provide for the common defense," as well as "secure the blessings of liberty" for the American people.

There is a simple fact underlying this dynamic: one cannot live free if one lives in danger. Safety is an essential prerequisite to being able to exercise one's freedoms. Rights and liberties on paper lack meaning if the people who hold these rights lack the security to exercise them.

To be sure, the need to be safe should not be used, as it sometimes has been, to justify policies or actions that clearly ignore or undermine our constitutional rights. The truth is, while we can significantly advance security without having a deleterious impact on individual rights, situations can arise where tradeoffs are inevitable.

And increasingly, in a world of fast-changing, ever-evolving threats, it is the Executive Branch that must deal with these issues. The speed at which the terrorist threat moves, which is much faster than the legislative or judicial processes, makes it necessary for the Executive to adopt a proactive posture to these issues during policy planning. I would like to present some examples of areas where these issues have arisen recently within the Department of Homeland Security.

One is the effort to expand the use of Advanced Imaging Technology at our nation's airports. This gets to the heart of a clear vulnerability in aviation security that we saw during the attempted bombing on Christmas Day, 2009. The reality is simple: al-Qaeda and other terrorist groups continue to target commercial aviation, and attempt to use explosive materials that do not contain metal and therefore cannot be detected by standard metal detectors. Consequently, improved technology is necessary to secure the safety of passengers on board planes.

The new technology, known as Advanced Imaging Technology, or AIT, is objectively better at doing this because it can pinpoint anomalies on a person's body, such as non-metallic weapons and explosives, as well as other dangerous materials.

The courts have clearly recognized the permissibility of security measures like AIT because they fall within the category of a special-needs or administrative search. The Supreme Court has not had occasion to rule on airport screening, but the circuit court precedent is clear. Since the 1970s, case law establishes that airport searches are constitutional if they are done for the right reasons (to detect the presence of threats to airplane safety) and in the right way (no more intrusively than necessary to accomplish that purpose). In one of the earliest of these cases, *United States v. Davis*, the U.S. Court of Appeals for the Ninth Circuit upheld airport screening, "provided that the screening process is no more extensive nor intensive than necessary, in the light of current technology, to detect the presence of weapons or explosives."[1]

Weapons and explosives have become harder to detect over time. Advanced imaging technology is a tool that can help detect them. It is reasonably fast and is not physically intrusive. This makes AIT an essential security technology—but also one that has raised privacy as well as civil rights and civil liberties concerns.

DHS has worked to accommodate privacy and civil rights and civil liberties through a number of steps when it comes to this new technology. DHS started by asking for assistance. We consulted with privacy and civil rights and civil liberties advocates from the outset about how to build in protections, which were incorporated into the resulting technology and operative policies.

First, the Transportation Security Officer who asks the passenger to walk through the machine never sees the passenger's image. Next, another security officer in a walled-off location in the airport views the black and white, chalk-like image generated by the technology. Once the officer reviews the image and resolves any anomalies, the image is immediately deleted. None of the AIT machines can store data because DHS requires the manufacturers to disable this function before these machines can be placed in airports. There are no identifiers and there are no records made. TSA employees are prohibited from bringing any kind of device capable of capturing an image, like a camera or cell phone, into any area where the images are being shown. TSA is now providing further privacy protections by utilizing automated target recognition on AIT machines, which displays anomalies on a generic stick figure outline of a person. Automated Target Recognition eliminates the need for the screener in the separate room, and does not resemble a photographic image, further strengthening security *and* privacy protections.

A second area that illustrates the interplay between our national security and national values is in determining which travelers should receive what kinds of searches before boarding a plane en route to the United States. It is critically important that we prevent dangerous people, including those with known connections to terrorism or terrorist groups, from boarding flights to the United States. But at the same time, we continually seek ways to ensure that we are not casting the net wider than necessary and running the risk of ensnaring innocent people.

Following the attempted terrorist attack on Christmas Day, 2009, the U.S. government implemented a new security process for all air carriers with international departures to the United States, based on real-time, threat-

---

[1] *United States v. Davis*, 482 F.2d 893 (9th Cir. 1973).

based intelligence. Developed in consultation with the intelligence community and law enforcement, with input from U.S. and international partners in government and industry, these new measures are designed to use our knowledge of the tactics and techniques used by terrorists and the latest intelligence and risk analysis to inform our law enforcement and security measures.

This program enables us to work with our partners abroad to act on specific intelligence the United States has about an active plot. While many of the operational details of this program are classified, it is possible to describe how it ensures proper respect for privacy, civil rights and civil liberties.

DHS' Privacy Office and Office for Civil Rights and Civil Liberties have been involved from the beginning in shaping the program. Every quarter, these Offices lead a review of the program's protocols to verify that they are appropriately matched to actual threat intelligence—in other words, checking to ensure that the program matches the scope of the intelligence, neither casting the net too narrowly nor too widely. This approach strengthens our ability to respond to threats while ensuring individual rights are protected.

A third area where careful balance must be struck is the need to secure our nation against violent extremism here at home. We must prevent terrorist acts that are conceived, plotted, and carried out by U.S. citizens on U.S. soil, while respecting the rights and liberties of Americans.

One of the significant threats facing our country in recent years is greater mobilization by violent extremists of people who are either U.S. citizens or legal residents. Indeed, al-Qaeda and other terrorist groups are actively and publicly recruiting U.S. citizens. There are cases like that of David Headley—the U.S. citizen who helped conduct preparatory work for the Mumbai attacks in 2008; Najibullah Zazi—the legal permanent U.S. resident who was arrested in 2009 for planning terrorist bombings of the New York City subway system; and Faisal Shahzad—a legal U.S. resident who attempted to set off a bomb in Times Square in 2010.

This type of internal threat presents a new challenge to the system our country set up post-9/11, which focuses heavily on targeting threats coming from abroad and from non-U.S. persons. It also opens up a range of new legal and constitutional questions.

At the root of homegrown terrorism is the problem of violent extremist ideology. The fact is that the First Amendment protects radical opinions, but it does not prohibit the government from responsible policing when it comes to the consequences of such statements or exhortations—such as legally monitoring the recruitment of terrorists over the Internet.

When young people are targeted by terrorist recruiters, we must view their communities as partners in prevention. DHS has begun important work with hundreds of communities across the country, seeking to collaborate with organizations already working to prevent and mitigate threats involving new recruits to terrorism. By doing so, we are demonstrating our respect for the civil rights and civil liberties of these communities, while also making important progress in keeping our country safe.

These are just three contemporary examples of how DHS, and the Executive Branch as a whole, approaches the relationship between our national security and our national values. Today's threats are growing and changing so quickly that we are often forced to take swift action, yet it is essential that we preserve and protect our national values as we do so. That is why the DHS Privacy Office and Office for Civil Rights and Civil Liberties are both active participants in formulating policies *before* they are implemented. The idea is that we do not attempt to shoehorn these considerations into policies after the fact; we consider them critical priorities from the beginning. In fact, these offices are robust and fully integrated into the decision-making process at the Department. They are each led by lawyers who are nationally respected leaders in their fields, and they are at the table throughout the policymaking process.

The American people should know that their safety and security comes first. That is what my Department focuses on every day and every week throughout the year. We face a determined set of ever-evolving adversaries, and, in light of the ever-changing threat environment, we need to evolve, too. We need to evolve in a way that puts to rest the old dichotomy that pits security against other values. We need to evolve in a way that recognizes a more complex and dynamic interrelationship—where we search hard for solutions in which rights and security work in tandem, and where those considerations are built strongly into every part of a fast-moving process.

While the threats we face are very unpredictable, we can predict one thing: securing ourselves will often present us with difficult decisions and force us to enter uncharted waters. We must embrace the fact that considering all of our rights—from security to privacy—in these challenging situations is not an impossible task, but rather a calling that our nation and its leaders must heed.

No one can make guarantees that we can protect against every threat or future attack. But, by holding fast to our guiding principles, we can—and we will—continue to make progress in securing our country and cultivating a safer and more resilient America. This is the true source of our great American strength, and the reason that, in the face of ever evolving threats, our nation will prevail.

9

Reframing the Affirmative Action Debate[*]

Lani Guinier

Lani Guinier is the Bennett Boskey Professor of Law at Harvard University. She was the first woman of color appointed to a tenured professorship at Harvard Law School. She was part of the Civil Rights Division of the U.S. Department of Justice and headed the NAACP Legal Defense Fund's voting rights project in the 1980s. Her many honors include the Champions of Democracy Award from the National Women's Caucus and ten honorary degrees.

Affirmative action has, at least in contemporary terms, been thought of as an issue exclusively concerning blacks and women. My goal in what follows is to try to reframe that debate so that all of us can begin to see the conversation about affirmative action, not as a wedge, but as a platform and an opportunity to start a much bigger conversation about democracy, justice, and fundamental fairness. To do this, I would like to use the image of the miner's canary.[1]

It is my understanding that miners used to take a canary with them into the mine to alert them when the atmosphere in the mine was beginning to get dangerous—poisonous. The canary's more fragile respiratory system was a signal to the miners, not just that it was dangerous for the canary to remain in the mine, but that the miners had better leave the mine, too. My central claim is that the experience of blacks and women in this country is the experience of the miner's canary. Let me explain what I mean by this.

Unfortunately, the way the present affirmative action conversation is framed, we talk about fixing the so-called beneficiaries of affirmative action—namely, black men and women of various ethnicities and races. But this is analogous to talk about fixing the miner's canary. Perhaps we should provide a lung transplant or some other medical intervention for the canary, or maybe we should outfit the canary with a pint-sized gas mask so it can continue to survive in its deadly environment.[2] But we know that it is not the canary that

---

[*] This chapter was originally published in 1998 in the *Kentucky Law Journal* (volume 86, number 1, page 3 (Fall 1998)).

[1] See Lani Guinier & Gerald Tones, *The Miner's Canary: Enlisting Race, Resisting Power, Transforming Democracy* (Cambridge, MA: Harvard University Press, 2002) (citing Felix S. Cohen, *The Erosion of Indian Rights, 1950-1953: A Case Study in Bureaucracy*, 62 Yale L.J. 348, 390 (1953) (race functions like the miner's canary, "mark[ing] the shift from fresh air to poison gas in our political atmosphere")).

[2] After I delivered this lecture, a gentleman approached me at the lectern to advise me that he found great irony in my application of the miner's canary metaphor to issues of racial

needs to be fixed; it is the atmosphere in the mines that is poisoning not just the canary, but eventually all of us. The same is true when we talk about race and gender in our society. That is, women and blacks need to be understood as our miners' canaries—their experiences signal us about the health of our social environment. In particular, the experiences of members of these groups make visible to us fundamental flaws in the way we are distributing opportunity to everyone, but we can't see the flaws except as they are revealed in the canary. Let me give you an example.

In 1976, the percentage of black high school graduates who went on to college was beginning to approximate the percentage of white high school graduates who went on to college—not the same number, but the same percentage.[3] That is, of blacks who graduated from high school, approximately the same percentage went on to college as the percentage of whites who graduated from high school. By 1986 that was no longer true. What happened between 1976 and 1986? One significant event was the election of Ronald Reagan as President. The Reagan administration decided to change the way college education was funded through something called the "Pell Grant."[4] In

---

justice. After all, he reminded me, a black man from Kentucky had invented the gas mask to replace the canary but because of racism had trouble marketing it until the U.S. Army began using the same design in its gas masks during World War I. *See* Black Firsts: 2,000 Years of Extraordinary Achievement (Jessie Carney Smith et al. eds., 1994) ("Garret Morgan (1875-1963) was the first black to receive a patent for a safety hood and smoke protector.... Born on a farm near Paris, Kentucky, Morgan became a very astute businessman and inventor in Cleveland. In 1923 he patented a three-way automatic traffic signal, which he sold to General Electric."). *See also Who Invented the First Traffic Light and Gas Mask?*, N.Y. Beacon (New York, N.Y.), Feb. 12, 1997, at 3:

> In 1916, [Garret] Morgan came to public attention in a big way when, using a breathing device he had invented two years earlier, he took part in a dramatic rescue. A disastrous explosion had occurred in a tunnel below Lake Erie [in Cleveland, Ohio], trapping nearly thirty [city waterworks] workers. Morgan and his brother, wearing his newly invented device, which he called a "Safety Hood," went into the smoke-filled shaft and pulled the workers to safety.
>
> When they heard about the rescue, fire officials around the country placed orders for the Safety Hood, but many canceled them when they learned that Morgan was an African American. At this point, the army saw the value of Morgan's invention, made some improvements on it, and the Safety Hood became the gas mask that saved thousands of lives in World War I.

3 *See* Gerald David Jaynes & Robin M. Williams, Jr., eds., A Common Destiny: Blacks and American Society 377-79 (Washington, DC: National Academy Press, 1989). In a comprehensive study, Jaynes and Williams found that blacks' status in higher education worsened or stalled since the mid-1970s. "After the mid-1970s, the college-going chances of black high school graduates have declined." *Id.* at 378.

4 "The purpose of the [Pell Grant] is to assist students from low-income families who would not otherwise be financially able to attend a post secondary institution." Margot A. Schenet, CRS Report for Congress: Pell Grants: Background and Issues (Apr. 4, 1997). The Pell Grant program was established to be the foundation of federal student aid to further the goal of access and to provide students with more choice among institutions. *See id.* at 16.

1976, the Pell Grant provided scholarship aid to needy students. In an effort to broaden the constituency that would be supported by Pell Grants and consistent with its "self-help" philosophy, the Reagan administration pushed to change Pell Grants from scholarships to primarily loans.[5]

Now, this may appear on its face as a race-neutral effort to expand the constituency for higher education. But it had a very distinct racial effect because the median net worth, or financial assets, of a black family is significantly less than the median net worth of a white family.[6] This is the cumulative effect of discrimination. We are not talking now about income; we are not talking about the amount of money coming in through salary. We are talking about the assets that a family has. In 1988, the net financial worth for a white family averaged about $43,000; for a black family, it averaged about $3700.[7]

---

[5] President Reagan introduced budget proposals throughout the 1980s to cut Pell Grants and other higher education subsidies. *See, e.g.,* Macon Morehouse, *House, Senate Bills Compared: Bills to Curtail Loan Defaults Would Also Expand Aid Rolls,* 46 Congressional Quarterly, Sept. 3, 1988, *available in* 1988 WL 2835183. "Pell Grants authorizations used to be open-ended. After Reagan came into office, however, the authorization was limited to a specific amount—$2.65 billion for that year." Also under the Reagan administration, the House proposed an expansion of budget authority for loans and other policies more likely to benefit students from middle income families. *See id.* (referring to H.R. 4986, 100th Cong. (1988)). In each of his budget proposals, President Reagan proposed a major philosophical shift in federal student aid: to return to the traditional emphasis on parental and student contributions as the basis of meeting college costs. *See* U.S. Dep't of Educ., Revised Fiscal Year 1982 Budget 3 (1981):

> The 1982 budget includes reforms of the major post-secondary student assistance programs to focus the aid on students who need it for the costs of attending college while controlling the rapidly escalating growth in Federal costs. In proposing these reforms, the Administration assumes that families and students—not the Federal government—should be the first source of funds for educational expenses.

President Reagan attempted to implement this goal by limiting grant aid and other federal subsidies and by increasing "self-help aid." In his 1982 proposal, Reagan attempted to underscore his "self-help" philosophical approach by proposing a slight reduction in Pell Grant aid while increasing National Direct Student Loans from $186 million to $286 million. *See id.* at 4; *see also* U.S. Dep't of Educ., The Fiscal Year 1984 Budget 6 (1983) ("Under the new proposal, self-help would come first. Students would be required to provide a minimum of 40 percent (or a minimum of $800) of their educational expenses through work or loans before obtaining any grants."). Reagan's 1988 budget proposal sharply cut back the Pell Grant program from $4.2 billion in 1987 to $2.7 billion. *See* David Rapp, *Education: Reagan Targets Student Aid for Deep Spending Cuts,* Congressional Quarterly, Jan. 10, 1987, at 59, *available in* 1987 WL 2647837 This budget proposal would have made up the difference in student aid by expanding "income-contingent" loans from their 1987 level of $5 million to $600 million in fiscal year 1988. Under this program, "borrowers would have to repay the loan without the benefit of federal interest subsidies, though on a repayment schedule geared to income after graduation." *Id., see also* U.S. Dep't of Educ., The Fiscal Year 1988 Budget, Summary and Background Information 2 (1987).

[6] *See generally* Melvin L. Oliver & Thomas M. Shapiro, Black Wealth, White Wealth (New York: Routledge, 1995, 1999).

[7] *See id.* at 86. To compare median net worth over time, see U.S. Bureau of the Census, Current Population Reports, Series P-70, No. 7, Household Wealth and Asset Ownership 1984, 22 (1986) (stating that in 1984, white families had a median net worth of $39,135,

Assets have a significant effect on one's ability to get a loan, and the consequence of this difference in financial status between black and white families was that many black families could not compete for Pell Grants. So the fact that the Pell Grant program appeared to be race-neutral masked the way in which the Pell Grants were having a very specific racial effect, namely, lessening the percentages of black high school students going to college. That's the miner's canary.

In this case, college-aged blacks provide us a visible sign that there is something wrong. The something wrong is manifested in terms of black families, but it is not only black families who have a net financial worth of $3700. There are many white families whose net financial worth is only $3700.[8] Part of the masked problem here is that the poverty of whites is hidden by the great affluence of other whites. It is only when we look at the effect of the Pell Grant on blacks that we begin to see that this decision, which initially appeared to be so neutral, actually had a very significant effect in determining who had access to higher education. By race? Yes.[9] But not only

black families had a median net worth of $3397, while families of Spanish origin had a median net worth of $4913); U.S. Bureau of the Census, Current Population Reports, Series P-70, No. 22, Household Wealth and Asset Ownership 1988, at 8 (1990) (stating that in 1988, white households had a median net worth of $43,279, while median net worth of black households was $4169; the median net worth for families of Hispanic origin was $5524); U.S. Bureau of the Census, Current Population Reports, Series P-70, No. 47, Asset Ownership of Households: 1993, at 8 (1995) ("In 1993, White households had a median measured net worth of $45,740, while the figure for Black households was $4418. Hispanic households had median holdings of $4656."). This census data is the result of the Survey of Income and Program Participation ("SIPP") that was first used in 1984. For a description of SIPP, see Oliver & Shapiro, *supra* note 6, at 55-58.

[8] In 1984, the total number of households with a white householder was 75,343,000. U.S. Bureau of the Census, Current Population Reports, Series P-70, No.7, Household Wealth and Asset Ownership 1984, at 18 (1986). Fourteen percent of these households, or 10,548,020, had a net worth of between $1 and $4999. In 1984, the total number of households with a black householder was 9,509,000. Of those, 23.9%, or 2,272,651, had a net financial worth between $1 and $4999. *Id.*

[9] See Oliver & Shapiro, *supra* note 6, at 37-45, for a discussion of racial effects of "neutral" policies. The current application of the tax code, the authors argue, is another form of the racialization of state policy *See id.* at 43. They argue that the *"lower tax rates on capital gains* and the *deduction for home mortgages and real estate taxes* flow differentially to blacks and whites because blacks generally have fewer and different types of assets, than whites with similar incomes." *Id.* at 43. The effect of this "'fiscal welfare' is to limit the flow of tax relief to blacks and to redirect it to those who already have assets. The seemingly race-neutral tax code thus generates a racial effect that deepens rather than equalizes the economic gulf between blacks and whites." *Id.* Oliver and Shapiro also discuss the FHA program under which the federal government places its credit behind private loans to homebuyers. *See id.* at 39. They explain that the "FHA's conscious decision to channel loans away from the central city and to the suburbs has had a powerful effect on the creation of segregated housing in post-World War II America." *Id.* The FHA even provided restrictive covenants that would be upheld in court to assist in the exclusion of blacks from white neighborhoods. *See id.* at 39. Though now unconstitutional, this "legacy of the FHA's contribution to racial residential segregation lives on in the inability of blacks to incorporate themselves into integrated neighborhoods in which the equity and demand for their homes is maintained." *Id.* When blacks move into white neighborhoods, white flight occurs,

by race, also by class. What is more, this process of making wealth or making financial assets a pre-condition for college is not just limited to the way we fund a college education. Consider the example of Cheryl Hopwood. Cheryl Hopwood is a white woman who applied to the University of Texas Law School (UTLS) but was denied admission. She claimed that the reason she didn't get in is that a number of black and Mexican-American students with lower Texas index scores were admitted pursuant to an affirmative action program then in place in the University of Texas Law School. Now, it is true that sixty-three of the ninety-two black and Mexican-American students who were admitted to UTLS did have lower Texas index scores than Cheryl Hopwood. But so did 140 white students who also got into UTLS when Cheryl Hopwood was denied admission. This fact consistently goes unnoticed in discussions of the case, but it turns out to be crucial in understanding it.[10]

Why was Cheryl Hopwood denied admission? Part of the reason she wasn't admitted goes back to the issue of using wealth or class or financial status as a credential. It turns out that Cheryl Hopwood had gone to both a state and a community college in Texas, and because of this, she was given a lower Texas index score than candidates who had gone to private colleges. Now, you may think that's odd since the University of Texas Law School is also a state institution. Nonetheless, it is a state institution that discounts the credentials of people who went to other state institutions. Points were taken off of Cheryl Hopwood's application because she went to both a state and a community college.[11] She went to those institutions in part because she is a

---

commencing the segregation process. This causes housing prices to fall, and the home appreciation seen by black homeowners slows relative to that of white homeowners in white areas. *See id.; see also* Michael Janofsky, *Report Finds Bias in Lending Hinders Home Buying in Cities,* N.Y. Times, Feb. 23, 1998, at A13 (citing report by the United States Conference of Mayors on discriminatory lending practices that disproportionately affect both urban dwellers and minorities; 71.3% of whites are homeowners, while only 43.6% of blacks and 41.7% of Hispanic Americans own homes). These figures are often the result of redlining.

Blacks also paid disproportionately more into the social security system and received less. *See* Oliver & Shapiro, *supra* note 6, at 38. Oliver and Shapiro note that "[b]ecause social security contributions are made on a flat rate and black workers earn less 'black men were taxed on 100 percent of their income, on average, while white men earned a considerable amount of untaxed income.'" *See id.* (quoting Jill Quadagno, The Color of Welfare: How Racism Undermined the War on Poverty (New York: Oxford University Press, 1994)). They also point out that black workers earn lower retirement benefits which do not last as long as those enjoyed by whites due to the shorter average life span for blacks. *See id.* Finally, they argue that the "tax contributions of black working women 'subsidize the benefits of white housewives.'" *Id.* (quoting Quadagno, *supra*). More black women are single, divorced, or separated. They must work now and many of them will not be able to one day share a spouse's retirement benefit. For these reasons, African-Americans have paid more to Social Security but receive less.

[10] *See* Susan Sturm & Lani Guinier, *The Future of Affirmative Action: Reclaiming the Innovative Ideal,* 84 Cal. L. Rev. 953, 961-62 (1996).

[11] *See id.* at 990. Many law schools do this by creating an admissions index based on the applicant's GPA and LSAT and then adding in the median LSAT of the college from which

working-class woman who couldn't afford a private institution. Yet the admissions protocol at UTLS discounted her degrees from public colleges in Texas as part of the process for denying her admission, as if going to a state or community college is not about class (although it was) but about competence. But commentators never talk about that. Instead, they talk simply about her Texas index scores in some abstract way, and look only at the black and Chicano students who got in with lower scores. But what do those scores actually tell us about the ability of any of these students to do well in law school? How do those scores relate not only to Cheryl Hopwood's class status, but to the class status of all the students who were applying to UTLS?

As it turns out, if we look at the SAT, the LSAT, and the GRE, within every race and ethnic group scores go up as income goes up—there is a direct correlation between family income and scores on these tests.[12] Part of that is because these are coachable tests. You can learn how to take them and you learn best how to take them if your parents can afford to send you to a review course that coaches you how to take them.[13] You also do very well on these

---

the applicant graduated. The rationale for including the median LSAT score of all those who took the LSAT from the applicant's college is to provide a uniform standard from which to assess the value of the applicant's GPA. Since there is a strong relationship between LSAT scores and parental income, however, applicants applying from prestigious private institutions (that also cost more to attend) are advantaged by the fact that they attended college with peers who test well, many of whom, not surprisingly, are also upper middle class students. *See infra* note 12.

[12] There is a correlation between income and SAT scores. *See* Sturm & Guinier, *supra* note 10, at 987-92. Generally, with each 100-point increase in SAT scores, average family income rises. *See id.* at 988 (citing Table 6.1, James Crouse & Dale Trusheim, The Case Against The SAT 125 (1988)); *see also id.* at 988 n.152 ("'There is a positive correlation between income level and standardized test scores.'") (quoting Robert G. Cameron, The Common Yardstick. A Case for the SAT 11 (1989)); Michael Scott Moore, *Three Hours on a Saturday Morning: UC May Drop the Flawed SAT as an Admission Requirement. But Are the Other Options Any Better?*, San Francisco Weekly, Dec. 10, 1997 ("The correspondence between family income and test scores has historically been as high as 80 percent. So choosing between scores of, say, 1100 and 1000 on the SAT is likely to amount to a decision based on class, not potential"); David K. Shipler, *A Leg Up: My Equal Opportunity, Your Free Lunch,* N.Y. Times, Mar. 5, 1995, at 4 (noting that within each racial or ethnic group, SAT scores increase as income rises); *University of California Weighs Optional S.A.T's,* N.Y. Times, Sept. 21, 1997, at 32 ("'The only thing the S.A.T. predicts well now is socioeconomic status.'") (quoting Eugene Garcia, Dean of the Graduate School of Education, University of California at Berkeley).

There is also a correlation between race and SAT scores. *See* Sturm & Guinier, *supra* note 10, at 992-97 "Blacks on average score 110 points below whites on the math portion of the SAT and 92 points below whites on the verbal portion." *Id.* at 992 (citing Robert B. Slater, *Ranking the States by Black-White SAT Scoring Gaps,* J. Blacks Higher Educ , Winter 1995/1996, at 71). *See also Larry P v. Riles,* 495 F Supp. 926, 954-60 (N.D. Cal. 1979) (noting persistent disparate impact of so-called aptitude or intelligence tests on blacks and noting existence of cultural bias), *aff'd in part and rev'd in part,* 793 F.2d 969 (9th Cir. 1984).

[13] *See, e.g.,* Neil L. Rudenstine, *The Uses of Diversity,* Harv. Mag., Mar.-Apr. 1996, 48, 57 ("Students who have had less consistent access to good education (and who lack the money to pay for extra 'prepping') will frequently do less well on standardized tests."). It is important to note the difference here between standardized achievement tests (which give

tests if you have gone to a school that teaches for a long period of time how to start doing the kind of strategic quick guessing that is rewarded on these tests. Yes, guessing! A case in point: Twins in Florida scored a perfect 800 on their SATs; they were the first set of siblings to take the SAT at the same time and each get an 800. The *New York Times* interviewed their mother, who was asked, "Aren't you proud that you have two kids both of whom got perfect scores?" She said she was proud. The *Times* interviewer then asked, "To what do you attribute this great success?" Her answer? They'd been practicing taking the SAT since the seventh grade.[14] Examples like these show clearly that we're using certain aptitude tests to credentialize a social oligarchy and we're mistakenly calling it merit. Then, when some working class or poor people don't have the attributes that we assume are part of the social oligarchy, we don't say, "Well, it's too bad you're poor," we say, "It's too bad you're stupid."

Once we begin to see these things, we have an opportunity to have a different kind of conversation. This conversation has taken place in the most polarized and divisive way in California. One of the reasons it began there was that California used to have one of the premier systems of higher education in the country. In 1984, California spent more than two-and-one-half times as much money on higher education as it spent, for example, on prisons.[15] Ten years later, California spent the same amount on higher education as it spent on prisons. In 1995, California spent more on prisons than it did on higher education. Now, 140 years ago Victor Hugo said that "every time we build a prison we close a school."[16] He was right. For the cost of imprisoning one person for one year, California could educate ten community college students, five California state university students, or two University of California students. But instead, California decided to pass a "three-strikes-and-you're-out" policy.[17] The decision to imprison a third-strike burglar for forty years means

---

[14] *See* Peter Applebome, *For Twins, Double Jackpot on the S.A.T.*, N.Y. Times, Nov. 10, 1995, at A16 (Twila Salthouse, the mother of fraternal twins who scored simultaneous 1600s—the highest possible score—said her children had benefited from taking the SAT repeatedly over time. Salthouse said, "The best preparation for taking the S.A.T. ... is taking the S.A.T.").

diagnostic information and feedback to the teacher and the students) and aptitude tests, which seek to predict future performance. It is the aptitude test format that I challenge here. *See infra* note 20.

[14] *See* Peter Applebome, *For Twins, Double Jackpot on the S.A.T.*, N.Y. Times, Nov. 10, 1995, at A16 (Twila Salthouse, the mother of fraternal twins who scored simultaneous 1600s—the highest possible score—said her children had benefited from taking the SAT repeatedly over time. Salthouse said, "The best preparation for taking the S.A.T. ... is taking the S.A.T.").

[15] Troy Duster, *The New Crisis of Legitimacy in Controls, Prisons, and Legal Structures*, The American Sociologist, Spring 1995, at 20, 24-25.

[16] *Id.* at 25 (paraphrasing Victor Hugo).

[17] *See* Cal. Penal Code § 667 (West 1998). This statute reads (emphasis added):

It is the intent of the legislature in enacting subdivisions (b) to (i), inclusive, *to ensure longer prison sentences and greater punishment* for those who commit a felony and have been previously convicted of serious and/or violent felony offenses.

For purposes of subdivisions (b) to (i), inclusive, and in addition to any other enhancement or punishment provisions which may apply, the following shall apply where a defendant has a prior felony conviction:

the state is foregoing the opportunity to educate two hundred community college students for two years.[18]

It is not surprising, when higher education becomes such a scarce resource, that people begin fighting over who can get in. As they begin fighting over who can get in, they also start looking around at who seems to be getting in, but they don't look at those like the 140 students with lower Texas index scores or lower SAT scores in California—they look instead at the vulnerable canary. They question the admission of minorities to their schools. They start saying, "Look, these people can't even do well on the SATs." They blame the canary. I've been on a number of television debates in which I was told, "You know, these black and Chicano students, they don't do well on the SAT." And I say, "Yes. Well?" And then I pull out an SAT question, and I say, "Melodian is to organist as (choose one) reveille is to bugler, solo is to accompanist, crescendo is to pianist, anthem is to choir master, kettle drum is to timpanist."[19] I asked that question, for example, of Professor Lino Graglia of the University of Texas Law School, who was making this argument, and he said, "Are you asking me if that question is on the SAT?" I said, "No. I'm telling you it's on the SAT and I want to know the answer." He didn't know the answer. And so what? What difference does it make whether you know the answer to that question? It makes no difference unless, perhaps, you are going to be a musician.

> (1) If a defendant has one prior felony conviction that has been pled and proved, the determinate term or minimum term for an indeterminate term shall be twice the term otherwise provided as punishment for the current felony conviction.
>
> (2) (A) If a defendant has two or more prior felony convictions as defined in subdivision d) that have been pled and proved, the term for the current felony conviction shall be an indeterminate term of life imprisonment with a minimum term of the indeterminate sentence calculated as the greater of:
>
>> (i) Three times the term otherwise provided as punishment for each current felony conviction subsequent to the two or more prior felony convictions.
>>
>> (ii) Imprisonment in the state prison for 25 years.
>>
>> (iii) The term determined by the court pursuant to Section 1170 for the underlying conviction, including any enhancement applicable to under Chapter 4.5 (commencing with Section 1170) of Title 7 of Part 2, or any period prescribed by Section 190 or 3046.

[18] *See* Duster, *supra* note 15, at 25. This costs all taxpayers, not just those unlucky enough to be tracked to prison. In 1995, California spent more money on prison construction than on building colleges for the first time. Between 1984 and 1994, California built 16 new prisons; in the same decade, the state built only one new campus for the California State University system. Furthermore, the Department of Corrections increased its personnel by 25,864 while higher education personnel dropped by 8082. *Id.*

[19] Asa G. Hilliard III, Testing African American Students 95 (1991) (providing examples of questions from SATs).

Now, I am not saying we don't want to have and maintain standards of excellence. I am committed to standards of excellence. I am committed to high expectations for all students. All I am questioning is whether performance on a single paper-and-pencil test in which the stakes are high, and in which a large part of what we measure is quick strategic guessing, represents excellence or whether it, in fact, represents wealth?[20] If you look, for example, at those black and Chicano students in California who weren't doing as well on the SAT, thirty-six percent of them came from households with incomes of less than $15,000 a year.[21] On the other hand, sixty percent of the white students taking the SAT in California came from households with incomes of

---

[20] Of course, this is an oversimplification. The SAT and other "norm-referenced" aptitude tests do tell us something about one's capacity to do analytic thinking. The problem is that such capacity is often improved by practice, which comes from coaching (which costs money), from taking practice tests (which means exposure to the opportunity of learning from previous mistakes), and from other kinds of exposure to travel, books, and unusual vocabulary words. Thus, while the tests do tell us something about those who do well, they often tell us less about those who do poorly; i.e., they do not tell us what a poor performer is actually capable of doing, only what that person has already learned or not learned to do. *See, e.g.,* Michael Feuer, *The Changing Science of Assessment: Issues and Implications* (remarks at Symposium held Jan. 30, 1998); *Rethinking Law in the 21st Century Workplace,* 1 U. Pa. J. Lab. & Emp. Law 429 (1998) (stating there is a non-trivial proportion of people who would be excluded from employment opportunities because of performance on a test who could nevertheless do the job; low-scoring test takers are more likely to be misclassified; and black applicants, in particular, are more likely to be misclassified). Feuer, the Director of the Board of Testing and Assessment at the National Academy of Sciences, explained that for many low-scoring individuals, differences in performance on a job are less than the differences in their test performance. This is because the tests only measure certain quantifiable traits and ignore "context, situation, training, teams and prior performance," which also affect job performance. *Id.* Feuer mentioned that the Academy supported research, published as "Fairness in Employment Testing," which included a study of the performance of 3500 Air Force pilots. The study found that previous performance of the pilots was the best predictor of their future performance. Feuer also gave the example of research on milk truck delivery drivers in New York who were able to do sophisticated mathematical calculations as part of their job, but the same drivers would not have been able to perform comparable calculations had they been asked first to take a test. Feuer concludes that some test-driven decisionmaking confuses prediction with merit, especially in light of research regarding the important role of practice and skill acquisition in the workplace itself. *See id.; see also* Sturm & Guinier, *supra* note 10, at 974 n.82 and accompanying text. A study of 300,000 recruits who failed the Army battery of tests in 1976, but because of a calibration error were admitted, was done. Longitudinal study of their subsequent performance showed little difference in re-enlistment and promotion rates compared to those who actually passed the test. *See id.*

[21] *Cf.* Stephanie Simon, *Education/An Exploration of Ideas, Issues and Trends in Education; Working to Compete; Latino Students Preparing for the SAT Want the Opportunity to Show They Can Succeed,* Los Angeles Times, Oct. 1, 1997 (citing The College Board, 1997) ("SAT tests taken in California show that scores rise with the income of students' families. Two-thirds of Mexican-American high school graduates come from families with incomes of less than $25,000 annually.") The article includes a table showing that students from families with a total annual income between $10,000 and $20,000 had an average combined SAT score of 906 (437 verbal and 469 math) and students whose family income was under $10,000 annually had an average combined SAT score of 859 (409 verbal and 450 math). Meanwhile, students from families with income of $80,000 to $100,000 had an average combined SAT score of 1082 (535 verbal and 547 math). *See id.*

more than $60,000 a year.[22] We use these scores to determine merit, but they are in many ways functioning as a wealth test. This is important because higher education has become a gateway to democratic citizenship: It is difficult to get a secure job without a college degree—and without a job, you are not treated as a contributing member of this society.[23] Yet, the gateway to citizenship is controlled by tests that tell us more about how much money your parents make than what kind of citizen you are ultimately going to be.

Now, we defend these tests by saying that they are efficient and, in any event, they predict first-year performance in college or graduate school. Well, they may be efficient, but they don't necessarily predict first-year performance. The average correlation between SAT scores and first-year college grades is about thirty percent.[24] In terms of the LSAT (and going back to those

---

[22] *See* Fair Test, 1996 California SAT Statistical Data (comparing household income in thousands of dollars with the percentage of Mexican-American, black, and white test-takers) (Fair Test National Center for Fair & Open Testing, Cambridge, Mass., Jan. 1998) (unpublished analysis on file with author). The data analysis was compiled from the Educational Testing Service's Profile of College-Bound High School Seniors data from 1996.

[23] *See, e.g.,* Robert B. Westbrook, *Public Schooling and American Democracy, in* Democracy, Education and The Schools 125 (Roger Soder ed., San Francisco: Jossey-Bass, 1996). Westbrook asserts:

> The relationship between public schooling and democracy is a conceptually tight one. Schools have become one of the principal institutions by which modern states reproduce themselves, and insofar as those states are democratic, they will make use of schools to prepare children for democratic citizenship.

Id. Some might argue that the exclusive, or at least primary, aim of schools should be to educate students "for the market." In President Clinton's 1994 State of the Union address, he declared, "We measure every school by one high standard: 'Are our children learning what they need to know to compete and win in the global economy'?" *Id.* at 126. Others, such as Benjamin Barber, suggest the important yet neglected goal of "'civic literacy,'" meaning "'the competence to participate in democratic communities, the ability to think critically and act with deliberation in a pluralistic world, and the empathy to identify sufficiently with others to live with them despite conflicts of interest and differences in character.'" *Id.* at 125 (quoting Benjamin Barber, *America Skips School,* 287 Harper's Mag. 39, 44 (Nov 1993)).

Westbrook agrees with Barber that public schools are public, not just because they are supported by public monies, but because they educate every student for the responsibilities and benefits of participating in public life. *See* Westbrook, *supra.* Professor Susan Sturm and I argue that both goals (of educating citizens for employment opportunities and for democratic participation) are critical, although we might restate them differently *See generally* Susan Sturm & Lani Guinier, *From Triage to Transformation: The Role of Multiracial Learning Communities* (arguing that learning how to collaborate with people who are different is an essential mission of education both because the workplace of the twenty-first century will demand such "teamwork" and because complex problems are often only solved when diverse perspectives are taken into account through the process of constructive conflict) (unpublished manuscript, on file with author). *See also infra* text following note 40 (summarizing values of democratic diversity).

[24] *See* Sturm & Guinier, *supra* note 10, at 971 (a "study of the correlation of SAT scores with freshman grades showed correlations ranging from .32 to .36") (citing Warren W Willingham, et al., Predicting College Grades: An Analysis of Institutional Trends Over Two Decades 43 (Princeton: NJ: U.S. Educational Testing Service, 1990)); *see also* Moore, *supra* note 12 ("According to most independent studies, the SAT's accuracy in predicting first-year college

black and Chicano students at the University of Texas), Martin Shapiro, a statistician, did an affidavit in the *Hopwood* case in which he said that the correlation between black students' LSAT scores and first-year UT law school grades was negative.[25] In other words, if we wanted to figure out how the students were going to do using the Texas index, we would have to assign a negative number to their undergraduate GPAs. There simply was no correlation that was worth considering. I've spoken to many people, including people at the Law School Admissions Council, who say that nationwide the LSAT is about nine percent better than random in predicting the variation in first year law school grades. Nine percent! Not even ten percent.

I did a study of women and legal education with Michelle Fine and Jane Balin. We got the academic performance records of 981 students, and we also looked at their undergraduate GPAs and their LSAT scores.[26] We found that at the University of Pennsylvania Law School, the LSAT did a little better—fourteen percent better than random.[27] However, that still means eighty-six percent of the variance in Penn's first-year grades is not explained by the LSAT scores. When we plotted out these scores on a graph they were all over the map. There were students with perfect LSAT scores who were among the students with the lowest course grades in the first-year class.

Now, if LSAT or SAT scores do not predict first-year grades, do they measure success in some other way? For example, do they measure success in life which, after all, seems a more important measure? A group at Harvard actually decided they were going to investigate this. They did a study of three different classes of alumni over a thirty-year period. They wanted to know what correlates with success. The researchers measured success as financial satisfaction, professional satisfaction, and contribution to the community. Within these three different classes of alumni the researchers found two things that did correlate with their criteria of success: low SAT scores and a blue-collar background. Part of the explanation, they said, is that the SAT does not account for a very important ingredient in achievement—ambition,

---

grades hovers around 30 percent, odds Ralph Nader once described as 'a little better than throwing dice.'").

25 *See* Sturm & Guinier, *supra* note 10, at 972-73 nn. 69-70 (citing Shapiro's affidavit that found weak correlations between LSAT scores and first-year law school performance for everyone, but particularly for African-American students).

26 Lani Guinier et al., Becoming Gentlemen: Women, Law School, and Institutional Change 31 (Boston, MA: Beacon, 1997).

27 *See id.* at 8 ("For students in their first and second years, the LSAT explains even less: 14% and 15% [of performance] respectively."); *see also id.* at 124 n.74 ("In other words, when LSAT is the only variable in a bivariate regression equation, it explains 14% of the variance in first-year law school GPA.").

drive, motivation, hunger to succeed.[28] Other variables that correlate with success, such as intense involvement in extracurricular activities,[29] willingness to ask for help,[30] the tendency to reflect on one's work and revise it,[31] the ability to prioritize and juggle tasks,[32] are not measured by the SAT. We do not measure these things when we give people a paper-and-pencil test and ask them to guess whether "melodian" is to "organist" as "kettle drum" is to "timpanist." And yet we are taking performance on these paper-and-pencil tests to be an accurate predictor of success. The discrepancy between test scores and actual performance in law school or ultimate success after graduation serves as the miner's canary. It is the miner's canary because black and Chicano students, despite their weak performance on these timed paper-and-pencil tests, have the capacity to succeed.[33] Their experience is the miner's canary because it is telling us that we are using the wrong instrument to measure *everyone's* capacity to succeed, not just theirs.

It is not just race that's the miner's canary, but also gender. The study I did with Michelle Fine and Jane Balin of women at the University of Pennsylvania Law School started when one of my students wanted to do a video. I told her I didn't know anything about video, but it seemed to me that the first

---

[28] *See id.* at 10. According to Marilyn McGrath Lewis, director of admissions for Harvard and Radcliffe, "We have a particular interest in students from a modest background. We know that's the best investment we can make: a kid who's hungry."

[29] *See id.*, further noting (*id.* at 10 n.17):

> Intense extracurricular involvement in high school reflects qualities of student leadership as well as initiative, and also usually means that the student has developed a long-term relationship with an adult mentor. The mentoring relationship is critical. It usually means an adult has expressed confidence in the student's ability and provides emotional and other support even after high school graduation.

[30] Other capacities associated with success that are not evaluated by high-stakes test include willingness to seek help. *See* National Commission on Testing and Public Policy, *From Gatekeepers to Gateway: Transforming Testing in America* 7-8 (Boston College, Chestnut Hill, MA, 1990).

[31] *See generally* David N. Perkins, Outsmarting IQ: The Emerging Science of Learnable Intelligence (1995); The Nature of Expertise (Michelene T.H. Chi et al. eds., 1988); Toward A General Theory of Expertise: Prospects and Limits (K. Anders Ericcson & Jacqui Smith eds., 1991).

[32] In addition to the ability to prioritize and juggle tasks, it is important to understand and be able to do what is valued within one's environment. *See* Robert J. Sternberg & R.K. Wagner, *The G-ocentric View of Intelligence and Job Performance is Wrong,* 2(1) Current Direction in Psychol. Sci. 1-5 (1993); Robert J. Sternberg & Wendy M. Williams, *Does the Graduate Record Examination Predict Meaningful Success in the Graduate Training of Psychologists?: A Case Study,* 52 (6) Am. Psychologist 630 (1997); *see generally* Mindy Kornhaber, *Some Means of Spurring the Equitable Identification of Students for Selective Higher Education* (Nov. 17, 1997) (unpublished manuscript on file with author).

[33] Indeed, this is Michael Feuer's point: that high-stakes aptitude tests may disadvantage low-scoring test-takers unfairly because the test results fail to tell us whether the person has the capacity to do the job, yet we rely on the tests to deny the applicant the chance to prove what he or she can in fact do. *See supra* note 20.

thing she should do would be to write a script. So she did. She wrote a script about various incidents of harassment that she had experienced. When she showed me the script, I said to her, "Ann, I don't doubt that all of this has happened. But you are the central figure in each of these incidents and if this is going to be a video that other people are going to learn from, perhaps it would help if you found out whether your experiences are representative of your classmates." So she did a survey. She distributed her survey to all the students. We got back some very discouraging results. On the one hand, over one-half of the students responded to the survey; on the other hand, disproportionate numbers of the women students who answered the survey were unhappy. They weren't speaking up in class and they felt alienated from their law school experience. One woman said, "Guys think law school is hard; we think we're stupid." Such comments revealed that they were internalizing their experiences. It reminded me of the razor company that was trying to conduct a study in which they observed (through a one-way mirror) men and women using defective razors. The men took the razor, shaved, cut themselves, declared the razor no good and threw it away. The women used the defective razor, shaved, cut themselves, and started to worry about what was wrong with their technique. So, like the razor study, part of what our study told us was that the women in our law school were internalizing something that everybody was experiencing. We then went from the self-reporting survey to the academic performance data, and we found that the women, despite identical entry level credentials—virtually the same GPAs, LSAT scores, and undergraduate majors—simply were not doing as well in law school.

I brought this information to some of my colleagues, one of whom said, "Varsity sports." "Well," I said, "that's an interesting theory. Play it out for me; what is it that you're saying?" He said, "Well, perhaps the men who attend law school were all very active in varsity sports as undergraduates. And maybe they were so distracted by their efforts in varsity sports that they didn't perform up to their potential in college so their undergraduate GPAs understate their capacity to perform in law school where there are no varsity sports." I did not pursue the theory.

On the other hand, my colleague may have had a point. Many of the men we interviewed said that they basically looked at law school as a game. Now, what do you do when you play a game? In our culture, you play to win. And if you're playing the game of law school and you're playing the game of winning in a law school class, you win by raising your hand first. You are the agenda setter. You get to talk and control how the rest of the class has to respond. The women, however, said that they did not look at law school as a game. Rather, they saw it as a conversation, and they wanted to say something relevant within that conversation. Part of this approach involves building on what the person before has said. So we found that women commonly edit their remarks. They want to make sure what they are saying is right. By the time they feel confident in what they have to say, however, the class has moved on. Or, they have been so efficient at editing their remarks that when they raise their hands, they essentially deliver a haiku poem. It can take many days to really figure out the significance of their comments.

Now, what does all of this have to do with affirmative action? And what does this have to do with the miner's canary? I think the women at Penn Law School are a miner's canary. They are telling us that there may be something wrong with an academic style of discourse in which we, the professors, are sages on the stage. We engage in a dialogue with students where we have complete information. But we purposely edit student casebooks so that our students have less-than-perfect information. This method of teaching demonstrates to students that they, unlike their professors, do not know the answer because students, of course, have not read the entire case with all its footnotes, and the cases that came before it and the cases that came after it. As one of my law school colleagues observed, the law school process is too often like learning how to ask rude questions. That is, in normal contexts when you ask a question, you ask it because you want to know the answer. That's the reason you ask the question. Lawyers are trained *never* to ask a question to which they don't already know the answer. Thus, law professors ask questions of students, but the professors already know the answer. It's an intimidating environment. Some people learn by intimidation. But not everyone does. And the women were our miner's canary. Their doing less well than their male counterparts suggests that we are using a one-size-fits-all pedagogy that may impair some students' capacity to perform and denies *all* of the students the value of genuine conversation.

Now why do I say that lawyers, of all people, need to know the value of genuine conversation? Think about lawyers in the 21st century, even lawyers in the late 20th century. Put out of your mind some of the lawyers on television, because they are exceptions. Most lawyers do not go to court, most lawyers do not litigate, most lawyers are not solo practitioners, most lawyers must function in a team.[34] And those who function in a team have to know

---

[34] *See* Lani Guinier, *Lessons and Challenges of Becoming Gentlemen,* N.Y.U. J. L. & Soc. Pol'y 18 (1998) (citing Law School Admission Council/Law School Admission Services, Law as a Career: A Practical Guide 17 (Newton, PA, 1993) (stating that many lawyers do not litigate at all)); Gary L. Blasi, *What Lawyers Know: Lawyering Expertise, Cognitive Science, and the Functions of Theory,* 45 J. Legal Educ. 313, 322, 325 (1995) (asserting that even in litigation what counts is judgment and experience, and many lawyers work as members of teams representing large organizations in multiparty transactions and disputes and only rarely go to court). "Lawyering is a 'bundle of skills' including the lawyer's ability to 'integrate factual and legal knowledge and to exercise good judgment in light of that integrated understanding.'" Guinier et al., *supra* note 26, at 107 n.27 (quoting Blasi, *supra,* at 326). For example:

> Often lawyers work as members of teams representing large organizations
> in multiparty transactions or disputes and only rarely go to court. The

how to cooperate, they have to know how to listen, they have to know how to build on what other people have said. These are skills that are valuable, not just for women lawyers, but for lawyering generally So the model of advocacy that we are using as the singular frame to teach how to be a lawyer—learning how to ask rude questions—probably isn't the best way to teach all potential lawyers. The Penn women students provide an opportunity to start rethinking the educational process for *everybody*. The women are the miner's canary— their experiences suggest that we can do better. We can do better by the women and we can do better by the men. We can make better lawyers.

I've said that there are certain skills that are valuable to lawyers in the 21st century, but I know that not everybody is going to be a lawyer. Uri Treisman had some African-American students who were studying math; they were studying calculus. They weren't doing as well as some of his Chinese-American students, and he wanted to know why.[35] He asked some of the other math professors at his college about this, and they offered all sorts of classic stereotypes: they came from single-parent households, they didn't study as hard, they weren't as motivated. But none of that was true. In fact, the African-American students were studying harder, longer than the Chinese-American students. The difference was that the Chinese-American students were studying as a group. They would talk calculus on their way to lunch. They would talk calculus on their way to the library. They would work through

---

> lawyer as aggressive litigator representing a single client may be outmoded in terms of what most lawyers actually do, and this paradigm may be dysfunctional in terms of 'the collection of competencies' lawyers need to possess in order to do their job well.

Id. at 15-16. Moreover,

> A study found that the three most important qualities of lawyers were oral communication, written communication, and "instilling others' confidence in you." After these, the skills or areas of knowledge considered most important were, in order, "ability in legal analysis and legal reasoning, drafting legal documents, and *ability to diagnose and plan solutions for legal problems*."

Id. at 107 n.27 (quoting Bryant G. Garth & Joanne Martin, *Law Schools and the Construction of Competence*, 43 J. Legal Educ. 469, 473 (1993)) (emphasis added).

[35] *See* Guinier et al., *supra* note 26, at 103 n.2 (citing Uri Treisman, *Studying Students Studying Calculus: A Look at the Lives of Minority Mathematics Students in College*, 23 C. Mathematics J. 362, 364-65 (1992), and Philip Uri Treisman, A Study of the Mathematics of Black Students at the University of California, Berkeley 13-15, 46 (1985)). Uri Treisman found that the

> collaborative approach of Chinese American students "provided them with valuable information that guided their day-to-day study"; these students "routinely critiqued each other's work" and thus discovered when study-mates also found problems unusually difficult; as a result, students learned that their failure "was not one of simple oversight" but could be addressed by asking a teaching assistant "without fear of appearing incompetent or ill-prepared."

Id. (quoting Treisman).

problems together. They engaged in a conversation about calculus and as a result of that conversation, they became better mathematicians. So the notion of engaged conversation, a communication of learning how to cooperate, is not just something that is good for lawyers. It's also something that is good for calculus students. When Uri Treisman designed a peer workshop in which he adapted some of the techniques he had seen his Chinese-American students use, he invited the African-American students into the workshop. These students drew some of the highest scores in his calculus class the next semester. The lesson was simple, easy to learn, easy to use—Chinese-American students had a better way of learning calculus. We can learn from bringing in new perspectives and new ways of thinking about old jobs. The miner's canary signals us that the atmosphere in the mine is dangerous, but the warning also tells us to start thinking about new ways of fixing, not the canary, but the mine.

One final example involves women. The New York City Police Department used to have a height requirement. One had to be almost six feet tall in order to be a police officer. A group of women challenged this, since there aren't many women who are six feet tall. Their challenge to the height requirement was successful. More women became cops; more Latino men became cops; more Asian men became cops; more short white men became cops.[36] Women of average height executed the first role of the canary—to signal that the standard didn't really make a lot of sense; it was arbitrary. But they also executed the second role of the canary—they became the instigators of a different kind of thinking about police work.[37] This was especially true of the black and Puerto Rican women who lived near some of the housing projects in New York. They made the projects safer by approaching the young, primarily African-American and Puerto Rican teenage males, who were the

---

[36] See id. at 18 ("New York City once used a height requirement pegged to tall men to select police officers. This discriminated against women, Asian men, some Latino men, and short white men and normalized a particular type of officer-tough, brawny, macho."). The Los Angeles Police Department had similar policies. See Sturm & Guinier, supra note 10, at 985 n.136 (citing Mary Anne C. Case, Disaggregating Gender from Sex and Sexual Orientation: The Effeminate Man in the Law and Feminist Jurisprudence, 105 Yale L.J. 1, 87 (1995) (noting report finding that LAPD training officers criticized female officers for a perceived lack of "stereotypically masculine qualities")).

[37] See Sturm & Guinier, supra note 10, at 984-85 n.134 (citing Telephone Interview with J. Phillip Thompson, Director of Management and Operations, New York City Housing Authority, 1992-93 (Jan. 25, 1996)):

> Thompson recounted that an internal evaluation conducted by the Housing Authority revealed that women housing authority officers were policing in a different, but successful, way As a result of this evaluation, the authority sought to recruit new cops based on their ability to relate to young people, their knowledge of the community, their willingness to live in the housing projects, and their interest in police work. They also offered free housing to any successful recruit willing to live in the projects.

likely trouble-makers, as mentors.[38] They offered these young men respect, and the young men, grateful for the attention of an adult, constrained their old behaviors so they could continue to earn that respect.[39] These women were developing a different style of policing. This is not to say that we want all police officers to become mentors, but it wouldn't hurt if more officers knew how to modify their command and control approach when appropriate. When the Los Angeles Police Department commissioned a study (headed by Warren Christopher, the former Secretary of State) to find out what they should do about excessive use of force by police officers, the answer that came back was, "Hire more women." Hire more women. Women, the study showed, were not reluctant to use force, but they didn't resort to force as their initial reaction to a situation involving conflict.[40]

Now, I have to say I am optimistic about conversations in which we think about the miner's canary as a signal and as a lesson. I am optimistic as more people begin to see diversity as something that benefits the entire society—in other words, as more people learn the lessons of the miner's canary. To summarize, these lessons include:

(1) the value of democratic legitimacy—that all taxpayers feel they have an opportunity to pursue the benefits they are subsidizing;

(2) the value of diversity as an important tool for solving complex problems in the information economy when no single individual can memorize all the available information (nor do we need anyone to memorize it when it keeps changing, yet is quickly accessible). In other words, what we really need is synthesis of information—being able to take information from diverse sources, then put it together in innovative and creative ways to solve problems; and

(3) that bringing in previously underrepresented or marginalized groups can help all of us rethink the nature of the job or the task (for example, the lesson of the women cops and Uri Treisman's Chinese-American calculus students).

I am optimistic as well because of my own experience raising my nine-

---

[38] *See supra* note 29 (describing importance of mentoring relationship with an adult during adolescence).

[39] *See* Sturm & Guinier, *supra* note 10, at 985 n.135 (noting that the "women officers showed the young men respect, which was critical to the social status needs of these males; and that the men in turn checked their own behavior, out of mutual respect for the women officers") (citing Telephone Interview with J. Phillip Thompson, *supra* note 37).

[40] *See id.* at 983 n.133 (citing Independent Commission on the Los Angeles Police Department, Report of the Independent Commission on the Los Angeles Police Department 83-84 (1991)) ("[F]emale LAPD officers are involved in excessive use of force at rates substantially below those of male officers. The statistics indicate that female officers are not reluctant to use force, but they are not nearly as likely to be involved in use of excessive force, due to female officers' perceived ability to be 'more communicative, more skillful at de-escalating potentially violent situations and less confrontational.'").

year-old son, Nikolas. When Nikolas was seven he was in second grade, and the teacher had him keep a journal. (I asked him if it was okay to share with you his journal, and he said it was okay as long as I told you it was written when he was in second grade. He's now in fourth grade.) The teacher said, "Tell us what your family does, you know, what does your mother do? What does your father do?" Nikolas talked about his mom. "My mom is a professor," he said. "I think it's boring. I think it's boring because you get to sit in front of a computer and you don't get to play games. On the other hand, I think it's fun because you get to stand in front of a class and you're the boss." I could hear in my son's journal an echo of conversations with a lot of the men in my Penn law school classes who also see things as a game; the goal is to win, to be powerful. On the other hand, my son also showed me that he, too, can learn to look at the world differently. His second-grade teacher subsequently told me that they were sitting around talking about what each of their parents did, and one of Niko's classmates said that his mom is the vice-president of a bank. At which point my son just looked at him and blurted out, "Well, why isn't *she* president?"

10

Will Our Children Live as Well?

Robert Reich

Robert Reich, who served as Secretary of Labor under President Bill Clinton, was named one of the ten most successful cabinet secretaries of the century by Time Magazine in 2008. In 2003, he was awarded the prestigious Vaclav Havel Vision Foundation Prize for his pioneering work in economic and social thought. Currently, Reich is Chancellor's Professor of Public Policy in the Goldman School of Public Policy, University of California, Berkeley.

A question on many people's minds the past few years asks us to explore the relationship between economic and social justice. It is a question I want to ask in such a way as to focus on where we have been and where we are going, drawing from my training and experience as both a lawyer and an economic policy maker and analyst. That question is, "Will our children live as well as we are living?"

To answer this question, we need to understand what has happened to the economy—not just in the Great Recession and its aftermath, but over the last several decades. We have to look at the relationship between our economic life and our civil life, between prosperity and social justice.

The Great Recession was worse than the garden variety recession—worse than any recession we have had, or at least different from the last five recessions. In depth and duration, it most closely resembled the Great Depression of the 1930s.

The previous recessions were brought on by the Federal Reserve Board (the Fed) raising interest rates too high to overcome inflation and, by doing that, indirectly bringing the economy to a grinding halt. That is what happened in 1980-82 when Paul Volker, the chairman of the Fed when Jimmy Carter was president, decided to break the back of inflation by raising interest rates so high that he almost broke the back of the economy. Unemployment zoomed up to ten percent of the labor force. But inflation was brought under control relatively quickly, the economy expanded, and unemployment fell.

The Great Recession was not created by the Federal Reserve Board, at least not directly, as in the past. It was precipitated by the bursting of a huge asset bubble that was based on speculation. It paralleled what happened in the 1920s, leading to the great crash of 1929. The received wisdom in 2008 was that the core problem lay in credit markets, and you could get credit moving again by inundating Wall Street banks with bailout money through the so-called "T.A.R.P." (Isn't a tarp something you use to cover things up?) It was assumed that this would provide banks enough liquidity to feel confident about lending again, and bank investors could be induced to take some of the toxic assets off the bank's balance sheets. The strategy appeared to work, but it did not deal with the core issue. There was a lot of blame to go around, including Wall Street and Wall Street traders and executives, regulators who failed to understand what was going on, and the credit rating agencies. But if you feel an overwhelming need to blame one person, I'd nominate Alan Greenspan, then Chairman of the Fed. I do not want to be unfair; Alan Greenspan has accomplished a lot of good things in his very long and distinguished career. But he did one thing very badly. He pushed short-term interest rates down to one percent by 2003. For the major Wall Street banks and lending institutions, that lowered the cost of borrowing money to effectively zero.

When money costs nothing, you are going to do with it as much as you possibly can. If you are a major Wall Street bank or other lending institution, you are going to find people to borrow it. In fact, you are going to lend it to anybody who can stand up straight and to many who cannot. You are just going to shove the money out the door, especially if you can use a device known as securitization; that is, once you lend the money and have a promissory note from the person who actually borrowed it, you can grind that promissory note up like sausage with a lot of other promissory notes and a lot of other loans, and you sell the "sausages" around the world.

Securitization took the risk off the backs of the banks. Free money combined with securitization allowed the banks to make lots of money by lending to virtually anyone, and they had every incentive to do so.

Greenspan's error was not to see this, and not to understand the necessity of increasing bank oversight under these circumstances. This was not the first time Greenspan punted on regulatory oversight. In 1998 there was a very important meeting between the Federal Reserve Board, the Commodity Futures Trading Commission, and the Treasury of the United States. At that meeting, the head of the Commodity Futures Trading Corporation warned of unregulated credit default swaps, insurance devices that were conveniently off the balance sheets of the major banks and lending institutions. In particular, an insurer called AIG was issuing huge amounts of such insurance, without any rules or regulations requiring that it hold a certain amount of capital against the possibility of default. At that meeting, Alan Greenspan and the Secretary of the Treasury, Bob Rubin, both said to the head of the Commodity Futures Trading Commission that no regulation was needed. Credit default swaps should be left to the market. Parties were sufficiently sophisticated to protect themselves. It was a bomb waiting to explode. And explode it did.

But if you take a closer look at the Great Recession you see that the bursting of the financial bubble was a symptom of a deeper problem—one that continues to haunt the American economy. The supply of credit was important, but the fundamental cause was on the demand side of the economy.

To understand why this is important, I turn to an economist named John Maynard Keynes. People paid a lot of attention to Keynes from the 1930s through the 1970s. Even Richard Nixon once said, "We are all Keynesians now." It was only later, after the double-digit inflation of the late 1970s, that economist Milton Friedman and his free market disciples superseded Keynes. We thereafter assumed that the central problem of the economy was its tendency toward inflation and over-consumption. We forgot Keynes' admonition that the central problem can be a tendency toward deflation and under-consumption. But Keynes is very much relevant to our current situation. He stood for a very simple proposition: when demand is substantially below the productive capacity of a nation, government has to be the purchaser of last resort. Keynes' ideas were forged in the crucible of the Great Depression of the 1930's. What finally got America out of the Great Depression was government spending on such a large scale—far larger than Franklin D. Roosevelt had ever anticipated—because the nation had to mobilize for World War II.

When I was a small boy my father said to me: "Bobby, you and your children and your children's children and their children will be paying for the debt created by Franklin D. Roosevelt." It scared me silly. I was only about four but I remember thinking: "How am I going to pay? My allowance won't cover them. I don't have any idea of how I am going to do this." In truth, I didn't even know what a debt was. By 1946 the U.S. debt was far greater than the nation's entire yearly production, running at about 160 percent of the GDP, gross domestic product. But in this instance, my father proved wrong. Those debts did not continue to burden the nation. What changed—and this is as important to understand now as it was then—was that the ratio of the debt to the GDP continued to drop as the GDP grew. The denominator of the equation proved more important than the numerator. The American economy grew in the 1950s because we had a huge middle class with money in their pockets, strong labor unions that could negotiate good wages and good benefits, and public investments in education and infrastructure that both put people to work and also laid the foundation for future growth. What a newly exhumed Keynes would say to people who are worried about a big debt today is the best way to get back on the path of growth—and indeed, this is the only way to get the debt GDP ratio down—is to do the same today.

Not only is the strategy we embarked on in the three decades after World War II good for the economy; it is also socially good and socially just. Those who are most badly hurt by unemployment are those at the lower end of the income ladder who can least afford long periods of unemployment, and who are, typically, the first to be laid off at signs of economic downturn. When government spending fills the shortfall in private spending in order to create more jobs, and invests in the building blocks of future growth, it spreads prosperity to everyone. Consumers are 70 percent of the national economy. If they don't have enough purchasing power to buy what the economy is capable of producing at or near full employment, there will be a tendency toward recession—or worse.

Some believe that the Great Recession—and, indeed, its antecedent, the Great Depression—were brought on by American consumers living beyond their means. But the real problem was that the means of most Americans didn't keep up with what the growing economy should have been able to provide them. Starting in the late 1970s, the median wage of male workers began to level off and then decline, adjusted for inflation. This is particularly true of the 80 percent of male workers who were hourly workers. Their pay began to drop due to technological changes, software, robotics, and globalization. Rarely has a word gone so directly from obscurity to meaninglessness without any intervening period of coherence as the word globalization, but when I say globalization in terms of jobs, what I mean is the combination of technology and the ability of many people around the world to do a lot of manufacturing and other production jobs much more routinely. This combination of factors meant that, for the first time, a lot of American blue-collared and middle-class workers without much education or college credentials started to feel great economic pressure.

How could average American middle-class and blue-collar families keep spending under these circumstances? They adopted three coping mechanisms. The first was for millions of wives and mothers to move into paid work. The second was for everyone to work longer hours. The third and final coping mechanism was to go ever more deeply into debt, taking advantage of rising home values to get home equity loans or to refinance. When the housing bubble burst, so did the last of the coping mechanisms.

A reasonable question at this juncture might be, "What happened to all the money?" Remember, the American economy doubled in size between the late 1970s and 2007. If the wages of average working Americans barely rose, who got the gains from growth? Overwhelmingly, the very rich. In the late 1970s, the top one percent took home 9 to 10 percent of total national income, but beginning in the 1980's, more and more of the total national income started to go to the top. By 2007, the top one percent took home 22.5 percent of total national income. In other words, their share of the pie more than doubled. The share going to the top one-tenth of one percent tripled.

Quite apart from questions of social justice, this lopsidedness creates an economic problem that Keynes would immediately understand. The very rich do not spend nearly as much of their income as people of more modest means. After all, if you're rich you have most of what you need. That's the definition of being rich. The rich save more of their income than people who earn less than they do, and their savings go around the world to wherever they can get the highest return. As a result, there's not enough demand in the system to keep the economy moving at full speed or full employment. The last time in American history that the top one percent took home anything close to 22 percent of total national income was the year 1928. And we all know what happened then.

Fairness and social justice are entirely consistent with a growing economy; indeed, they are essential to it. Even if the government were to stimulate the economy with billions of additional dollars of public spending, that would not be enough to keep the economy moving unless the vast middle class has a sufficient share of the gains of growth. Whenever you hear public officials, the media or any pundit talk about needing to "get the economy back on track," you should be mindful that it was that very track we were on that got us into the problem in the first place. So rather than get back on that track, we need to embark on a new one that's more economically sustainable. That path requires a progressive tax system that better spreads the benefits of economic growth, and a system of public investment that helps guarantee that almost everyone has a fair chance of becoming a fully productive member of society.

This approach is exactly the antithesis of what's come to be known as "trickle-down economics." This school of economic thought—if one can charitably characterize it as a school of thought—holds that the rich must get even richer in order that the rest of us benefit. Their salaries must be far higher; their taxes far lower. All this will encourage them to work harder and invest in such a way that everyone else benefits. But trickle-down economics has been proven wrong. As we have seen, during the past thirty years those at the top of the economic ladder have become far richer than ever before, taking home a far greater share of total national income. And yet little or nothing has trickled down. The way to rebuild the national economy is not from the top; it is from the bottom.

This is not a zero-sum game, a kind of reverse Robin Hood. To the contrary, the best-off members of society are likely to do far better with a smaller share of a faster-growing economy than with a larger share of an economy that is barely growing at all. We learned this in the first three decades after World War II. It is a tragedy that we have forgotten it.

The key is not financial capital. It is human capital. Indeed, we are seeing that in the global economy, nations have essentially only two ways of attracting global capital in order to create jobs: "come here because we are cheap" or "come here because we are so productive." But the first strategy, "Come here because our labor is so cheap, and we have no regulations or taxes to speak of," leads to a lower standard of living, because a nation that embarks on it inevitably finds itself competing with places in the world that are far cheaper—where labor is less costly, where taxes are lower, and where regulations hardly exist. There is no way to out-compete Bangladesh in these terms. Instead, we must say, "Come here, global capital, build good jobs. You will get a high return on your investment because we are so productive."

If we change tracks—investing in good schools, job training, efficient and results-oriented health care, superb research and development, excellent infrastructure—we will be on the road to widespread prosperity. This is the choice we face—the high road or the low road. The only road to broad-based prosperity and sustainable economic growth is through bottom-up, trickle-up economics in which public investment is central, and economic gains are widely shared.

Will our children live as well as we do? It depends on the choices we make over the next years. The answer could easily be yes, but not necessarily so; it depends on us.

11

Change and Continuity on the Supreme Court[1]

Linda Greenhouse

Linda Greenhouse is the Knight Distinguished Journalist in Residence and Joseph M. Goldstein Senior Fellow at Yale Law School, and a Pulitzer Prize-winning reporter. She has served as Supreme Court correspondent for The New York Times. *She earned her B.A. from Radcliffe College of Harvard University in 1968, as well as a Master of Studies in Law in 1978 from Yale Law School.*

When two new Justices joined the Supreme Court during the 2005 term, the longest period of membership stability in the Court's modern history came to an end. The eleven years without personnel change, from 1994 until 2005, made this the longest "natural court," as scholars call the period during which the same Justices serve together, since the 1820s. And not since the 1971 Term, a generation ago, when Justices Lewis Powell and William Rehnquist took their seats, had two new Justices joined the Court during a single term.

With personnel change, of course, comes institutional change. Justice Byron White, who served on the Court for thirty-one years and witnessed the arrival of thirteen new colleagues, once said that "every time a new justice comes to the Supreme Court, it's a different court."[2] My interest today is actually better expressed not so much by that comment of Justice White's, but by a question posed years earlier by Justice Robert Jackson. "Why is it," Jackson asked in the preface to his book *The Struggle for Judicial Supremacy*, published shortly before he joined the court in 1941, "that the Court influences appointees more consistently than appointees influence the Court?"[3]

Indeed, what makes the Court so fascinating as an exercise in small group dynamics is the relationship between personal and institutional change. Justices have an impact on the institution, obviously. That is why a Supreme Court nomination is such a major event, and why it is so often followed by a contentious process. But the impact of the institution on the individual justice is a bit more elusive, less obvious, but no less important.

---

[1] This chapter is adapted from an essay originally published in 2007 by the Washington University (St. Louis) *Journal of Law & Policy* (volume 25, number 1, page 39 (2007)).

[2] Dennis J. Hutchinson, *The Man Who Once Was Whizzer White* 467 (New York: Free Press, 1998).

[3] Robert H. Jackson, *The Struggle for Judicial Supremacy: A Study of a Crisis in American Power Politics* vii (New York: Knopf, 1941).

My own work in the papers of Justice Harry Blackmun, which led to my book, *Becoming Justice Blackmun: Harry Blackmun's Supreme Court Journey*, published in 2005,[4] brought this subject home to me and whetted my appetite for a broader ranging examination of personal change on the Supreme Court. It is a very rich subject, and obviously a timely one. I plan to explore it with you, first by looking in some detail at the case, and career, of Harry Blackmun, and then by offering some general observations that might be worth keeping in mind as we watch the unfolding of the new Roberts Court, a Court that is still very much a work in progress as we await the decisions that will define at least this early period.

Robert Jackson had no reason to suppose, when he raised his provocative question, how close to home it would come, in that he himself would personify the kind of personal and intellectual change that can occur on the Supreme Court. So before turning to more current events, let me speak for a few moments about one of the 20th century's most interesting Supreme Court justices.

Robert Jackson took his seat on the Supreme Court on July 11, 1941, and served until his death on October 9, 1954, at the age of sixty-two.[5] Thirteen years is not a long tenure on the Supreme Court, and Jackson's thirteen years included a year of service as the chief prosecutor at the Nuremberg war crimes trials.[6] It was an amazingly consequential period in the life of the country, with Pearl Harbor at the beginning, World War II and the start of the Cold War, including the Korean War, in the middle, and *Brown v. Board of Education*[7] at the end. The country changed, the Court changed, and there is no doubt that Robert Jackson changed as well.

Two opinions, one from the beginning of his tenure and one from near the end, demonstrate how much Jackson changed. The later opinion, his concurrence in the steel seizure case of 1952, *Youngstown Sheet & Tube Co. v. Sawyer*,[8] is very famous. The earlier one is almost unknown except to scholars, because it was never issued. It was a separate opinion he wrote and then decided not to publish in the summer of 1942, when the Court was considering *Ex parte Quirin*,[9] concerning the constitutionality of the wartime military commission that tried and sentenced to death eight Nazi saboteurs who were captured after entering the United States in June of that year.

---

[4] Linda Greenhouse, *Becoming Justice Blackmun: Harry Blackmun's Supreme Court Journey* (New York: New York Times, 2005).

[5] Eugene C. Gerhart, *Robert H. Jackson: Country Lawyer, Supreme Court Justice, America's Advocate* 233 (Buffalo, NY: Hein, 2003).

[6] *See* Gerhart, *supra* note 5, at 253, 467.

[7] *Brown v. Board of Education*, 347 U.S. 483 (1954).

[8] *Youngstown Sheet & Tube Co. v. Sawyer*, 343 U.S. 579, 634 (1952) (Jackson, J., concurring).

[9] *Ex parte Quirin*, 317 U.S. 1 (1942).

As a case about the dimensions of the wartime powers of the President, *Quirin* remains relevant. The Court unanimously upheld President Roosevelt's use of the military commission that tried the saboteurs, finding, in contrast to the Court's conclusion in June 2006 in the *Hamdan* case,[10] that the commission had been lawfully constituted by Congress. The Court in *Quirin* thus did not have to reach or resolve the deeper question of whether, in the absence of congressional authorization, the President would have possessed the inherent authority to proceed as he wished.

Jackson believed that the Court should have reached this question and should have decided it in the affirmative.[11] The saboteurs, he wrote in his unpublished opinion, "are prisoners of the President by virtue of his status as the constitutional head of the military establishment."[12] And, he added, "[t]he custody and treatment of such prisoners of war is an exclusively military responsibility."[13] In other words, it was the President's business, not the business of Congress or the federal courts. Jackson's suggestion was that the Supreme Court should not even have undertaken to review Roosevelt's exercise of his commander-in-chief authority.

Yet just ten years later—a blink of an eye in Supreme Court terms, or maybe that is just my perspective, having covered the court for twenty-nine years—Robert Jackson expressed a very different view of presidential authority. During the Korean War, acting in what he deemed to be the national interest, President Truman seized the steel mills to prevent the nation's manufacturing capacity, especially its wartime armaments-manufacturing capacity, from being crippled by a steel industry strike. Truman invoked his inherent authority as chief executive and commander-in-chief. The Supreme Court ruled that, lacking congressional authorization, the action was invalid.[14] Justice Jackson wrote a concurring opinion that has come to be seen as the most eloquent expression of limitations on presidential authority, an opinion that has lost none of its relevance and that was cited in the Supreme Court as recently as the final day of its 2005 term.[15] When the President acts pursuant to an express authorization from Congress, Jackson said, his power is at its peak, "for it includes all that he possesses in his own right plus all that

---

[10] *Hamdan v. Rumsfeld*, 548 U.S. 557 (2006).

[11] *See* Jack Goldsmith, *Justice Jackson's Unpublished Opinion in Ex parte Quirin*, 9 Green Bag 223 (2006) (the author reproduces and analyzes Justice Jackson's draft opinion in *Ex parte Quirin*); *see also* Dennis J. Hutchinson, *"The Achilles Heel" of the Constitution: Justice Jackson and the Japanese Exclusion Cases*, 2002 Sup. Ct. Rev. 455, 458-59 nn.21-24 (2002).

[12] Goldsmith, *supra* note 11, at 237.

[13] *Id.*

[14] *See Youngstown Sheet & Tube Co.*, 343 U.S. at 579.

[15] *Hamdan*, 548 U.S. at 638 (Kennedy, J., concurring in part).

Congress can delegate."[16] When the President acts without congressional authorization, Jackson said, he enters a "zone of twilight" and uncertainty.[17] And "when the President takes measures incompatible with the expressed or implied will of Congress, his power is at its lowest ebb."[18]

Was this the same Robert Jackson, the President's man in the *Quirin* case? Clearly, his trajectory calls for some sort of explanation. One explanation is that in the *Quirin* case, arising as it did during the first year of his tenure on the Court, Jackson was still very much President Roosevelt's man. Arriving in Washington from Western New York, early in the Roosevelt administration, to be chief counsel of the Internal Revenue Service, he had spent his entire Washington career in the administration's service, quickly becoming head of the Justice Department's Tax Division; then head of its Antitrust Division; then Solicitor General; and then Attorney General.[19] It was certainly natural for him to view the exercise of government authority from the perspective of the executive branch.

However, by 1952, he was a seasoned Supreme Court Justice who had seen at first hand, during his year at Nuremberg, the dire consequences of concentrated and unchallenged executive power. Not to equate Harry Truman with Adolf Hitler, as obviously Jackson did not, but Jackson certainly had a different perspective by the time he encountered the steel seizure case. As he had so presciently observed eleven years earlier, the institution and the life experience he had gained while serving there had changed him.

The topic of personal change on the Supreme Court, although of obvious interest, largely has been ignored in scholarly literature. The study of judicial behavior long has been in the grip of political science theories that go under the names of "partisan entrenchment" or "the attitudinal model."[20] Political scientists had assumed, despite abundant evidence to the contrary, that judges go on the bench with fixed ideas that they strive to implement for the remainder of their careers. But scholars have recently begun to apply some welcome and overdue skepticism to these assumptions. "[M]any, if not most, Justices on the Supreme Court exhibited some degree of preference shifting during their careers," Professor Theodore Ruger of the University of Pennsylvania Law School wrote in a 2005 law review article.[21] He proposed that instead of the "entrenchment" image, which suggests hard rocks and geology,

---

[16] *Youngstown Sheet & Tube Co.*, 343 U.S. at 635.

[17] *Id.* at 637.

[18] *Id.*

[19] *See* Gerhart, *supra* note 5, at 62-229.

[20] *See, e.g.*, Richard J. Lamb et al., eds., Harold J. Spaeth, *Supreme Court Policy Making: Explanation and Prediction* (1979).

[21] Theodore W. Ruger, *Justice Harry Blackmun and the Phenomenon of Judicial Preference Change*, 70 Mo. L. Rev. 1209, 1217 (2005).

we should use a nautical metaphor, in which judicial preferences are "anchored not in stable bedrock but rather a softer bottom that permits a meaningful, if slow, movement as currents change with time."[22]

Lee Epstein, Jeffrey A. Segal, and their co-authors have concluded in a recent empirical study of "ideological drift" among Supreme Court justices that change is the rule, not the exception, and that "contrary to the received wisdom, virtually every Justice serving since the 1930s has moved to the left or right or, in some cases, has switched directions several times" during their tenure on the Court.[23] The database compiled by Epstein and her co-authors provides support for a phenomenon that has been obvious to the most casual court-watcher, one that led President Bush to declare, defensively, when he nominated his White House counsel, Harriet Miers, to the Court that "I know her well enough to be able to say she's not going to change."[24] With a barely disguised reference to conservatives' disappointment in his father's nomination of Justice David H. Souter, the President said: "I don't want to put somebody on the bench who is this way today, and changes."[25]

To see how Supreme Court justices change, we do not have to go back as far as Robert Jackson, or even as far as Harry Blackmun, who retired from the court in 1994.[26] We can look at Justice Sandra Day O'Connor, whose tenure on the Court at twenty-four years was almost exactly as long as Blackmun's, and who retired in January 2006. Justice O'Connor ended her tenure on the Supreme Court as a very different Justice from the one who arrived from Arizona in 1981, or the one who spoke disparagingly of *Roe v. Wade* in 1983,[27] or even the one who in 1992 published a tribute to the newly retired Thurgood Marshall in which she described Marshall as an embodiment of "moral truth."[28] The experience of knowing and working with Thurgood Marshall, O'Connor said then, of sitting with him at conference for ten years, listening

---

[22] *Id.* at 1225.

[23] Lee Epstein et al., *Ideological Drift among Supreme Court Justices: Who, When, and How Important?*, 101 Nw. U. L. Rev. Colloquy 127 (2007).

[24] Press Release, President George W. Bush, Press Conference at the Rose Garden (Oct. 4, 2005), http://www.whitehouse.gov\news/releases/2005/10/print/20051004-1.html.

[25] *Id.*

[26] *But see* David A. Strauss, *It's Time to Deal With Reality: The Myth of the Unpredictable Supreme Court Justice Debunked*, Chicago Trib., Aug. 7, 2005, at C9 ("The idea that judges change their basic philosophical views once they are on the bench is a myth").

[27] *Compare Akron v. Akron Ctr. for Reprod. Health*, 462 U.S. 416, 458 (1983) (O'Connor, J., dissenting) (criticizing the "Roe framework" as "clearly on a collision course with itself" in the first abortion-related case she encountered after joining the Court), *with Planned Parenthood of S.E. Pa. v. Casey*, 505 U.S. 833 (1992) (participating in the joint opinion, O'Connor reaffirmed the "Roe framework").

[28] Sandra Day O'Connor, *Thurgood Marshall: The Influences of a Raconteur*, 44 Stan. L. Rev. 1217 (1992).

to him tell stories from his amazing life, "would, by and by, perhaps change the way I see the world."[29]

It seemed an odd sentiment from a Justice whose jurisprudence at that time appeared to bear little of Thurgood Marshall's imprint, certainly not in the core areas of voting rights and racially conscious affirmative action.[30] Yet "by and by," as we all know, came to pass. In 2003, Sandra O'Connor led the Court in reasserting a role for affirmative action in university admissions in *Grutter v. Bollinger*,[31] the University of Michigan Law School case. Now, with Justice O'Connor gone, it may be no coincidence that the Court quickly agreed to revisit the question of race and education, in the two cases it decided in June 2007 on the constitutionality of race-conscious student assignment policies adopted by public school systems struggling to maintain hard-won integration.[32] I do not have much doubt that early in her career, Justice O'Connor would have found these policies highly problematic if not constitutionally unacceptable. Later, however, she would probably have agreed with Judge Alex Kozinski's view, expressed in an opinion concurring with the en banc Ninth Circuit in the Seattle case, that this was the kind of pragmatic policy decision, taken by democratically accountable officials, with which federal judges should be very reluctant to interfere.[33] If my assumption is correct, the cases would have been decided 5 to 4 the other way: the challenged plans in Louisville and Seattle would have been upheld rather than invalidated under the Fourteenth Amendment.

I will return in a moment to Harry Blackmun, but first, it must also be acknowledged that change during a justice's career on the Supreme Court is not universal. Let me offer you a dissenting opinion from the 2004 Term that bears the name of Justice Clarence Thomas. The question in *Deck v. Missouri*[34] was the constitutionality of shackling a defendant in the presence of the jury during the capital sentencing phase of a criminal trial. The defendant had been convicted of shooting an elderly couple to death in the course of robbing them.[35]

The routine use of visible shackles during the guilt phase of a criminal

---

[29] *Id.* at 1220.

[30] *See, e.g., Adarand Constructors, Inc. v. Pena*, 515 U.S. 200 (1995); *Miller v. Johnson*, 515 U.S. 900 (1995).

[31] *Grutter v. Bollinger*, 539 U.S. 306 (2003).

[32] *Parents Involved in Cmty. Sch. v. Seattle Sch. Dist. No. 1*, 426 F.3d 1162 (9th Cir. 2005), *cert. granted*, 74 U.S.L.W. 3676 (U.S. Jun. 5, 2006) (No. 05-908); *Meredith v. Jefferson County Bd. of Educ.*, 416 F.3d 513 (6th Cir. 2005), *cert. granted*, 74 U.S.L.W. 3676 (U.S. Jun. 5, 2006) (No. 05-915).

[33] *Parents Involved in Cmty. Sch.*, 426 F.3d 1162, 1193 (9th Cir. 2005) (en banc), (Kozinski, J., concurring).

[34] *Deck v. Missouri*, 544 U.S. 622 (2005).

[35] *Id.*

trial has long been forbidden under a rule that has deep roots in English common law, based on the presumption that the sight of a defendant tied up like a mad dog would naturally prejudice the jury. But surprisingly, the use of shackles during the punishment phase of a capital case was an open question in American law. By a majority of seven to two, Thomas and Scalia dissenting, the Court ruled in *Deck v. Missouri* that for constitutional purposes, the two situations were the same, and that the use of shackles during the sentencing phase without special justification violates the defendant's right to due process.[36]

We know that Justice Thomas is a traditionalist and self-described "originalist," but he argued in his dissenting opinion that tradition should not apply.[37] Modern day shackles were different from the pain-inducing shackles of olden times, he said.[38] "The belly chain and handcuffs are of modest, if not insignificant weight," he wrote.[39] "Neither they nor the leg irons cause pain or suffering, let alone pain or suffering that would interfere with a defendant's ability to assist in his defense at trial."[40] Given that a defendant during a sentencing hearing stands before the jury as one who has already been found guilty, he said, "the court's holding defies common sense."[41]

I found this opinion quite startling, yet it received very little attention in the press, on the blogs, or among academic commentators. Perhaps that is because we are all inured to Justice Thomas. After all, it was in *Hudson v. McMillian*,[42] during his first term on the Court, that he dissented from a decision holding that the use of excessive force against a prison inmate can violate the Eighth Amendment's prohibition of cruel and unusual punishment even if no serious injury results. The Framers, Thomas said, "simply did not conceive of the Eighth Amendment as protecting inmates from harsh treatment."[43] The forty-five year-old Clarence Thomas let us know then, in the opening months of his tenure, what kind of Justice he would be.

This brings us back to Harry Blackmun, and the Justice he became. Harry Blackmun was sixty-one years old when Richard Nixon, in an increasingly desperate search for a confirmable law-and-order nominee, named him to the Supreme Court in 1970. Before the choice was final, Attorney General John Mitchell had asked a young Justice Department lawyer to vet Black-

---

[36] *Id.* at 635.

[37] *Id.* at 635-51.

[38] *Id.* at 640.

[39] *Id.*

[40] *Deck,* 544 U.S. at 640.

[41] *Id.* at 636.

[42] *Hudson v. McMillian,* 503 U.S. 1, 17-18 (1992) (Thomas, J., dissenting).

[43] *Id.* at 19.

mun's record on the Eighth Circuit. Assistant Attorney General William H. Rehnquist, discharging that assignment, pronounced Blackmun acceptable— that is, professionally respectable and reliably conservative.[44]

Indeed, the early Justice Harry Blackmun offered few surprises. The first major constitutional confrontation during his tenure on the Supreme Court was over the death penalty, and when the Court invalidated every death penalty statute in the country in *Furman v. Georgia* in 1972,[45] Blackmun dissented. When the Court ruled against the Nixon Administration's effort to stop publication of the Pentagon Papers,[46] Blackmun dissented.

In 1973, he wrote the opinion for the Court in *United States v. Kras*,[47] a bankruptcy case that challenged the constitutionality of requiring a fifty dollar fee as a condition of filing for bankruptcy. Could the statute be applied to one who was too poor to pay? Blackmun was skeptical of respondent Robert Kras's claim that he could not afford the fifty dollars. Blackmun noted in the memo he wrote to himself before the argument in the fall of 1972, that Kras had turned down the chance to pay the fee in installments, $1.28 a week for nine months.[48] In his opinion for the Court rejecting the constitutional challenge to the filing fee, he wrote dismissively that Kras could have paid the fee for a weekly installment of "less than the price of a movie and little more than the cost of a pack or two of cigarettes."[49]

The dissents were stinging. "[T]he desperately poor almost never go to see a movie, which the majority seems to believe is an almost weekly activity," Thurgood Marshall wrote.[50] William O. Douglas, another of the four dissenters, wrote about the case some months later in his memoir, *Go East, Young Man*, observing: "Never did I dream that I would live to see the day when a court held that a person could be too poor to get the benefits of bankruptcy."[51]

Blackmun was undeterred. He was gratified more than a year later to hear from the government lawyer who had argued the case that Kras had paid the fifty dollars in full barely a month after the decision. "I always had a feeling that there was something wrong with this case," Blackmun responded

---

44 Greenhouse, *supra* note 4, at 46-47. *See* Harry A. Blackmun, Harry A. Blackmun Papers (1970) (unpublished manuscript, on file with Library of Congress, Manuscript Division Box 1360) [hereinafter HAB Papers].

45 *Furman v. Georgia*, 408 U.S. 238, 405 (1972) (Blackmun, J., dissenting).

46 *New York Times v. United States*, 403 U.S. 713, 759 (1971) (Blackmun, J., dissenting).

47 *United States v. Kras*, 409 U.S. 434 (1973).

48 *See* Greenhouse, *supra* note 4, at 108; HAB Papers, *supra* note 44, at Box 156.

49 *Kras*, 409 U.S. at 449.

50 *Id.* at 460 (Marshall, J., dissenting).

51 William O. Douglas, *Go East, Young Man: The Early Years* 175 (New York: Random House, 1974).

to the lawyer.[52] In an "I-told-you-so" gesture, he then circulated the lawyer's letter to the dissenters.

Yet barely four years later, we see a very different Harry Blackmun, one who confronted the rights of the poor in another context that evoked from him a much different response. A trio of cases reached the Court during the 1976 term on the question of the government's obligation to pay for abortions for women who could not afford them. The *Roe v. Wade* majority of three years earlier, Potter Stewart, Lewis Powell, and Warren Burger, fractured over this question and left Blackmun alone in dissent. John Paul Stevens, the newest member of the Court, who had succeeded Douglas, also abandoned Blackmun. Blackmun was left to speak for the poor in his dissenting opinion in *Beal v. Doe*,[53] one of the most powerful dissents of his career. "There is another world 'out there,' the existence of which the Court, I suspect, either chooses to ignore or fears to recognize," he wrote.[54] Was this the same Justice whose tone had been so dismissive, even smug, in the bankruptcy case just four years earlier? What was happening to Harry Blackmun?

It is the thesis of my book that what transformed him was the fortuity of having been assigned by his childhood friend, Chief Justice Burger, to write for the Court in *Roe v. Wade*.[55] Blackmun was shocked by the public response to *Roe*—not only by the criticism of the opinion and its outcome, but by the way in which he personally was vilified and lionized. He was the one who got the hate mail, letters by the tens of thousands (he saved them all and gave them to the Library of Congress, which decided to preserve only a random sample), the death threats, and the pickets wherever he went for the rest of his career.[56] Yet on the other side, he was the one who became a hero to women's groups in whose cause he was at most a reluctant foot soldier, if that: *Roe*, after all, was about the rights of doctors, and only incidentally about the rights of women.

Initially, Blackmun resisted the efforts by both sides to attach *Roe* to him personally. It's not my opinion, he would say. It was the opinion of the Court. The vote was seven to two. He received the assignment and he fulfilled it. But the personification was so relentless that eventually, perhaps inevitably, Blackmun did incorporate *Roe v. Wade* into his self-image in a profound way. He was not only the father of abortion rights in America, in his own mind, but he devoted himself to becoming the defender of those rights as the climate changed both outside the Court and within it. I say "perhaps inevitably" because someone with a different personality structure might have reacted

---

[52] *See* Greenhouse, *supra* note 4, at 109-10; HAB Papers, *supra* note 44, at Box 156.

[53] *Beal v. Doe*, 432 U.S. 438 (1977) (Blackmun, J., dissenting).

[54] *Id.* at 463 (Blackmun, J., dissenting).

[55] *See* Greenhouse, *supra* note 4, at 82.

[56] *Id.* at 134-35.

differently. It is hard to imagine a William Brennan collecting his hate mail and brooding over it. But throughout his life, Blackmun displayed a tendency to personalize events around him.[57] He dwelled, he brooded, he was in pain—and in the process, he became attuned to the pain of others: to "poor Joshua" of the *DeShaney* case,[58] tragic victim of an abusive father and an inadequate government safety net; to those who found their way to death row through incompetent legal counsel and judicial shortcuts; to women who were victims of sex discrimination, a concept for which the Court had no constitutional language at the time it confronted the abortion cases, and to which Harry Blackmun eventually came around in a quite grudging and ultimately rather improbable alliance with his future colleague, Ruth Bader Ginsburg.

How might the Harry Blackmun of 1970 have evolved had Warren Burger chosen someone else for the assignment in *Roe v. Wade*,[59] if *Roe* never became for Blackmun more than just another case? Or if *Roe* had not become so embattled both inside the Court and out, leading Blackmun to assign himself the mission of defending it against all enemies? Of course we will never know the answer to any of those questions,[60] but there are major areas of his jurisprudence that can plausibly be seen as grounded in *Roe,* or at least in how he experienced *Roe.* Commercial speech is one example.

Without *Roe,* would the commercial speech claim in *Bigelow v. Virginia*[61] have caught his interest? The speech at issue in that case was an advertisement for an abortion referral service.[62] In writing for the Court that the advertisement was deserving of First Amendment protection, Blackmun launched a reappraisal of commercial speech that went on to bring us, for better or worse, advertising by lawyers, doctors, and other professionals, and the robust and sometimes controversial corporate speech that fills the airwaves today.[63] It was one of his most important doctrinal contributions.

I think it is unlikely, based on his earlier opinions, that he would have so passionately taken up the cause of poor women except for the context in which the question arose: abortion funding. Nevertheless, these later cases helped move him away from his initial doctor-centered view of the abortion right and toward his eventual embrace of a unified jurisprudence of women's rights and abortion rights. How he eventually got there is a long story, but I

---

[57] *See* Greenhouse, *supra* note 4, at 134-35.

[58] *DeShaney v. Winnebago County Dep't of Soc. Serv.,* 489 U.S. 189 (1989).

[59] *Roe v. Wade,* 410 U.S. 113 (1973).

[60] The concept of "path dependence," from economics, comes to mind; see Linda Greenhouse, *Harry Blackmun, Independence and Path Dependence,* 56 Hastings L.J. 1235 (2005).

[61] *Bigelow v. Virginia,* 421 U.S. 809 (1975).

[62] *Id.*

[63] *See* Greenhouse, *supra* note 4, at 116-21.

will give you just one example from his papers of how far he had to come. Early in the Court's 1973 term, a pair of cases arrived at the Court challenging the then common practice by public school systems of requiring teachers to take unpaid maternity leaves midway through their pregnancy, before their vulnerable young students could notice anything. Presumably, it was less traumatic for the students if their invisibly pregnant teachers suddenly disappeared rather than grow visibly larger and give birth.[64] Most of the Justices thought these policies were unfair, but three years before *Craig v. Boren*[65] made sex discrimination subject to heightened judicial scrutiny, these Justices lacked the constitutional vocabulary to express what, exactly, the problem was. In a memo that Blackmun wrote to himself while preparing for argument, we can see him struggling to get a handle on the issue:

> It is easy to say initially that any regulation which relates to pregnancy is automatically and per se sex discriminatory. I am not at all certain that this is necessarily so. Actually, what the regulation does is to draw distinctions between classes of women, that is, those who are pregnant and those who are not pregnant, rather than between male and female. It is somewhat similar to an Army regulation requiring that enlisted men be shaved and not wear beards or mustaches. Such a regulation discriminates between one class of men and another class of men, and not as between men and women.[66]

At the top of this typewritten memo, Blackmun added a handwritten note: "Not sex related."[67] He eventually joined a majority opinion that invalidated the mandatory leave policies on the basis of due process. The word "discrimination" did not appear in Potter Stewart's majority opinion in *Cleveland Board of Education v. LaFleur.*[68] So, Blackmun did have far to go, but so did the Court. Blackmun did not instinctively grasp what the young Ruth Bader Ginsburg was trying to convey to the Court during her carefully constructed strategic litigation campaign of the 1970s, but neither did he close his eyes and turn away from it, even when his law clerks advised him to do so.[69] During this period, the Court was gradually constructing a language and jurisprudence of women's rights. Blackmun was not a leader. However, it is fairly clear that the more entrenched he became in his defense of *Roe*, the

---

[64] *See* Greenhouse, *supra* note 4, at 213-15. *Cleveland Bd. of Educ. v. LaFleur* and *Cohen v. Chesterfield County Sch. Bd.* were consolidated for decision at 414 U.S. 632 (1974).

[65] *Craig v. Boren*, 429 U.S. 190 (1976).

[66] HAB Papers, *supra* note 44, at Box 203.

[67] *Id.*

[68] *Roe*, 414 U.S. at 633.

[69] *See, e.g.*, Memorandum from law clerk to Justice Blackmun, on *Weinberger v. Wiesenfeld*, 420 U.S. 636 (1975) (Dec. 23, 1974) (unpublished manuscripts, on file with Library of Congress); *see also* Greenhouse, *supra* note 4, at 216-17 (discussing the law clerk's memorandum).

more receptive he became to the claims of women's equality. By 1986, in his opinion in the *Thornburgh*[70] case, we see a description of what it means to a woman to have the right to decide whether to terminate a pregnancy, a description very different in tone from the doctor-centered language of *Roe:* "Few decisions are more personal and intimate, more properly private, or more basic to individual dignity and autonomy...."[71]

Toward the end of his career, Blackmun would occasionally deny that he had changed very much, but the statistics tell the story. In closely divided cases, he voted with Burger 87.5% of the time during his first five terms and with Brennan only 13%.[72] During the next five years, 1975-1980, he voted with Brennan 54.5% of the time and Burger 45.5%.[73] During the final five years that Blackmun and Burger served together, 1981-1986, Blackmun joined Brennan in 70.6% of the divided cases and Burger in only 32.4%.[74]

So this is the question: Which types of Justices are open to change, and which are not? Can we draw conclusions from our recent and not so recent experience as we wait for the Roberts Court to reveal itself more fully?

Predictions are as dangerous as they are irresistible. As a starting point, we might do well to consider a new Justice's stance toward the body of law of which he or she is now a guardian. Although Blackmun developed a sense of mission and was propelled by it in the way I have just described, it is important to note that he did not arrive at the Court with any agenda (beyond survival, which early in his tenure, he doubted). Neither did Justice O'Connor; instead she concentrated on climbing the steep learning curve required to make the transition from the Arizona Court of Appeals and her earlier career in elective politics.

Both Blackmun and O'Connor experienced the personal disruption of a midlife move to a distant city and culture with which they were almost entirely unfamiliar. This mind-bending experience, and their lack of a personal agenda, left each of these Justices open to new and unexpected influences in a way that Clarence Thomas, for example, has not been. The world of Clarence Thomas, a product of bureaucratic Washington by the time he was named to the Court at the age of forty-three, has become more insular and self-

---

[70] *Thornburgh v. Am. Coll. of Obstetricians & Gynecologists*, 476 U.S. 747 (1986).

[71] *Id.* at 772.

[72] Greenhouse, *supra* note 4, at 186 (citing Joseph Kobylka, "Speech at the Midwest Political Science Association: Discovering Judicial Compassion: The Evolving Egalitarianism of Harry A. Blackmun" (Apr. 2001) (on file with author) (compiling data based on annual statistical summary)); *see also* Ruger, *supra* note 21, at nn. 21, 27, 35, 36 (collecting statistical studies of voting patterns).

[73] Greenhouse, *supra* note 4, at 186.

[74] *Id.* (citing data compiled by Joseph F. Kobylka, based on the annual statistical summary in the *Harvard Law Review*); Ruger, *supra* note 21, at nn. 21, 27, 35, and 36 (collecting other statistical studies of voting patterns).

reinforcing, while the worlds of Harry Blackmun and Sandra O'Connor became ever more open.

For seventeen summers, Blackmun left Washington for the Aspen Institute, where he would conduct a seminar in which people from around the country and the world would wrestle with age-old debates about justice and society.[75] Justice O'Connor traveled widely, interacting with judges of other constitutional courts and spending many hours working with the American Bar Association's project on the rule of law in central and eastern Europe.[76] She became a champion of the idea that American courts benefit from studying and acknowledging legal developments in the rest of the world.[77]

I should note that I am not the first or only observer of the Court to see a correlation between a mid-life move to Washington and a new Justice's amenability to change. "Newcomers to Washington are risks," one conservative commentator, Terry Eastland, observed in 1993 with reference to Anthony Kennedy, David Souter, and Sandra Day O'Connor.[78] Lawrence Baum, a political scientist who specializes in judicial behavior, notes in an interesting 2006 book that a statistical analysis of the voting patterns by Republican-appointed Supreme Court Justices since Earl Warren demonstrates that "residency had a greater impact on voting change than initial ideological positions."[79] Justices appointed from outside Washington were more likely to become more liberal on civil liberties issues, Baum observes, noting that on this scale, "the difference between the most conservative and least conservative Republican appointee in voting change was not nearly as great as the difference between Washington residents and newcomers."[80]

Professor Michael Dorf of Columbia Law School has come to the same conclusion through a slightly different lens. Looking at the twelve Justices appointed by Republican Presidents beginning with Richard Nixon's appointment of Warren Burger, he observes that the six who had Executive Branch experience before joining the Supreme Court (Burger, Rehnquist, Scalia, Thomas, and—projecting—Roberts and Alito) changed very little,[81] while the six who had never served in the Executive Branch of the federal

---

[75] *See* Dennis J. Hutchinson, *Aspen and the Transformation of Harry Blackmun,* 2005 Sup. Ct. Rev. 307, 310-11 (2005).

[76] *See, e.g.,* Elizabeth F. Defeis, *A Tribute to Justice Sandra Day O'Connor from an International Perspective,* 27 Seton Hall L. Rev. 391 (1997).

[77] *See, e.g., Roper v. Simmons,* 543 U.S. 551 (2005) (O'Connor, J., dissenting).

[78] Terry Eastland, *The Tempting of Justice Kennedy,* Am. Spectator, Feb. 1993, at 37 n.3, *cited in* Lawrence Baum, *Judges and Their Audiences: A Perspective on Judicial Behavior* 144 (Princeton, NJ: Princeton University Press, 2006).

[79] Baum, *supra* note 78, at 150-51.

[80] *Id.* at 150-51.

[81] Michael Dorf, *Does Federal Executive Branch Experience Explain Why Some Republican Supreme Court Justices 'Evolve' and Others Don't?,* 1 Harv. L. & Pol'y Rev. 457-76 (2007).

government (Blackmun, Powell, Stevens, O'Connor, Kennedy, and Souter) became more liberal during their Supreme Court service.[82] It is an interesting chicken-and-egg problem. Executive Branch service, at least among ambitious young conservatives, seems to serve as a proxy for Washington experience. These individuals engaged in self-selection and were then, of course, selected by Presidents who might have seen their Executive Branch service as a good indicator of ideological commitment and reliability.

Our current Chief Justice, John Roberts, fits this pattern to a striking degree. He does not face a notably steep learning curve. Few people have come to the Court as familiar with the institution and the docket. Between his service as a government lawyer—in the Justice Department and the White House—and his distinguished career in private practice before the Court, there are few issues he has not confronted.[83] He did not have to go through the challenging experience of a mid-life move to a distant city.[84] In moving from one federal courthouse to another, his daily commute from his close Maryland suburb grew by only six blocks.

For Roberts, the forces for change that confronted Justices Blackmun and O'Connor may be absent. David Strauss of the University of Chicago, for one, wrote shortly after Roberts was nominated that "whatever his views are now, the Senate, and the American people, should count on his being the same person throughout the thirty or so years he is likely to spend on the Court if he is confirmed."[85] I think that is a little categorical, but it is not completely unfounded. Although Samuel Alito came to the Court after fifteen years as a federal appeals court judge with chambers in New Jersey, the formative period of his early legal career was spent in Washington, including arguing before the Supreme Court as a young lawyer in the Solicitor General's office.[86] The discourse of the Court, and the legal community that centers around it, is certainly familiar to him. Whether by the Baum residency measure, or Michael Dorf's focus on prior Executive Branch service, neither of the new Justices fit the pattern of those likely to display significant ideological drift.

Of course, that tentative conclusion begs the question of the location of their starting points. While there is little doubt that they are on the conservative side of the Court's current spectrum, are either of these new Justices on a mission, in service of a personal agenda to remake constitutional law? I strive to remain agnostic. On the one hand, I see insiders, comfortable with the

---

[82] *Id.*

[83] Supreme Court of the United States, Biographies of Current Justices 1 (2006), available at http://www.supremecourtus.gov/about/biographiescurrent.pdf.

[84] *Id.*

[85] *See* Strauss, *supra* note 26.

[86] Supreme Court of the United States, *supra* note 83, at 3.

status quo that has brought them success and professional fulfillment. I do not sense the anger and axe-grinding of a Thomas or Scalia. Or, to go back just a bit further, I do not see a Warren Burger, who had been at war with the liberals on the D.C. Circuit while he served there, and approached the Chief Justiceship girded for continued battle and seeing enemies all around him, as his correspondence at the time with his friend Harry Blackmun makes dramatically evident.[87] Nor do I see a young William Rehnquist, who emerged from a Supreme Court clerkship and lived through the 1950s and 1960s deeply persuaded that constitutional law was on the wrong course and needed to be wrenched back.[88] On the other hand, I see young Justices in a hurry to reshape the law to their liking across doctrinal areas from Equal Protection to standing.[89]

Another new book, not about the Court at all, offers some insight as we consider the forces for personal change that operate on Supreme Court Justices. In *Private Lives, Public Consequences: Personality and Politics in Modern America,* historian William Chafe presents portraits of national leaders from Franklin D. Roosevelt to Bill Clinton and tries to identify the connection between the personal and the political.[90] Most of these individuals endured some crisis that had the result of causing or forcing them to see things in a new way. Looking at the Supreme Court through the same lens, I think it is clear that for Blackmun, the crisis was the trauma of his early years at the Court, a period that included *Roe v. Wade*[91] and its aftermath. I am not aware of a crisis in the lives of John Roberts or Sam Alito that would have shattered their received notions of how the world works.

Let me conclude on a note of modesty about the dangers of predictions and generalizations. The Court's very recent history should warn us against jumping to quick conclusions about what lies ahead, especially when we are considering the future tenure of relatively young men who are likely to still be on the Court when my twenty-one year-old daughter is approaching middle age. We thought we knew William Rehnquist pretty well by the time he approached his third decade on the Court. Who would have imagined that it would have been Rehnquist, at war with the *Miranda* doctrine for much of his judicial career, who on a June morning in 2000 would announce the Court's

---

[87] Greenhouse, *supra* note 4, at 44; HAB Papers, *supra* note 44, Boxes 50 and 51.

[88] *See generally* Craig Bradley, *The Rehnquist Legacy* 1-5 (Cambridge, MA: Harvard University Press, 2006).

[89] *See Hein v. Freedom from Religion Foundation,* 551 U.S. 587 (2007).

[90] William H. Chafe, *Private Lives, Public Consequences: Personality and Politics in Modern America* (Cambridge, MA: Harvard University Press, 2006).

[91] *See generally Roe v. Wade,* 401 U.S. 113 (1973).

judgment in *Dickerson v. United States*,[92] reaffirming the *Miranda* decision and describing it as "part of our national culture"?[93]

I was equally surprised four years later to hear Chief Justice Rehnquist announce the Court's judgment in *Locke v. Davey*,[94] rejecting the argument that a state that provided financial aid at the college level to needy and deserving students had to provide the same basis of support for students studying for the ministry. This underestimated decision put the brakes on the school voucher movement, of which Chief Justice Rehnquist was the doctrinal godfather in a series of Establishment Clause rulings going back to *Mueller v. Allen*,[95] decided twenty years earlier, and continuing through the Ohio school voucher case, *Zelman v. Simmons-Harris*,[96] in 2002. And recall Chief Justice Rehnquist's surprising opinion for the Court in the 2003 Family and Medical Leave Act case, *Nevada Department of Human Resources v. Hibbs*,[97] in which the Court rejected the state's claim of Eleventh Amendment immunity from suit after having accepted such claims in a series of cases challenging congressional efforts to extend federal civil rights protections to state employees.[98]

The William Rehnquist of the final years of his tenure, in other words, was not necessarily the Justice we thought we knew from the beginning, middle, or even late middle of his career.[99] The question is, what happened? I do not think Rehnquist changed his views in any fundamental way; in fact, I don't think he changed his views about anything that was really important to him during his adult lifetime. What I think he acquired, however, was a different perspective, one that included not only his personal agenda, but also the long-term institutional interests of the Supreme Court. He was a very smart man whose effectiveness derived in no small part from his ability to see around corners, and in the cases I have mentioned, that kind of vision told him that it was time to hold back—to mix metaphors, that it was not the time to follow the logical implications of the Court's recent precedents right off a cliff. The last few years of the Rehnquist Court provide us with a case study of the impact of the institutional on the personal. It is worth noting, of course,

---

[92] *Dickerson v. United States*, 530 U.S. 428 (2000).

[93] *Id.* at 443.

[94] *Locke v. Davey*, 540 U.S. 712 (2004).

[95] *Mueller v. Allen*, 463 U.S. 388 (1983).

[96] *Zelman v. Simmons-Harris*, 534 U.S. 1111 (2002).

[97] *Nevada Dep't of Human Res. v. Hibbs*, 538 U.S. 721 (2003).

[98] *See, e.g.*, Robert C. Post and Reva B. Siegel, *Protecting the Constitution from the People: Juricentric Restrictions on Section Five Power*, 78 Ind. L. Rev. 1 (2003).

[99] *See, e.g.*, Linda Greenhouse, *Foreword to Craig M. Bradley*, The Rehnquist Legacy, at xiii to xii (2006); Erwin Chemerinsky, *Just Right? Assessing the Rehnquist Court's Parting Words on Criminal Justice: The Rehnquist Court and the Death Penalty*, 94 Geo. L.J. 1367 (2006).

that Chief Justice John Roberts clerked for Rehnquist, who became his mentor, and Rehnquist himself clerked for Robert Jackson, so we are back where we started.[100]

It is also worth observing of another Chief Justice, Earl Warren, that his first term was a very poor predictor of the kind of justice that he would become. Warren had spent twenty-three years of his life as a local prosecutor and state attorney general.[101] During his first term on the Court, 1953, he voted against criminal defendants and civil rights litigants most of the time.[102] But over the next fifteen years, as we know, he became their champion.[103]

That is, of course, another story.[104] The point is that every Supreme Court Justice will have his or her own story—a story that, just maybe, will surprise us.

---

[100] Supreme Court of the United States, *supra* note 83, at 1.

[101] *See* Jim Newton, *Justice For All: Earl Warren and the Nation He Made* 45-87 (New York: Riverhead Books, 2006).

[102] Lee Epstein et al., *Ideological Drift Among Supreme Court Justices: Who, When, and How Important?*, 101 Nw. U. L. Rev. 1483 (2007).

[103] Epstein, *supra* note 23, at Fig. 6.

[104] *See* Newton, *Justice For All: Earl Warren and the Nation He Made* (2006).

12

Reconceptualizing Federalism

Erwin Chemerinsky

Erwin Chemerinsky is the Founding Dean and Distinguished Professor of Law, University of California, Irvine School of Law. Legal Affairs named him one of "the top 20 legal thinkers in America" in 2005. Professor Chemerinsky is the author of seven books and over 150 law review articles. His most recent book, The Conservative Assault on the Constitution, *was published in 2010. He frequently argues appellate cases, including in the U.S. Supreme Court and U.S. Courts of Appeals.*

Since the country's earliest days, federalism has been used as a political argument primarily in support of conservative causes. During the early 19th century, John Calhoun argued that states had independent sovereignty and could interpose their authority between the federal government and the people to nullify federal actions restricting slavery.[1] During Reconstruction, Southern states claimed that the federal military presence was incompatible with state sovereignty and federalism.

In the early 20th century, federalism was successfully used as the basis for challenging federal laws regulating child labor, imposing the minimum wage, and protecting consumers.[2] During the Depression, conservatives objected to President Franklin Roosevelt's proposals, such as Social Security, on the ground that they usurped functions properly left to state governments.[3] During the 1950s and the 1960s, objections to federal civil rights efforts were phrased primarily in terms of federalism. Southerners challenged Supreme Court decisions mandating desegregation and objected to proposed federal civil rights legislation by resurrecting the arguments of John Calhoun.[4] Segregation and discrimination were defended less on the grounds that they

---

[1] See, e.g., Samuel H. Beer, *To Make a Nation: The Rediscovery of American Federalism* (Cambridge, MA: Harvard University Press, 1993), 224.

[2] See, e.g., *Carter v. Carter Coal Co.*, 298 U.S. 238 (1936) (invalidating federal regulation of employment, including a minimum wage); *Hammer v. Dagenhart*, 247 U.S. 251 (1918) (invalidating the federal regulation of child labor); *United States v. E.C. Knight*, 156 U.S. 1 (1895) (holding that the Sherman Antitrust Act could not be applied to businesses engaged in production).

[3] See Forrest McDonald, *A Constitutional History of the United States* (New York: Franklin Watts, 1982), 193; William Manchester, *The Glory and the Dream* (Boston, MA: Little, Brown, 1974), 164-66.

[4] Beer, *supra* note 1, at 19-20.

were desirable practices, and more in terms of the states' rights to choose their own laws concerning race relations.

In the 1980s, President Ronald Reagan proclaimed a "new federalism" as the basis for attempting to dismantle federal social welfare programs.[5] In his first presidential inaugural address, President Reagan said that he sought to "restore the balance between levels of government." Federalism was thus employed as the basis for cutting back on countless federal programs.

No area of constitutional law has changed more dramatically in the last 20 years than federalism. In 1995, for the first times in 60 years, the Supreme Court declared a federal law unconstitutional as exceeding the scope of Congress' commerce clause power, and twice in the 1990s the Court declared a federal law unconstitutional as violating the Tenth Amendment (something that had happened only once since 1936 and that case had been overruled).[6] At the same time, the Court has used federalism to enlarge the states' immunity to suit in federal court for violations of federal statutes.[7] These decisions have spawned literally hundreds of lower court decisions concerning federalism and ensure that federalism will be a constant issue before the Supreme Court for years to come. Although it is unclear how far the Court will extend these rulings, the cases signal a major change in constitutional law and American government. There is no mistaking the Court's ardent desire to use federalism to limit the powers of Congress and the federal courts.

Federalism was often invoked in the Republican-controlled Congress of the 1990s. Soon after the Republican triumph in the 1994 elections, the new Congressional leaders, Bob Dole and Newt Gingrich, held a press conference where they displayed a large poster board containing the words of the Tenth Amendment and proclaimed a return to principles of federalism.[8] In fact, one of the first laws adopted by the new Congress was the "unfunded mandates law," which prohibits Congress from enacting statutes that impose substantial costs on state and local governments.[9] Another example of a law with im-

---

[5] *Id.* at 2.

[6] The first of these two cases was *United States v. Lopez*, 514 U.S. 549 (1995), invalidating the Gun-Free School Zone Act, which prohibits possessing a firearm within 100 feet of a school. The second was *Printz v. United States*, 521 U.S. 898 (1997); *New York v. United States*, 550 U.S. 144 (1992). The earlier decision was *National League of Cities v. Usery*, 426 U.S. 833 (1976), which was overruled in *Garcia v. San Antonio Metropolitan Transit Authority*, 469 U.S. 528 (1985).

[7] See, e.g., *Federal Maritime Commission v. South Carolina Port Authority*, 535 U.S. 743 (2002) (state governments cannot be sued in agency adjudicatory proceedings); *Alden v. Maine*, 527 U.S. 706 (1999) (state governments cannot be sued in state court, even on federal claims, without their consent).

[8] See generally Ed Gillespie and Bob Schelihas, eds., *Contract with America: The Bold Plan By Rep. Newt Gingrich, Rep. Dick Armey, and the House Republicans to Change the Nation* (New York: Times Books, 1994).

[9] *Unfunded Mandates Reform Act of 1995*, 2 U.S.C.A. § 1501 (West Supp. 1997).

portant federalism implications is the Anti-terrorism and Effective Death Penalty Act of 1996, which greatly restricts the ability of federal courts to grant habeas corpus relief to those convicted in state courts.[10]

Not surprisingly, these changes occurred at times when conservatives were in control of both the Supreme Court and Congress. In the Supreme Court, recent federalism rulings usually have been decided by a 5-4 margin, with the majority comprised of the five most conservative Justices: Chief Justice William Rehnquist and Justices Sandra Day O'Connor, Antonin Scalia, Anthony Kennedy, and Clarence Thomas. The shift from Justice O'Connor to the more conservative Justice Alito offers the likelihood of even greater limits imposed by the Supreme Court based on federalism. In Congress, of course, it has been the conservatives who have invoked federalism in a wide variety of areas, such as in support of radical changes in welfare law enacted in 1996.[11]

Once more, federalism is at the core of the issues before the United States Supreme Court. In the October 2011 Term, the two most high-profile cases—concerning the constitutionality of the Patient Protection and Affordable Care Act[12] and Arizona's immigration law, SB 1070[13]—were about federalism. In the coming, October 2012, Term, the Court seems likely to decide whether there is a right to marriage equality for gays and lesbians. This, too, involves federalism, though also equal protection and the right to marry.

In this essay, I argue, first, that the conservatives' approach to federalism has little relationship to the underlying values that federalism is supposed to advance. States' rights is simply the way in which conservatives argue against federal efforts they don't like or for protection of state efforts they do like. Second, an alternative conception of federalism is preferable—one that focuses on empowering government at all levels to meet society's problems. The benefit of having three levels of government is that there are multiple power centers capable of acting. Federal and state courts, from this view, both should be available to protect constitutional rights. Federal, state, and local legislatures should have the authority to deal with social problems, such as unsafe nuclear wastes, guns near schools, and criminals owning firearms. Finally, I want to apply this view of federalism as empowerment to the most recent federalism issue confronting the Court—the constitutionality of the Patient Protection and Affordable Care Act—and show what this alternative vision of federalism should mean.

The debate about allocation of power between the national government

---

[10] 28 U.S.C. §§ 2249-2266 (Supp. 1997).

[11] Personal Responsibility and Work Opportunity Reconciliation Act of 1996, Pub. L. No. 104-193, 110 Stat. 2105.

[12] *National Federation of Independent Businesses v. Sebelius*, 132 S. Ct. 2566 (2012).

[13] *Arizona v. United States*, 132 S. Ct. 2492 (2012).

and the states began with the Articles of Confederation and is as recent as the Court's most high-profile decisions in June 2012. My central point is that positions on federalism are not about the best allocation of power between the national and state governments, but instead reflect differing views on social policy. Federalism is simply the constitutional rhetoric that conservatives use to oppose progressive social change.

The Disconnect Between The Values of Federalism and Supreme Court Decisions

The Constitution says remarkably little about federalism. Article I begins by stating that Congress is limited to those powers "herein granted," which implies that Congress only can do that which is authorized, while states can do anything that is not prohibited. This distinction is made explicit in the Tenth Amendment, which declares that all powers not granted to the United States, nor prohibited to the states, are reserved to the states and the people respectively. Article VI makes the Constitution, and laws and treaties made pursuant to it, the supreme law of the land, thus establishing a hierarchical relationship between the federal government and the states.

But other than this, there is little about federalism in the text of the Constitution. The scope of Congress' powers—whether to regulate commerce among the states, or to tax and spend, or under the "necessary and proper" clause—is not spelled out. Nor was there any consensus at the Constitutional Convention or in the state ratifying conventions about this, even assuming that the views of that era should be controlling over 200 years later.

And even if it could be known what the framers of the Constitution thought in 1787, the reality is that the Civil War and the amendments after it dramatically changed the Constitution with regard to federalism. I often have thought that when conservatives argue for states' rights—or proclaim as Justice Scalia did in his dissent in *Arizona v. United States* that states are sovereign—they are ignoring how much the conception of state sovereignty was altered by the Civil War and the Thirteenth, Fourteenth, and Fifteenth Amendments.

Therefore, the only way to discuss federalism issues—whether about the commerce clause, or the Tenth Amendment, or state sovereign immunity—is relative to the underlying values that federalism is supposed to serve. In teaching constitutional law, I have been continually struck by the absence in the case law of careful exploration of the values of federalism. From time to time, the Court does allude to the underlying benefits of federalism: limiting tyranny by the federal government; enhancing democracy by providing governance that is closer to the people; providing laboratories for experimentation; protecting and advancing liberty. But these values are seldom more than just slogans. Rarely, if ever, is there any explanation of how these values are compromised by the federal law in question.

The first justification for protecting states from federal intrusions is that the division of power vertically, between federal and state governments, lessens the chance of federal tyranny. Professor Rapaczynski noted that "[p]erhaps the most frequently mentioned function of the federal system is the one it shares to a large extent with separation of powers, namely the protection of the citizen against governmental oppression—the 'tyranny' that the Framers were so concerned about."[14] The framers of the Constitution relied primarily on the structure of government as a protection against tyrannical government. The Constitution itself, apart from the amendments, has relatively few protections of individual rights. Instead, the framers saw the separation of powers horizontally, among the branches of the federal government, and vertically, between the federal and state governments, as the best safeguard against autocratic rule.

How do state governments prevent federal tyranny? Perhaps most importantly, the framers thought that the possibility of federal abuses could be limited by restricting the authority of the federal government. The framers envisioned that the vast majority of governance would be at the state and local levels and that federal actions would be relatively rare and limited. Alexander Hamilton explained that "[the] necessity of local administration for local purposes would be a complete barrier against the oppressive use of such power."[15] If the powers of the federal government are limited, most governing, of necessity, must be done at the state and local levels.

Yet, the notion of radically limited federal powers seems anachronistic in the face of a modern national market economy and decades of extensive federal regulations. The Supreme Court appears to recognize this problem. It has approved increased federal power during times of great economic distress and war. The Rehnquist Court's decisions of the 1990s restricting federal power in the name of federalism, on the other hand, occurred during a time of economic prosperity and peace. There was less focus on federalism in the rhetoric of the Bush administration than during the Reagan presidency. This, in part, is likely due to the events of September 11 and the perceived need for federal actions of many sorts to deal with the terrorist threat.

There has been a major shift over time as to how abusive government is best controlled. Now it is thought that if a federal action intrudes upon individual liberties, the federal judiciary will invalidate it as unconstitutional. We tend to see judicial review as an important check against tyrannical government.

The mismatch between the rhetoric of federalism and the cases to which it is applied is most evident when federal authority is used to advance rights

---

[14] Andrzej Rapaczynski, "From Sovereignty to Process: The Jurisprudence of Federalism After Garcia," 1985 *Sup. Ct. Rev.* 341, 380 (1985).

[15] Alexander Hamilton, Federalist No. 32, *The Federalist Papers* 199 (J. Cooke ed. 1961).

and equality, such as through the Religious Freedom Restoration Act or the Violence Again Women Act or the Age Discrimination in Employment Act. In cases like these, it is perverse to justify restricting federal power on the grounds that it inherently risks tyranny. Did the Rehnquist Court's federalism decisions in any way lessen the likelihood of federal tyranny? How does the federal government forcing states to clean up nuclear wastes—the issue in *New York v. United States*—increase in the slightest the chances of a tyrannical government? Nor do federal laws prohibiting guns near schools or requiring state and local background checks for firearms seem related in the slightest to lessening tyranny, unless, of course, one believes that such laws violate the Second Amendment. I do not have this view, but if I did, then the objection would be on that basis and not about increasing the chances of tyranny. I could go through each and every one of the Rehnquist-era federalism decisions and raise the same question because none has the slightest relationship to preventing tyranny.[16]

A second frequently invoked value of federalism is that states are closer to the people and thus more likely to be responsive to public needs and concerns. Professor David Shapiro clearly summarizes this argument when he writes: "[O]ne of the stronger arguments for a decentralized political structure is that, to the extent that the electorate is small, and elected representatives are thus more immediately accountable to individuals and their concerns, government is brought closer to the people and democratic ideals are more fully realized."[17] This argument has intuitive appeal. It suggests that the smaller the area governed, the more responsive the government will be to the interests of the voters.

However, it must be recognized that this value of federalism does not necessarily work this way. Voters at the state and local level might prefer what might be regarded as tyrannical decisions—or might favor rules that abuse a particular minority group. In this case greater responsiveness increases the dangers of government tyranny. In other words, the substantive result of decreasing tyranny will not always be best achieved by the process approach of maximizing electoral responsiveness; indeed, the reverse might well be the result.

In fact, there is a greater danger of special interests capturing government at smaller and more local levels. James Madison wrote of the danger of "factions" in Federalist 10 and modern political science literature offers sup-

---

[16] Perhaps that is the underlying issue with regard to the individual mandate in the Affordable Care Act, that individuals should have the freedom to not purchase health insurance. But no lawyer, at any level of court, made that argument because it is untenable under post-1937 constitutional law, which provides that the government can regulate economic transactions so long as its action meets a rational basis test.

[17] David Shapiro, *Federalism: A Dialogue* 92 (Evanston, IL: Northwestern, 1995).

port for his fears.[18] In *J.A. Croson v. City of Richmond*, the Supreme Court emphasized the dangers of special interest capture at the local level in invalidating a city's affirmative action to benefit minority businesses.[19]

Arguments about responsiveness must rest on one of two assumptions. One is that voters more closely monitor the conduct of representatives at more local levels. Yet, this is an empirical proposition and it is at odds with reality. Presidential and Senatorial elections usually attract more voter interest and more knowledgeable electoral decisions than elections for purely local offices. An alternative justification for favoring local decision-making is that the smaller the governing unit, the greater the likelihood of voter homogeneity, making it easier for officials to ascertain the will of the voters. But where do we find such homogeneity? For example, could a state the size of California or a city the size of Los Angeles, be considered homogeneous enough to increase the likelihood of responsive government? Professor Shapiro writes: "[T]he goal of realizing democratic values to the maximum extent feasible may not be significantly enhanced by reducing the relevant polity from one of some 280,000,000 (the United States) to one of, say 30,000,000 (the State of California)."[20] He explains that "[i]n either case, the size of the electorate and its heterogeneity tend to dwarf participation by the individual and to frustrate the recognition of small group preferences."[21] The point is that assertions about the responsiveness of government are descriptively shaky and normatively not necessarily desirable. There is little historical evidence that one level of government is inherently more responsive than any other.

Interestingly, if the real concern is with responsiveness, the concern should be with protecting *local* governments much more than state governments. But as Professors Rubin and Feeley point out, "federalism only protects the autonomy of states, not the autonomy or variability of local governments."[22] For example, sovereign immunity protects state governments from suits, but cannot be invoked by cities, counties, or other local governments.[23] Nor do the Supreme Court's recent federalism decisions have anything to do

---

[18] James Madison, Federalist No. 10, *The Federalist Papers*.

[19] 488 U.S. 469 (1989).

[20] Shapiro, *supra* note 17, at 93.

[21] *Id.*

[22] Edward L. Rubin and Malcolm Feeley, "Federalism: Some Notes on a National Neurosis," 41 *UCLA L. Rev.* 903, 919 (1994). There is one Supreme Court decision, *Printz v. United States*, which mentions protection of local governments as part of safeguarding federalism. *Printz* invalidated a federal law that required state and local governments to do background checks before issuing permits for firearms. The other Supreme Court decisions about federalism have all been about safeguarding state governments.

[23] See *Mt. Healthy School Dist. v. Doyle*, 424 U.S. 729 (1977) (sovereign immunity does not apply to local governments).

with protecting the autonomy of local government. What is striking, and often overlooked, is that the rulings of the last decade have, almost without exception, invalidated very popular federal laws that clearly were responsive to the public's desires. Several of these statutes, such as the Religious Freedom Restoration Act, the Americans with Disabilities Act, and the Violence Against Women Act, were passed overwhelmingly and sometimes almost unanimously.

A third argument that is frequently made for protecting federalism is that states can serve as laboratories for experimentation. Justice Brandeis apparently first articulated this idea when he declared: "To say experimentation in things social and economic is a grave responsibility. Denial of the right experiment might be fraught with serious consequences to the Nation. It is one of the happy incidents of the federal system that a single courageous State may, if its citizens choose, serve as a laboratory and try novel social and economic experiments without risk to the rest of the country."[24]

More recent federalism opinions, too, have invoked this notion. Justice Powell, dissenting in *Garcia*, lamented that "the Court does not explain how leaving the States virtually at the mercy of the federal government, without recourse to judicial review, will enhance their opportunities to experiment and serve as laboratories."[25] Likewise, Justice O'Connor, dissenting in *Federal Energy Regulatory Commission v. Mississippi*, stated that the "Court's decision undermines the most valuable aspects of our federalism. Courts and commentators frequently have recognized that the 50 states serve as laboratories for the development of new social, economic, and political ideas."[26]

It must be conceded that any federal legislation preempting state or local laws limits experimentation. For that matter, the application of constitutional rights to the states limits their ability to experiment with reducing individual liberties. The key question is when is it worth experimenting and when should experimentation be rejected because a national mandate would be better.

Who is in the best position to decide when further experimentation is warranted? A strong argument can be made that the decision to use states as laboratories should be made by Congress, not by judges to justify invalidating federal laws. Professors Rubin and Feeley take this argument even further. They argue that political realities mean that relatively few experiments will be done at the state and local levels:

> To experiment with different approaches for achieving a single, agreed-upon goal, one sub-unit must be assigned an option that initially seems less desirable, either because that option requires

---

[24] *New State Ice Co. v. Liebman*, 285 U.S. 262, 311 (1932) (Brandeis, J., dissenting).

[25] 469 U.S. at 567-68 n.13 (Powell, J., dissenting).

[26] *Federal Energy Regulatory Commission v. Mississippi*, 456 U.S. 741, 787-88 (1982) (O'Connor, J., dissenting).

changes in existing practices, or because it offers lower, although still-significant chances of success.... As a result, individual states will have no incentive to invest in experiments that involve any substantive or political risk, but will prefer to wait for other states to generate them; this will, of course, produce relatively few experiments.[27]

Professors Rubin and Feeley also contend that Congress has far more incentive to structure and monitor experiments. They thus conclude "that most significant 'experimental' programs in recent years have in fact been organized and financed by the national government."[28]

Have the Supreme Court's recent federalism decisions promoted positive experimentation? Does anyone really believe that states should be able to experiment with not cleaning up the nuclear wastes in their midst, or with allowing children to bring guns near schools, or with failing to provide an adequate remedy for women who are victims of gender-motivated violence? The Court often mentions the value of experimentation, but for obvious reasons, never even hints that these are areas where experimentation is a good thing.

The final justification often invoked for protecting federalism is, I believe, the most important: that federalism protects liberty. Perhaps this is just another way of presenting the first justification, that federalism avoids tyranny. But I think that the Justices invoking this value have something else in mind: they see freedom being increased by enforcing a particular conception of the proper structure of American government. For example, Chief Justice Rehnquist wrote: "This constitutionally mandated division of authority was adopted by the Framers to ensure protection of our fundamental liberties."[29] Similarly, Justice Scalia declared: "The separation of the two spheres is one of the Constitution's protections of liberty."[30] Justice O'Connor wrote: "Just as the separation and independence of the coordinate branches of the Federal Government serves to prevent the accumulation of excessive power in any one branch, a healthy balance of power between the States and the Federal Government will reduce the risk of tyranny and abuse from either front."[31] It is striking that so many of the Supreme Court's recent federalism decisions repeat the same language as a premise for judicial invalidation of federal laws.[32]

---

[27] Rubin and Feeley, *supra* note 22, at 925.

[28] *Id.* at 925.

[29] *United States v. Lopez*, 514 U.S. 549, 552 (1995).

[30] *Printz v. United States*, 521 U.S. 898, 921 (1997).

[31] *Gregory v. Ashcroft*, 501 U.S. 452,458 (1991).

[32] Scholars, too, have made this claim. See Martin A. Feigenbaum, "The Preservation of Individual Liberty Through the Separation of Powers and Federalism: Reflections on the Shaping of Constitutional Immorality," 37 *Emory L. Rev.* 613 (1998).

Unfortunately, none of the cases explains how federalism enhances liberty. The idea expressed is the simple one that limiting federal power means restricting the ability of the federal government to enact laws inimical to individual freedom. The problem with this claim is that the federal government can use its authority to advance liberty, not only to restrict it. The Court's assumption is that federal actions limiting liberty are more likely than federal laws significantly enhancing individual rights. The Court never has justified this premise.

Actually, to prove the majority's claim with regard to individual freedom would be quite complicated. In all likelihood, over time, limiting the federal government's power in the name of federalism probably will be used to strike down some laws that advance liberty and some that restrict it. The majority needs to offer some reason to believe that, on balance, federal actions will be more harmful than beneficial to liberty. Nothing of this sort is found in any of the Supreme Court's federalism decisions, or for that matter in any of the scholarly literature that champions federalism. Let us consider whether the Supreme Court's decisions protecting federalism actually have advanced liberty. Over the course of American history, and particularly in the last decade, have the Supreme Court's federalism decisions been "rights progressive," advancing rights, or "rights regressive," limiting individual liberty?[33] Looking at the decisions, it is startling how often they are rights regressive and how rarely the federalism rulings have ever expanded the scope of rights.

Perhaps the Court's most rights regressive actions have been the decisions limiting the scope of Congress's powers under section five of the Fourteenth Amendment. Section five broadly empowers Congress to enact laws to enforce the Fourteenth Amendment. In the last five years, the Court has greatly narrowed this authority in two respects: first, it has held that Congress cannot expand the scope of rights—it can only provide remedies for rights recognized by the judiciary; and second, it has held that Congress under section 5 may not regulate private conduct.

As to the former, in a series of decisions beginning with *City of Boerne v. Flores*,[34] the Court has held that Congress under section five of the Fourteenth Amendment cannot expand the scope of rights. Rather, Congress only can enact laws to prevent or remedy violations of rights recognized by the courts and these laws must be "proportionate" and "congruent" to the violations.

---

[33] I recognize, of course, that in many instances there could be debate over what is "rights progressive" as opposed to "rights regressive." For example, supporters and opponents of affirmative action would disagree as to whether it is rights progressive or rights regressive. But, as explained below, the Court's decisions do not raise hard questions as to what is rights progressive and what is rights regressive. The invalidation of laws, such as the Religious Freedom Restoration Act and the civil damages provision of the Violence Against Women Act, seem unquestionably rights regressive.

[34] 521 U.S. 507 (1997).

Individually and collectively, these decisions are tremendously rights regressive. They dramatically limit the ability of Congress to expand the scope and protections of individual liberties. Thus, the Supreme Court's federalism decisions—the states' rights position championed by conservatives—cannot be seen as advancing the underlying goals of federalism. Federalism is the rhetoric that conservatives, including conservative justices, use to oppose progressive federal legislation.

An Alternative Vision of Federalism

Conservatives always have looked at federalism as being about limiting government power. An alternative view would be to conceptualize federalism in terms of empowerment. The central thesis of federalism as empowerment is that the genius of having multiple levels of government is to have alternative actors equipped to deal with society's problems and needs. If one level of government fails, another is there to take over the responsibility. For example, if state governments can't or don't require the cleanup of radioactive wastes, the federal government can act to ensure their safe disposal.[35] If states fail to provide adequate remedies to deter gender-motivated violence and to compensate victims, the federal government can create a cause of action in federal court.[36] If the federal government fails to require insurance companies to disclose their Holocaust-era policies, state governments may do so for insurance companies doing business within their boundaries.[37]

To be clear, this does not mean that government at any level has unlimited powers and that there is no judicial role. Quite the contrary, I believe that courts should aggressively enforce the Constitution's protections of individual liberties and civil rights. This is the primary protection against tyranny, not federalism-based limits on government power, which have actually been rights regressive.

What, then, are the tenets of federalism as empowerment? They can be summarized in the following list.

1. Congress under the commerce clause may regulate any activity that it reasonably believes has an effect on commerce with foreign nations, Indian tribes, and among the states. The effect may be found from the cumulative impact of the activities in question across the country.

Here, I am arguing for the approach to the commerce clause that was followed from 1937–1995. I would reject the test for the commerce power that the Court developed in *United States v. Lopez*, that limits Congress to regulat-

---

35 This, of course, was the issue in *New York v. United States*.

36 This is exactly what Congress did in the Violence Against Women Act, which the Court declared unconstitutional in *United States v. Morrison*, 529 U.S. 528 (2000).

37 *American Insurance Assn. v. Garamendi*, 539 U.S. 396 (2003).

ing in three circumstances: the channels of interstate commerce, the instrumentalities of interstate commerce and persons or things in interstate commerce, and activities that have a substantial effect on commerce.[38] Likewise, I would reject any distinction between economic and non-economic activity in defining the commerce power, such as the Court drew in *United States v. Morrison*[39] or that five justices drew in *National Federation of Independent Business v. Sebilius*.

Or put another way, I am arguing for exactly the position urged by the four dissenting Justices in cases such as *Lopez* and *Morrison*. Their view, and the law that was controlling for almost 60 years, allowed Congress to regulate under the commerce clause so long as there was a reasonable basis for believing that the activity, looked at cumulatively across the country, had an effect on commerce. I urge a return to this approach.

2. Congress, under its taxing and spending power, should continue to have the power to tax and spend for the general welfare. In other words, Congress can adopt any tax to raise revenue or any spending program to expend it that Congress believes will serve the interests of the country. This is the approach taken by the Court in *United States v. Butler* in 1936 and followed ever since.[40]

Moreover, Congress should be able to put strings on grants to state and local governments to induce their action. In *South Dakota v. Dole*, the Supreme Court upheld a federal law that conditioned a percentage of federal highway money to state governments on their setting a 21-year-old drinking age.[41] Chief Justice Rehnquist, an ardent advocate for states' rights, wrote the opinion for the Court, and said that Congress may put strings on grants so long as the conditions are clearly stated and so long as they relate to the purpose of the program. This approach should be continued.[42] Conditions should not be found coercive so long as a state can say no to the federal money, regardless of how difficult that might be.

3. Congressional powers under the post-Civil War Amendments should be broadly defined in terms of whom Congress may regulate and what laws Congress may enact. These powers, of course, refer to Congressional powers under section two of the Thirteenth Amendment, section five of the Fourteenth Amendment, and section two of the Fifteenth Amendment. These

---

[38] 514 U.S. 549, 558 (1995).

[39] 529 U.S. 848 (2000).

[40] 297 U.S. 1 (1936).

[41] 483 U.S. 203 (1987).

[42] I thus very much disagree with those who would impose limits on Congress's ability to put strings on grants to state and local governments. See Lynn Baker, "Conditional Federal Spending and States' Rights," 574 *Annals* 104 (2001) (urging restrictions on congressional power to put strings on grants to state and local governments).

powers should be defined broadly to equip Congress with the authority to advance the goals of these amendments. First, Congress should be able to regulate both government *and* private actors. Second, Congress should have the power to expand the scope of rights and not be limited to providing a remedy for rights already recognized by the Court.

4. The Tenth Amendment should be understood as declaring that Congress may act only where there is constitutional authority, that is, states may do anything except that which is prohibited by the Constitution. This is the approach that the Court followed throughout the 19th century and from 1937 until 1992, with one exception that was overruled. It should be followed again.

The Tenth Amendment states: "The powers not delegated to the United States by the Constitution, nor prohibited by it to the States, are reserved to the States respectively, or to the people." Federalism as empowerment would take the language of the Tenth Amendment literally. It does not speak of a zone of activities for the states. It just says that Congress can exercise only powers granted, while states can do all that is not prohibited.

5. Sovereign immunity should not be a bar to suits. The Eleventh Amendment should be interpreted to preclude suits only if the sole basis for jurisdiction is diversity of citizenship between the parties. In other words, cases based on federal question jurisdiction, that is, suits for violation of the Constitution and laws of the United States, should not be deemed barred by the Eleventh Amendment. Nor should sovereign immunity be a bar to suits against state governments in state courts or in federal administrative agencies.

The structure of government exists to achieve two objectives: providing an effective government and advancing liberty. The crucial question is which approach to federalism will maximize the likelihood of attaining these goals. Is effective government better achieved by limiting federal and state government powers in the name of federalism, or by federalism as empowerment in the way I have described it here? Is liberty better ensured by limiting federal and state government powers in the name of federalism, or by federalism as empowerment?

The answer is clear. As for effective government, using federalism to limit federal and state power inevitably prevents government from successfully acting to deal with social problems. This has been so whenever the Supreme Court has used federalism to restrict government power. For example, during the first third of the 20th century, the Supreme Court's use of federalism and dual sovereignty prevented government from achieving important objectives. When Congress sought to prohibit child labor, undoubtedly a desirable goal with which few could disagree, the Supreme Court declared the law unconstitutional as violating the Tenth Amendment.[43] In adopting its child-labor

---

43 *Hammer v. Dagenhart*, 247 U.S. 251 (1918).

prohibition, Congress had been concerned that market pressures would prevent state governments from being able to act effectively. States that prohibited child labor would find that their manufacturers were at a competitive disadvantage relative to those in states that allowed child labor. The result would be an inevitable downward pressure to allow child labor across the country. The Supreme Court's invalidation of this statute meant that child labor continued for decades until ultimately the Court shifted course. Surely, no one could see the use of federalism as advancing effective government in this case.

The other Supreme Court decisions of the time that used federalism to limit federal power are similar in the way they thwarted effective government. The Court used a narrow definition of commerce to strike down federal laws regulating monopolies in agricultural production,[44] regulation of wages and hours in the coal industry,[45] a pension system for railroad workers,[46] and agricultural price supports.[47] These examples are striking because all are instances where few citizens would deny that the government objectives were desirable. Simply put, effective government was thwarted by using federalism as a limit on Congress's powers. Had the Court seen federalism as about empowering government, all of these laws would have been upheld and the country would have been better for it.

The same is true of federalism in the modern era. It is striking that the Supreme Court's use of federalism as limits has invalidated laws that are enormously desirable. The Rehnquist Court, for example, used federalism to strike down federal statutes prohibiting guns near schools,[48] allowing victims of gender-motivated violence to sue,[49] protecting intrastate waters from pollution and degradation,[50] requiring the clean-up of radioactive wastes,[51] and requiring background checks before the issue of firearm permits.[52] Can it really be argued that government was more effective because these laws were struck down? Few, I think, would argue for guns near schools, or uncompensated victims of violence, or degradation of wetlands, or dangerous radioactive wastes being uncontained, or for dangerous individuals having guns. It must be remembered that in each instance, Congress acted because it per-

44 *United States v. E.C. Knight*, 136 U.S. 1 (1895).

45 *Carter v. Carter Coal Co.*, 298 U.S. 238 (1936).

46 *Railroad Retirement Bd. v. Alton R.R. Co.*, 295 U.S. 330 (1935).

47 *United States v. Butler*, 301 U.S. 548 (1937).

48 *United States v. Lopez*, 514 U.S. 549 (1995).

49 *United States v. Morrison*, 529 U.S. 548 (2000).

50 *Solid Waste Agency of Northern Cook County v. United States Army Corps of Engineers*, 531 U.S. 159 (2001).

51 *New York v. United States*, 505 U.S. 144 (1992).

52 *Printz v. United States*, 521 U.S. 898 (1997).

ceived at least some state and local governments as failing to do so.

Under federalism as empowerment, all of the cases would have come out differently. Government would have been much more able to deal with the serious social problems that the legislatures were trying to tackle. It does not make sense to say that government will be more effective if its powers were significantly limited. That is why federalism as empowerment is far more likely to produce effective government than federalism as limits. In fact, I cannot think of any example of a Supreme Court decision invalidating a law on federalism grounds that made government more effective in dealing with social problems.

The response, of course, can be that even though the use of federalism to limit government power might frustrate effective government, it is still desirable because it enhances individual liberties. From this perspective, enforcement of the limits on government power in the name of federalism is a necessary evil in order to maximize freedom and equality. But the effect of the Supreme Court's enforcement of federalism as limits has not been to enhance liberty. Quite the contrary, the Supreme Court's federalism decisions have been rights regressive. The Court has invalidated numerous laws that enhance liberty and has, through the expansion of sovereign immunity, thwarted deterrence of government wrongdoing and compensation of its victims. To pick a couple examples, when the Court's invalidated the civil damages provision of the Violence Against Women Act,[53] and when it struck down the Religious Freedom Restoration Act,[54] it undermined, rather than enhanced, liberty. These were statutes advancing civil rights and both were invalidated based on federalism as limits. Similarly, the expansion of sovereign immunity has meant that victims of age and disability discrimination by state governments have been left without damage remedies.[55]

Put more generally, using federalism to limit government power prevents government from enacting laws to advance civil liberties and civil rights. Expanding state sovereign immunity inevitably means that victims of unconstitutional or illegal government action will not be able to secure a damages remedy from the state.

Applying Federalism as Empowerment

There were three parts to the Court's holding in *National Federation of Independent Business v. Sebelius.*[56] First, by a 5-4 margin, the Court upheld

---

[53] *United States v. Morrison*, 529 U.S. 548 (2000).

[54] *City of Boerne v. Flores*, 521 U.S. 507 (1997).

[55] *Kimel v. Florida Board of Regents*, 528 U.S. 62 (2000) (state governments cannot be sued for violating the *Age Discrimination in Employment Act*); *University of Alabama v. Garrett*, 531 U.S. 356 (2001) (state governments cannot be sued for violating Title I of the *Americans with Disabilities Act*).

[56] 132 S. Ct. 2566 (2012).

the individual mandate, the centerpiece of the Act. There are 50 million Americans without health insurance and the Affordable Care Act seeks to remedy that. A crucial mechanism is to require that almost all individuals have health insurance. Those that don't must pay a penalty to the Internal Revenue Service. Insurance companies are required to provide coverage to all and no longer can deny policies based on preexisting conditions, or charge higher premiums based on health conditions, or impose yearly or lifetime caps on payments.

In this case the Court embraced an approach entirely consistent with what I describe above as federalism as empowerment. Chief Justice Roberts, joined by Justices Ginsburg, Breyer, Sotomayor, and Kagan, said that the individual mandate is a tax and within the scope of Congress's taxing power. Chief Justice Roberts explained that the mandate is calculated like a tax; for example, in 2014, it is one percent of income or $95 for those who do not purchase insurance. The Internal Revenue Service collects these funds, an estimated $4 billion in 2014, which then go to the federal treasury. The Court said that it was irrelevant that the Obama administration never called it a tax; the labels used by the government are not determinative. The Court's decision does not change the scope of Congress's taxing and spending power or how the Court determines if something is a tax. At most, it is a reminder that if Congress wants to discourage behavior, it has the power to tax it.

At the same time, five justices—Chief Justice Roberts and the four dissenters (Justices Scalia, Kennedy, Thomas, and Alito)—said that the individual mandate was not a constitutional exercise of Congressional power under the commerce clause. They said that while Congress may regulate economic activity that has a substantial effect on interstate commerce, the individual mandate regulates *inactivity* and thus exceeds the scope of Congress's power.

I think that this part of the Court's decision is fundamentally misguided because all of us are engaged in economic activity with regard to health care. As Justice Ginsburg pointed out, over 99% of people will receive medical care in their lifetimes and 60% of the uninsured do so each year. Everyone is engaged in economic activity in that they are either purchasing insurance or self-insuring.

The five justices have created a new distinction limiting Congress's commerce power: it can regulate activity, not inactivity. How much will this matter? Perhaps little in that Congress rarely is going to compel economic transactions. On the other hand, any distinctions like "activity/inactivity" or "direct/indirect"[57] are an open invitation to litigation where a great deal turns on labels and characterizations. Consider an example: Title II of the 1964 Civil Rights Act, which was adopted under Congress's commerce clause power,

---

[57] *See A.L.A. Schecter Poultry v. United States*, 295 U.S. 495 (1936) (drawing a distinction between direct and indirect effects on commerce).

prohibits hotels and restaurants from discriminating on the basis of race.[58] Does that law regulate the "inactivity" of hotels and restaurants that refuse to serve African-Americans, or does it regulate "activity"? I am not suggesting that the Court will strike down Title II, but it does illustrate how much can turn on a label. The distinction between activity and inactivity is inherently incoherent. If a person does not stop at a stop sign is that activity or inactivity? If a person does not pay child support is that activity or inactivity? The approach of the five justices in the part of the opinion that limits Congress to regulating "activity" is inconsistent with the notion of federalism as empowerment.

In this same decision seven of the justices held that Congress lacked power to deny all Medicaid funding to states that do not comply with the new conditions for Medicaid. The Act requires states to cover those within 133% of the federal poverty level with the federal government paying 100% of these costs until 2019 and 90% thereafter. The law prescribes that any state that fails to comply loses all of its Medicaid funds. The ruling of the Court is that it is unduly coercive to tie existing Medicaid funds to a failure to comply with a new requirement. The reasoning was that there are in essence two Medicaid programs, the old one and the new requirements, and that it is impermissible to link them in this way. But why see this as two programs rather than one? Why see this as Congress coercing, or to use Chief Justice Roberts' word "dragooning," the states? Admittedly, given the huge amount of money involved, any state would face a hard choice to turn it down. But there is a basic difference between being forced to do something and facing a very difficult choice. The Court ignores this basic distinction.

It is this part of the opinion that is likely to have the broadest implications. This is the first time that the Court ever has found conditions on federal funds to be so coercive as to be unconstitutional. Countless federal statutes provide funds to state and local governments on the condition that they comply with requirements. There likely will be challenges to many of these laws on the ground that the requirements are too coercive. For example, the federal Solomon Amendment provides that if any law school refuses to allow the military to recruit on campus, its university will lose all federal funds. Similarly, federal law provides that if a university program discriminates based on race, the entire university, and not just that program, will lose its federal funding. Many federal environmental laws operate through conditions on state and local governments receiving money. The Court gave little guidance as to when conditions are too coercive to survive constitutional attack, and this will lead to a great deal of litigation. Using state sovereignty to limit federal power in this way is decidedly inconsistent with the notion of federalism as empowerment.

---

[58] This was upheld in *Katzenbach v. McClung*, 379 U.S. 294 (1964).

Conclusion

The Supreme Court's recent decision about the Affordable Care Act provides a useful time to rethink federalism. Under the approach urged in this essay, the answer should have been clear and easy: the individual mandate, and the entire Act, are clearly constitutional. It is time to get past conservative rhetoric about federalism and states' rights and press hard for an alternative vision of federalism.

John P. Frank

John P. Frank:
A Man for Justice

James P. Walsh

James P. Walsh practices law in Oracle, Arizona. He recently served 5-1/2 years as the Pinal (Arizona) County Attorney, and before that was Chief Deputy to the Arizona Attorney General. A graduate of the University of Chicago Law School, he practiced law with John P. Frank, who was his friend and mentor. Walsh and many of Frank's friends established the John P. Frank Lecture at Arizona State University, which has generated the contents of this volume.

Ask most lawyers and historians to identify the five most important, socially significant Supreme Court decisions of the last century and you are likely to find that the list includes *Brown v. Board of Education* and *Miranda v. Arizona*.[1] John P. Frank made a significant contribution to *Brown* and, with his partner John Flynn, was the principal architect of the defense brief in *Miranda*. These cases are important because they changed the way justice is perceived and implemented in our democracy. John P. Frank's professional life was dedicated to the effective pursuit of justice. His work inspired some of his friends and colleagues to envision and bring to life a lecture series that bears his name. The John P. Frank lecture series, which began in 1999, became the genesis of this volume.

The outline of John P. Frank's life and career is simple. He was born and educated in Wisconsin, earning both undergraduate and law degrees from the University of Wisconsin. He graduated from law school in 1940 and then attended Yale University for an additional year, graduating with a Doctor of Juridical Science. After clerking for Justice Hugo Black, he worked for Harold Ickes and Abe Fortas in various wartime Washington assignments.

In 1944, he married Lorraine Weiss. Lorraine was a partner and collaborator with John in many community and political endeavors, serving as the Democratic National Committeewoman for over 20 years and as the founding director of the Arizona Humanities Council. They had five children.

John Frank began his teaching career at Indiana University in Bloomington in 1946, doing legal work in the summers to cover his growing family's expenses. While in Bloomington he and the dean of the law school brought several civil-rights suits to end racial segregation of public accommodations

---

[1] *Brown v. Board of Education,* 347 U.S. 483 (1954); *Miranda v. Arizona,* 384 U.S. 436 (1966).

there. In the process, he met Thurgood Marshall, who was a young lawyer in charge of the NAACP legal staff at the time. The two became lifetime friends. In 1949, suffering from asthma, he left the area to join the Yale Law School faculty. While there, he worked with Dean Thomas Emerson to prepare a Law Professors' Amicus Brief in *Sweatt v. Painter*, which successfully challenged Texas' attempt to create a "separate, but equal" law school for African Americans.[2] John, a graduate of a state-supported law school, clearly recognized the importance of a legal education unfettered by racial segregation.[3]

John's interests and past connection with Thurgood Marshall led to his involvement with *Brown v. Board of Education*. Marshall wanted an amicus brief to demonstrate that the idea of "separate but equal" facilities had been rejected by the framers of the Fourteenth Amendment and by those who drafted other early civil-rights legislation. If that were not possible, Marshall at a minimum wanted a brief that neutralized any argument that "separate, but equal" was consistent with the historical record. John, at the time still a member of the Yale law faculty, was one of the principal drafters of the brief. He brought to that job his skills as a lawyer and as an expert on the history of the Court. The task was difficult because there was ambiguity in the historical documents surrounding the adoption of the post-Civil War amendments. Nevertheless, he was able to fashion the key argument that separate but equal was not part of the plan, thus strengthening the case for racial integration. The result in *Brown* was far-reaching, ending the long practice and legal structure of segregation in public facilities, from schools to bus stations.

By 1954, John was considering a move from teaching to practicing law full-time. He met Orme Lewis when both were in Washington. In light of John's continuing problems with asthma, Orme suggested that John give Arizona a try. John came out and worked at the Lewis and Roca offices while completing some projects. He met Paul Roca and the deal was struck for John to join the young firm. The family followed soon after and a beautiful desert home that Lorraine designed became the new center of their world. His former partner and later Ninth Circuit Judge Mary M. Schroeder remembers that the Franks

> entertained the world from their backyard on Arcadia Lane. It was there that I met legendary public figures like Hubert Humphrey, Alfred Knopf, Geraldine Ferraro, Charles Alan Wright, Erwin Griswold, and theologians Hans Kung, and Martin Marty.[4]

---

[2] *Sweatt v. Painter*, 339 U.S. 629 (1950).

[3] See John P. Frank, *A Sort of Professional Autobiography* (Phoenix, AZ: Lewis and Roca, 2001).

[4] Mary M. Schroeder, "John P. Frank," in *John P. Frank: November 10, 1917–September 7, 2002* (Phoenix, AZ: Lewis and Roca, 2002), 33.

John Frank's practice was general, with appellate work predominating. At the same time, he continued his active scholarly interests, authoring eleven books. His focus, however, was on practicing law, which he did for more than the next half century. Vice Chief Justice Scott Bales of the Arizona Supreme Court, who joined Lewis and Roca shortly before John died, observed:

> As far as my own career, his major impact was as an example of how lawyers should be engaged in their communities beyond the immediate demands of their practice and also how one can be a vigorous and effective advocate while also being gracious and collegial towards opposing counsel.... In 2002, upon the 60th anniversary of his practice of law, John Frank said that he wanted to encourage young lawyers to 'share the spirit of joy and satisfaction' he had found from 'performing socially useful work.' He warned that our professional values are threatened by the pressures of 'competitive commercialism' that would reduce law firms to factories where people merely punch the time clock for the business they serve.[5]

John Frank was often able to affect policy, not only through his Supreme Court advocacy, but also through his participation in the American Law Institute and in the activities of both the state and national Democratic Parties. These endeavors involved the minutiae of drafting rules of procedure and acting as the state party's lawyer and parliamentarian. Yet these constant and continuing activities are how John taught and practiced the ways of justice. Others also follow these paths, but John had the talent and creativity to make essential differences in the way people envision justice.

A prime example is *Miranda v. Arizona*. John and his law partner, John Flynn, undertook the appeal of Ernesto Miranda at the request of the Arizona ACLU. Flynn was best known for his trial work, but he and John formed a formidable team. In a typically generous gesture, John insisted that Flynn argue the case before the Court in 1966. The issue was protecting the criminally accused from coerced confessions in violation of the Fifth Amendment to the U.S. Constitution. The Supreme Court agreed with the defense position, holding that a suspect in custody must be advised of his or her constitutional rights, including the right to remain silent and the right to assistance of a lawyer. From this time forward, the encounters between law enforcement and suspected lawbreakers were fundamentally changed. *Miranda* has evolved in many ways, but John's work minimized, if not ended, the backroom sweatings, and even beatings, that used to sometimes occur in the pursuit of questionable incriminating statements.[6]

---

[5] Judge Scott Bales, personal correspondence on file with Ms. Eva Lester, June 2012.

[6] For a detailed account of the case, see Gary L. Stuart, *Miranda: The Story of America's Right to Remain Silent* (Tucson, AZ: University of Arizona Press, 2008).

As a lawyer, John practiced with a diverse, if not quirky, group of partners who were as talented as he was. But to many around the country, Lewis and Roca became known as John Frank's firm. He gave the credit due the founders, but his reputation on a national level identified the firm.

John wrote extensively about the Supreme Court, from the popular *The Marble Palace*, to Justice Hugo Black's biography and an edited edition of Black's letters.[7] He was called on regularly during the confirmation process for U.S. Supreme Court justices. One of these experiences led to his admiring study of Judge Clement Haynsworth, who failed to be confirmed.[8] In other instances, such as the appointments of Robert Bork and David Souter, John was asked to appear before the Senate Judiciary Committee or to supply written testimony concerning the confirmation process or the particular nominee's qualifications.

During the confirmation proceedings for Justice Clarence Thomas in 1991, a witness, Professor Anita Hill, testified that the nominee had engaged in sexual harassment. Hill had worked for Thomas when he was with the U.S. Department of Education and the Equal Employment Opportunity Commission. This testimony sensationalized the hearings. Professor Hill was summoned to appear before the Senate Judiciary Committee and a defense/advisory team was pulled together on her behalf. John Frank was a part of that team. He flew to Washington with his young colleague, Janet Napolitano, to help prepare Professor Hill for the hearing. In the end, Thomas was confirmed. Napolitano went on to become U.S. Attorney for Arizona, Arizona Attorney General, Governor of Arizona, and U.S. Secretary of Homeland Security.

John had many protégés whom he mentored inside and outside the firm. In addition to Secretary Napolitano, he mentored several Arizona judges, including a few who have served on the Arizona Supreme Court.

John's support for women lawyers was especially noteworthy, given the era. At the time, no major Arizona firm had any women partners. One of the lawyers whom John championed was Mary M. Schroeder, who began her Arizona legal career in 1970 as a Lewis and Roca associate and became the firm's first woman partner. Later she became an Arizona Court of Appeals judge on her way to an appointment to the prestigious U.S. Circuit Court of Appeals for the Ninth Circuit, where she later served as its chief judge. Similarly, Professor Toni Massaro remembers John's support for her pioneering

---

[7] *The Marble Palace: The Supreme Court in American Life* (New York: Knopf, 1958); *Mr. Justice Black: The Man and His Opinions* (New York: Knopf, 1949); "Hugo L. Black: Free Speech and the Declaration of Independence," in *Six Justices on Civil Rights*, ed. Ronald Rotunda (New York: Oceana, 1983).

[8] *Clement Haynsworth, the Senate, and the Supreme Court* (Charlottesville, VA: University Press of Virginia, 1991).

appointment to head the James Rogers College of Law at the University of Arizona:

> As for his influence in my career, he was among the most support-
> ive, influential bar leaders for me when I began as Dean of the Uni-
> versity of Arizona College of Law in 1999. He offered sage advice,
> moral support, and his insight into the profession and its higher
> goals. He was generous with his time and his resources. As the first
> woman dean of a major public law school, I had my work cut out
> for me. John was one of the blue ribbon lawyers who made clear
> from the start that they were completely enthusiastic about women
> in leadership roles. This mattered, to me and to everyone else he
> helped to mentor and support over the many years of his storied
> career.[9]

John's role as a mentor and teacher was significant in its generosity of spirit and recognition that law is only part of who we are. His law partner Susan Freeman acknowledges that aspect of his long-term influence:

> John loved celebrations with family and friends and colleagues. He
> arranged for big 4th of July celebrations in his backyard with firm
> lawyers and their families invited, and with fireworks requiring
> special legal authority. He arranged for impromptu lunches at
> Encanto Park for everyone working on a case with him, junior law-
> yers and paralegals and secretaries. He ended most days in the of-
> fice with Vespers, where lawyers at the firm and those who had left
> congregated around John's desk—including Mary Schroeder at the
> Court of Appeals and Janet Napolitano from her posts as U.S. At-
> torney, Attorney General or Governor, when they were in town and
> had the time. He kept wine and spirits in a small refrigerator, and
> we would unwind from the day and share each other's company.
> The practice of law is time-consuming and stressful, and so is rais-
> ing a family. John's most important lesson to me, and one which I
> continue to remind myself to follow, is to make the time to stop and
> celebrate life and enjoy your colleagues and friends and family.[10]

John P. Frank led an extraordinary life in very interesting times. As one of his law partners said upon his death in 2002: "John was a man of extra-ordinary breadth and scope so that when lunch counters are open to every-one, when professions are open to everyone, when rights are read to everyone, his legacy is there."[11] His life journey was a quest for justice and he was always on the lookout for those who would join him in that high endeavor. Once you were recruited, you bent your energy to the task and hoped to hear John's

---

[9] Professor Toni Massaro, personal correspondence on file with Ms. Eva Lester, June 2012.

[10] Ms. Susan Freeman, personal correspondence on file with Ms. Eva Lester, July 2012.

[11] Peter Baird, in "Noted Valley Attorney John P. Frank, 84, Dies" (article by Lindsey Collom), *Arizona Republic,* Sept. 8, 2002.

highest compliment: "very satisfactory." The lectures you have read are an effort to meet John's standard and continue the quest.

qp

Visit us at *www.quidprobooks.com*.

www.ingramcontent.com/pod-product-compliance
Lightning Source LLC
Chambersburg PA
CBHW061736270326
41928CB00011B/2254